PRESCRIPTION GAMES

OTHER BOOKS BY JEFFREY ROBINSON

FICTION

A True and Perfect Knight
The Monk's Disciples
The Margin of the Bulls
The Ginger Jar
Pietrov and Other Games

NON-FICTION

*The Merger: How Organized Crime
Is Taking Over Canada and the World*
The Manipulators
The Hotel
The Laundrymen
Bardot: Two Lives
The End of the American Century
The Risk Takers: Five Years On
Rainier and Grace
Yamani: The Inside Story
Minus Millionaires
The Risk Takers
Teamwork
Bette Davis

PRESCRIPTION GAMES

MONEY, EGO, AND POWER INSIDE THE GLOBAL PHARMACEUTICAL INDUSTRY

JEFFREY ROBINSON

M&S

National Library of Canada Cataloguing in Publication Data

Robinson, Jeffrey, 1945

Prescription games: money, ego and power inside
the global pharmaceutical industry

Includes bibliographical references and index.
ISBN 0-7710-7566-9

1. Pharmaceutical industry.   2. Pharmaceutical industry – Canada.
I. Title.

HD9665.5.R62 2001   338.4'7615   C2001-930068-9

We acknowledge the financial support of the Government
of Canada through the Book Publishing Industry
Development Program for our publishing activities.

We further acknowledge the support of the
Canada Council for the Arts and the Ontario
Arts Council for our publishing program.

Text design by Ingrid Paulson
Typeset in Bembo and Univers by Gordon Robertson
Printed and bound in Canada

McClelland & Stewart Ltd.
The Canadian Publishers
481 University Avenue
Toronto, Ontario
M5G 2E9
www.mcclelland.com

1 2 3 4 5   05 04 03 02 01

For my old pal
Trudy Desmond
jazz singer

New York, 1945 – Toronto, 1999

Dollar amounts given in the text are in United States currency unless specified as Canadian (C$).

CONTENTS

1. Big Pharma 1

2. The Third Wave 17

3. Money, Ego, and Power 32

4. In a Perfect World 44

5. Secret Science 63

6. Just Taking Care of Business 83

7. A Tale of Two More Drugs 98

8. Nancy O Talks Fast 115

9. The Street Fighter's Lament 136

10. Playing Hardball 154

11. Whatever It Takes 174

12. Taking Aim at the Doctors 193

Epilogue 216

Acknowledgements 221

Selected Bibliography 225

Index 255

CHAPTER 1

BIG PHARMA

[bɪg ˈfɑrmɛ] n. the drug industry's own term to describe a global collective of 75 to 100 research-based pharmaceutical companies.

Brenda never lived to see her daughter's first communion.

Diagnosed with ovarian cancer at the age of thirty-one, Brenda might have been able to extend her life by twelve to fourteen months with drugs – which would have been enough so that she could watch her only child receive God's blessing – but she couldn't afford them, and no one in the United States was willing to pay more than $2,300 every three weeks for her treatment.

This, at a time of unprecedented corporate prosperity.

The drug she needed, Taxol, had been developed by the U.S. government with the taxpayers' money and handed as a gift to Bristol-Myers Squibb (BMS) to commercially exploit as a prescription drug. The year Brenda died, BMS's worldwide sales on Taxol came to $1.27 billion.

Several thousand miles away in sub-Sahara Africa, more than 23 million people are HIV-positive. That's 70 per cent of the total HIV-infected population on the planet. Until the summer of 2000, Big Pharma had flatly turned its back on those people. Its excuse was that the Africans didn't have an infrastructure through which the pharmaceutical companies could work, and if the Africans wanted help, they had to begin by doing what they could for themselves.

When an AIDS conference in South Africa convinced the world's media to spotlight Big Pharma's intransigence, the industry's legions of press and public relations managers went to work. Almost in unison they said, "Of course we're willing to do something. We've always been willing to help, but what's really required is patent protection in the Third World and more respect for intellectual property rights because without that, if we give our drugs away for free, they'll only wind up being sold on the black market back in the West."

The media laid on more heat.

Glaxo Wellcome was first to blink. The company announced that, as a gesture of genuine concern, it would reduce the daily price of its AIDS drug, Combivir, from $16.50 – which is the retail price in the United States – to a mere $2, which is presumably at, or somewhere above, cost. Could that be an inadvertent admission that drug companies work on an 800 per cent markup?

Still, even at $2, those drugs weren't going to help a lot of people, not when you understand that most of them were living in countries where annual health-care expenditures were under $10 per person.

Several thousand miles away, in New York, *Fortune* magazine was rating thirty-eight industries in many different commercial categories. Big Pharma placed first in return on revenues, first in return on assets, and first in return on equity. It rated fifth for profit growth, sixth for total return to investors over one year, and fourth for total return to investors over ten years.

For much of the final decade of the twentieth century, and now into the twenty-first century, the pharmaceutical industry has continued to pay shareholders a higher percentage of revenues than any other sector. Drug companies have surpassed almost all other Fortune 500 companies in profit rates, outperforming the Standard & Poor's 500 Index by 90 per cent and averaging profits more than three times that of the other industries in *Fortune*'s survey. Pharmaceuticals have been rated either first or second in the list of the most profitable sectors for more than thirty of the past forty years.

There is a very deep and very wide philosophical canyon that runs through the centre of this industry, and nowhere is this divide more plainly visible than in Basel, Switzerland.

In the days before the two Swiss pharma-giants Ciba-Geigy and Sandoz merged to form Novartis – now the seventh largest drug company in the world – Ciba was already a major international player. The company's headquarters were spread out along the Rhine in a most telling way. Research and development (R&D) had its own building: that's where the scientists were. Corporate affairs were dealt with down the block: that's where the commercial people were. The top floor of corporate affairs was for executive offices, the legal department, and a group of strategic planners called the pharma-policy unit. Those were the people who drove the corporation towards what they intended would be ever-increasing profits. Below them was medical, the doctors who evaluated the commercial aspects of R&D and oversaw regulatory reporting requirements. Below them was sales and marketing – the people whose only role in this was to move product – close enough to the chief executive to be under his thumb but purposely far enough away from the scientists.

In other big pharmaceutical companies, even when marketing and R&D are not separated by a few streets, they are still kept miles apart. The reason why is fundamental to the industry – scientists should not worry about marketing, and marketing people must never confuse their own issues with medicine and science. The first group is soberly dedicated to changing the world, to finding that one molecule that might, somehow, cure the incurable; the second group is about making money for the company. If a drug cures the incurable but doesn't sell, it may be great science but it's lousy business. If a drug sells but doesn't cure much of anything, it's still good business.

This elementary principle – call it Big Pharma's theme song – drives the commercial side.

We need to make a lot of money in order to pay for the research that will produce the next blockbuster drug that will provide a lot of people with a lot of benefit.

It's a tune the stock exchange happily whistles with them. But *a lot of people* doesn't inevitably mean patients, and *a lot of benefit* doesn't automatically mean better health. Typically, the people are shareholders and, customarily, the benefit is financial reward. That isn't, in and of itself, sinister. Except when it results in such a massive energy force that commercial velocity nourishes group-think, which then feeds off itself by rewarding ruthlessness. Sometimes referred to as the tyranny of the bottom line – *small evils occasionally happen so that, in the end, there is something worthwhile* – it is how and why corporations in general, and the pharmaceutical industry in particular, can wind up making good people do bad things.

For Dr. Peter Mansfield, it is, in one way, akin to marriage. "You accept the faults of your partner so that you can get the benefits."

Mansfield is an Australian GP who runs a non-profit pharmaceutical industry watchdog group called the Medical Lobby for Appropriate Marketing (MaLAM). In 1981, as a young medical student, he'd travelled to Bangladesh, where he was appalled to see drug companies promoting anabolic steroids and glucose solutions for children with slow growth, tetracycline syrups for children, and breast-milk substitutes, all of which his training told him perverted the objectives of scientific medicine. He created MaLAM on a shoestring budget, hoping to pressure the industry into more ethical behaviour by grouping together fifty-three equally concerned health-care professionals.

It was 1986 when the group had its first significant success. It challenged a manufacturer's promotion of an anti-stress concoction – a mixture of arsenic, strychnine, vitamins, and alcohol – and got it withdrawn. Over the next five years, MaLAM forced drug companies to yank a total of eleven unsuitable medicines off the market, including the top-selling over-the-counter product for diarrhea in the Philippines. Around the same time, MaLAM began publicly attacking the quality of evidence used by pharmaceutical companies to justify efficacy claims.

Today MaLAM has six thousand subscribers in thirty countries, with a very strong presence in Canada, and has earned its place as a constant thorn in Big Pharma's side.

"To understand the way the commercial people in this industry think," says Mansfield, "you need to consider the nature of the beast. These are huge corporations, and the people working for them, just like the corporations themselves, are trying to survive and prosper. To avoid discord, people don't express their concerns. So, you've got a drug that's very important for the survival of the company and also for everybody's year-end bonus, and maybe there's a little concern about that drug, but nobody expresses it. Instead, they prefer to talk about the good things, to reinforce the positive view of the drug. To promote it they need to believe in it, so they convince themselves that their drug is superior to the competition's, even if the evidence shows otherwise. They trust the company's information. They accentuate the positive, and if there are negatives, they talk about how those negatives could be benefits. If a drug causes sedation, for instance, then they point out that it helps you sleep."

Adding to commercial pressures is the turmoil created in this industry by almost two decades of consolidation.

"They're called mergers," Mansfield explains, "but in a sense they're really the takeover of the weaker company by the dominant company. Underlying it is a tone of bitterness. It's an environment of uncertainty. There is a driving need to perform better, to sell more. If you're a drug company representative and your job is at risk, forgetting to tell a doctor about a contraindication that might worry him is easily rationalized away. You think to yourself, 'The literature spells out the contraindication, let him read the literature, my job is at stake.' Let's face it, in a high-paid, job-insecure atmosphere, people aren't going to say things that will upset their boss or cost a sale."

Mansfield sees it as a consequence of evolution. "If you've got an environment where survival relies on getting the leaves at the top of the trees, then you're going to produce giraffes. If you've got an environment where you're only going to survive by producing increased sales at the end of every quarter, then this is the kind of creature you're going to get."

In any other business, all this might not matter so much. If you don't like Coke, you can drink Pepsi. If the jeans don't fit, you can return them for another pair. If you want to buy a television, you compare different brands and choose what you think is the best value for your money. If one television has some little gadget that's been patented that's different from another television, that doesn't automatically mean the manufacturer can charge more than it's worth. Having a patent isn't a licence to gouge.

But that's not the way life works in the pharmaceutical industry. The products are not interchangeable at the level of the consumer unless they are exactly the same product. Unless they're the same compound, the same molecule. What's more, the person who pays for the product is not the person who chooses the product. We go to a doctor and the prescription we get represents someone else making a purchasing choice for us. Nor is there any discussion of price. The product must be paid for by us, or through an insurance plan, or out of government coffers. And yet there is hardly ever a cost consideration made when the product is chosen. Doctors may well ponder several similar drugs and, all things being equal, deliberately prescribe the least expensive. It's a rare doctor who actually discusses the price of a drug with a patient before writing that prescription, especially when the bill for it falls on an insurance plan. The question of cost may, at least in theory, be pertinent when you're standing at the pharmacy counter and there's the possibility of substituting a less expensive, bioequivalent generic drug. But it's a rare patient who, before accepting a prescription from a doctor, is in the least concerned with how much the drug is going to cost.

The industry is unique.

That's partially because there is a certain inevitability about prescription medicines. Many people go through life without soft drinks, jeans, or televisions, but everybody, at some point, needs medication. Frequently, life depends on it.

Stephen Schondelmeyer, doctor of pharmacology and director of the Prime Institute at the College of Pharmacy of the University of Minnesota, is a staunch believer that drugs are "public goods" in much the same way that public utilities are.

"Drugs are in limited supply," suggests Schondelmeyer. "That's why we, as a society, grant patents to the companies that discover new drugs because we want to encourage and stimulate innovation. To some degree, patents do that. But if I have a debilitating disease that affects the length of my life, I need that drug. If it's in limited supply because that company has a patent, which means no one else can manufacture it, and if I can't afford it because they have no competition and can charge whatever they want, then the result is that I have a shortened life. I argue that drugs meet that criteria of a public good. There is universal demand. There is limited supply. There is limited access to the product. It is essential to the health of the population."

But that's not how the Big Pharma marketing people see it.

"To these guys, drugs are just commodities," notes Dr. Larry Sasich, pharmacologist with the Health Research Group of the watchdog organization Public Citizen in Washington, D.C. "They don't look at drugs as something people need in order to live or to make their lives better when they face a disease. For them, drugs are just like a pair of shoes or a tennis racket."

This attitude leads Sasich to use the word "amoral." "Not immoral but amoral," he explains, "even if some people inside the industry may act in immoral ways when faced with stiff competition. The public's general view of the industry is that it exists for the public's best interest. And I think the industry has done a great PR job in portraying this image. What the public doesn't know is a lot of the background, about what goes on inside, about information that's withheld, about the spin that's put on drugs that aren't very effective, about how people get hurt. The public doesn't think of pharmaceutical companies as being amoral because the PR people have made certain that they don't hear about things like that."

Research and development is the nucleus of the pharmaceutical business and also the rationale the industry uses to justify much of what it does.

New molecules must be discovered and new drugs must be developed from them. Once in the development pipeline, these new drugs must be tested and approved – admittedly, a long and expensive process. It is not unheard of for a drug to take eight to twelve years to make its way through this maze of hurdles – two to four years for screening and discovery phase, another six to eight years for clinical testing – and to cost $300 million to $500 million before it can finally be brought to market. It is estimated that for every 4,000 to 7,000 molecules that get looked at, only one winds up as a drug in a package on a pharmacist's shelf.

That's not to say that only one drug is possible out of every 4,000 to 7,000 molecules. It's likely that dozens, if not hundreds, could be developed. But only one emerges and therein lies the massive contradiction that underscores this industry: the drugs that are needed are not necessarily the drugs that sell.

The World Health Organization has maintained for years that "there is an inherent conflict of interest between the legitimate business goals of manufacturers and the social, medical and economic needs of providers and the public to select and use drugs in the most rational way."

Not surprisingly, the industry sees it differently. Its battle cry is "Innovation has a price." And while no argument is possible with that basic premise, legitimate questions remain, such as, "How much? And what do we get for it?"

Big Pharma's answer to the first is very little, to the second, quite a lot.

The increasing cost of drugs is a topic that won't go away, despite Big Pharma's extensive efforts to downplay it. Don't look at the cost, it urges, look at how much innovative drugs can save. For example, drug therapy to treat coronary artery disease costs around C$1,000 a year, which is considerably less than the C$25,000 to C$41,000 that it costs Health Canada for bypass surgery. And the cost of drugs to treat depression is C$5,000 a year, but the cost of keeping someone in an institution is C$75,000 a year. Of course, the treatment of illness, like most things in life, is hardly ever an either-or situation. A bottle of Aspirin costs much less than brain surgery, but no one is seriously going to accept the argument that brain surgery is the best way to cure a headache any more than someone might suggest Aspirin is the best way to treat brain tumours. Then too, if all the drugs on the market were as cost-effective as Big Pharma insists they are, health-care expenditures would be going down. But that's not the case. Certainly not in Canada, where drugs now cost Canadians more money every year than doctors. Clearly not in the United States, where three out of every four people over the age of sixty-five rely on prescription drugs and where, today, some 5 million people in that age category are forced to choose between medicine and food.

Not in any country.

Drug company spin doctors would also have the public believe that drug costs reflect the competitive nature of science. They are fast to point out that theirs is an industry where breakthrough drugs soon find rivals, and generic alternatives take a growing share of the market. The cost of innovation, they claim, must take those factors into account.

Both arguments are, at best, only half true.

Breakthrough drugs eventually do find competitors, but that's largely because the industry itself continues to sink limited R&D funds into breakthrough imitations. When one company has a huge success in a major market, the commercial people make a bottom-line calculation to decide how much of that market they can pry loose. If it isn't big enough for a second or third competing drug, they don't bother. But if it is, they develop what is known as a "me-too" drug. Because it's an imitation and not an exact copy, me-toos require separate patents and separate clinical testing and separate regulatory approval. It's an expensive gamble, especially since me-toos also have to be heavily promoted. When Searle launched Celebrex in early 1999, the company expected its "Cox-2 inhibitor" – a new class of arthritis treatment – to enjoy unparalleled market share. But Merck was right behind with Vioxx. Warner-Lambert thought much the same when it launched its ill-advised diabetes treatment, Rezulin. SmithKline followed closely with Avandia, and Eli Lilly showed up with Actos. Me-toos traditionally take a backseat to the first drug entering the market, but it's not for the lack of trying and competition gets fierce. So for any company to complain about breakthrough competition, when everyone is doing it, is nothing more than bitching about what Big Pharma inflicts on itself.

The second contention, referring to generic competition, simply contravenes the rules of the game. It's as if one football team were to argue that the only reason it can't score against another team is because the other team is still on the field.

Patent protection is for a limited time only. Everybody understands that. Once it's over, the market is open to anyone. To fight that, Big Pharma spends tens of millions of dollars lobbying politicians to move the goalposts and hundreds of millions developing what are known as "line extensions." Those are variations on its originally patented drug that allow it to get new patents and, basically, to re-exploit its original market.

Eli Lilly, for example, has spent several hundred million dollars defending Prozac from patent expiration. Arguably the most successful drug in history – with the possible exception of penicillin – nearly 40 million people worldwide have taken Prozac since it came onto the market in 1988. In all that time, it has never been off of the top-ten most-prescribed-drug list. More than 10 million new prescriptions were written for it in 1999. Sales exceeded $2.5 billion. Needless to say, it's a cash cow that Eli Lilly does not want to give up. The company has developed a once-a-week version and patented that. The idea is that as the original patents expire on the old daily Prozac, Lilly will have moved that market onto the patent-protected weekly pill and kept the cash registers ringing.

What Big Pharma is essentially saying about generic competition is that, where its profits are at stake, it will pull every rabbit it can out of the hat and, by the way, that's included in the price of innovation too.

What Big Pharma is not saying is that me-toos and line extensions typically take up around 80 per cent of R&D spending.

Granted, it's an extremely competitive world. But commercial aggression is not unique to the pharmaceutical industry. It is, however, a uniquely fragmented market. No single company commands a very large share. The combined Glaxo SmithKline tops the list with 7 per cent. Pfizer with Warner-Lambert is next with 6.9 per cent. Then there is Merck and AstraZeneca (tied with 4.4 per cent) and Bristol-Myers Squibb (4 per cent). The next five companies – Aventis, Novartis, Johnson & Johnson, American Home Products, and Pharmacia & Upjohn – are all in the 3 per cent range. But these figures are slightly misleading because they imply that drug companies compete in all areas. They don't. The commercial powers pick and choose the fields where they want to compete and there, the market is anything but splintered.

It's called "disease management."

Disease is a business, and disease management is both a marketing technique to make that business profitable and a philosophy to make that marketing technique businesslike.

Drug companies view health care illness by illness, which allows them to examine the interrelated elements of any specific disease, establish a distinct pattern of cost elements unique to each illness, and then to create treatments that will, in effect, give the company a start-to-finish market. This is not about modelling R&D to fit the needs of the patient, it is about roping off territory for which particular companies stake a claim. Once a company has a dominant share of the drugs prescribed for a particular disease, competition recedes, because moving in on it becomes cost prohibitive.

Glaxo SmithKline may have but 7 per cent of the overall market, but it controls an estimated 46 per cent of the anti-migraine market. Warner-Lambert controls nearly half of the market for drugs in the cholesterol-lowering category. Schering-Plough, which isn't even a top-ten company in terms of sales, controls about 40 per cent of the anti-allergy market just with its drug Claritin.

Enter now the financial markets and the concept of great expectations.

The bigger pharmaceutical companies become, the more marketing clout they amass. Smaller companies are either taken over by the bigger ones or forced to retreat into smaller markets. In turn, the bigger companies must spend ever-increasing sums to protect their established positions. The real battleground now becomes the stock market.

It is possible that there is a CEO at a top-twenty-five drug company who doesn't keep one eye permanently on his share price. But even if you found one who said he didn't, chances are you'd be able to catch him peeking. After all, his business life depends on it. Share price values the company and a company's market value is a report card on the CEO's stewardship. But several factors determine share price and one of them is expectations. That's where the market believes the company is heading.

The yardstick used to determine expectations is the company's pipeline. Those are the drugs in various stages of development, all of which the company hopes will come onto the market over the course of the next ten years. In reality, most of them will fail. The trick is to figure out as early as possible which ones will become drugs and what impact they'll have. Analysts who get that right can make a lot of money for investors. Touting a strong pipeline can also boost the share price of a company. Those same analysts, casting doubts about a pipeline, can drive share prices down.

Expectations play their role every quarter when results are announced. If the analysts' expectations are lower than the results, the share price usually rises. If, on the other hand, the company has led analysts to believe that the results will be good, and the "whisper price" is too high, the share price can nose-dive.

Maintaining a pipeline full of promise – and eventually delivering on expectations – is one way that savvy CEOs keep a company from becoming a takeover target. With survival at stake, it's not surprising that the CEO's instincts tell him to bet on marketing rather than science.

Which is why survival in the pharmaceutical industry is not about curing the incurable. If that happens, it's a fortunate and happy coincidence. Instead, it's about blockbusters.

In 1990, a blockbuster drug was defined as one with $500 million annual sales. Ten years later, the figure was up to $1 billion and there were already twenty-three drugs on the list. By 2005, some industry sources expect the figure to be set at $2.5 billion, with as many as fifty drugs making the list.

The top-selling blockbusters at the turn of the millennium were Zocor (manufactured by Merck, with sales of $4.9 billion); Losec (AstraZeneca, $4.4 billion); Prozac (Eli Lilly, $2.6 billion); Norvasc (Pfizer, $2.34 billion), and Lipitor (Parke-Davis/Warner-Lambert, $1.9 billion), which was also the first drug to hit the $1 billion mark within a year of coming on the market.

To understand how blockbusters shape the industry, you have to realize that not every therapeutic category lends itself to blockbuster potential. Blockbusters are harvested out of chronic illnesses, as opposed to acute illnesses, because the real money is in drugs that must be taken every day for years and not in one-pill miracles. You also need very large disease populations located in countries where sufferers have the money to pay for expensive drugs.

Chief among the categories that meet those criteria are cancer, hypertension, psychiatric disorders, osteoporosis, rheumatoid arthritis, and thrombosis. Also included are almost anything that alleviates constant pain and treatments that lower cholesterol. Added in are lifestyle medications, the drugs people take because they want to, which includes diet drugs, sexual enhancers – Viagra, launched in sixty countries in its first year, is the prime example – and stuff that grows hair.

Big Pharma openly admits that's what everyone is after. But by directing R&D budgets to target blockbusters – approximately four-fifths of Big Pharma's total R&D budget is aimed at providing for one-fifth of the world's population – research on less profitable diseases is simply discarded. Drug companies are more and more financially captive to blockbusters. Dependence on billion-dollar drugs requires more billion-dollar drugs to support that dependence. The next big drug has to outsell the last big drug or the quarterly results will start to go backwards. Consequently, somewhere, somehow, someone has to determine the "floor," a quantifiable figure for projected sales, below which the company will simply refuse to develop a drug.

One report from corporate analysts Standard and Poor's suggests, "Most companies' primary strategy is to focus on products with minimum peak sales potentials of $500 million per year." Another floor number informally bandied about is $200 million. Whatever the number is, the thinking remains that if a drug is going to sell less than that, the money is better invested elsewhere. Oddly, six phone calls to six Big Pharma press spokespersons, in which this question was posed – "Is there a quantifiable amount that a drug must sell before you put it onto the market?" – prompted these responses: No; absolutely not; don't be daft; it doesn't work that way; anybody who says there is doesn't understand how this business works; and no.

Except there is all sorts of anecdotal evidence that floors exist. At some point, someone has to make a decision as to whether their company is going to proceed with the development of a drug and, at that point, commercial considerations include projected sales. It's hardly surprising that, according to several people inside the industry, commercial priorities always win out over scientific priorities.

"Board meetings," noted one company executive, "are not about science, they're about shareholder value."

In well-run companies it almost never gets to the point where someone in a board meeting has to say, "Here's this drug for which we have no market, now what?" The decision is very clinical and happens long before a drug can become either a public relations disaster or a profit drain. It happens as early in gestation as possible – the commercial equivalent of an abortion – when R&D is simply stopped before too many people can find out about it.

In January 2000, the CIA put together a National Intelligence Estimate entitled "The Global Infectious Disease Threat and Its Implications for the United States." The gist of it was that twenty well-known diseases – including malaria, TB, cholera, and dengue – are fast reaching epidemic levels, spreading to new regions, and are deadlier than ever before.

And no one is doing much about them.

The seven infectious diseases the CIA credited with the highest number of deaths in 1998 were HIV/AIDS, TB, malaria, hepatitis B and C, lower respiratory infections, diarrheal diseases, and measles.

Each of them remains a threat well into the twenty-first century.

As the CIA report noted, "Almost all research and development funds allocated by developed country governments and pharmaceutical companies, moreover, are focused on advancing therapies and drugs relevant to developed country maladies, and those that are relevant to developing country needs usually are beyond their financial reach."

Advanced sleeping sickness, which scientists believed had been wiped out half a century ago, is on the rise again – estimated to be killing 150,000 people a year – and the only drug currently available to treat it is a seventy-year-old mixture of melarsen oxide and propylene glycol that has been likened to arsenic in antifreeze. The treatment itself kills 5 per cent of the people injected with it.

There used to be alternatives, made by Aventis and Bayer, but both companies are backing away from producing them. In the meantime, one strain of sleeping sickness is becoming resistant to the only drug left on the market and no major pharmaceutical company reports new research on the disease.

Again, the numbers tell the story and point to a floor.

North America, western Europe, and Japan are 80 per cent of the world's drug market. Africa is 1 per cent. The industry claims to invest $27 billion a year in R&D. What it does with that money is what any business does with any investment, it puts it where the consumer power is and caters to the market. The sad thing is that even if it spent its budgets proportionately, and dedicated 1 per cent of its R&D to finding solutions for problems in Africa, that would only put $270 million in the pot, about half the money it takes these days to develop just one new drug.

When you ask about a "floor," they say it doesn't exist. That's because the term they use is "cost-effective illnesses."

Prime Institute's Schondelmeyer explains, "When it's cost-effective, they find a cure. The opposite, non-cost-effective illnesses, is where there is no economic incentive for anyone to go find a cure. Where you have rare diseases in developed countries with resources, they're likely to get taken care of. But if you have diseases, even with large populations in Africa, but no resources, people die."

Sasich at Public Citizen agrees: "Just look at the drugs that are being developed for malaria."

He points to Glaxo's Malarone, which won approval in Europe in mid-2000. The first new anti-malarial developed by a drug company in forty years – the others had all come from institutions – Malarone is preventative, meaning that its main market is the estimated 7 million tourists, businesspeople, and military personnel who travel annually into malaria-affected regions.

"They're marketed to treat travellers from rich western nations going to sub-Saharan Africa," he adds, "not to deal with malaria in Africa. New anti-malarials could probably be used to treat the problem in Africa, but those people don't have any money. So they don't get the drugs."

Glaxo announced it would be donating some quantities of Malarone to Kenya and Uganda. Malaria, nonetheless, remains the perfect example of Big Pharma's cost-effective neglect.

One of the most ancient diseases known to man and named by the Romans, who believed it came from evil air – hence, *mal aria* – it is transmitted by mosquitoes. In the past it has been contained by spraying swamps to kill the mosquitoes and had been widely treated with quinine compounds. But several strains have become resistant to standard drugs, and today, with approximately 500 million cases around the world, there are three thousand children dying of the disease in Africa every day.

It has taken several gifts from the Bill and Melinda Gates Foundation to offer some real hope to those people in Africa. First there was $50 million given to Malaria Vaccine Initiative. Then $25 million for Medicines for Malaria Venture. In July 2000, $40 million was offered to the London School of Hygiene and Tropical Medicine. That money will be spent on insecticides, vaccines to treat the disease, and the development of new drugs to prevent it.

Sadly, malaria is far from the only disease adversely affected by the cost-effective equation.

Bacterial meningitis was once treated cheaply and easily with something called "chloramphenicol in oil." The drug was manufactured by Roussel Uclaf – later merged into the Hoechst group to become HMR – but in 1995 Roussel stopped making it. Now, no one does.

A disease called leishmaniasis comes from a parasite and causes severe skin lesions and, sometimes, death. The treatment for it is said to exist in a drug company laboratory. None of the companies suspected of holding the cure will admit to it. But all of them say that they have no plans to market any such drug.

The Nobel Peace Prize–winning group, Médecins Sans Frontières, says that somewhere in the world, someone dies of tuberculosis every ten seconds. The group also points out that of the more than twelve hundred molecules brought to market by Big Pharma between 1975 and 1997, a mere thirteen wound up in trials for the treatment of tropical diseases. However, nine of the thirteen had nothing to do with Big Pharma and human disease R&D. Five came out of veterinary research – to cure animal illnesses, which is also a hugely profitable business –

while the other four came out of U.S. army research during the Vietnam War.

In other words, if you suffer from erectile dysfunction in the industrialized West, Big Pharma is there to help you out with Viagra. If you suffer from malaria, diarrhea, or measles in Africa, it's likely you will die.

Kurt Briner was fed up.

As CEO of the Swiss pharmaceutical company Sanofi, he didn't like criticism aimed at Big Pharma. He took it personally. So he used his keynote address at a management conference in Paris to lash back at the critics. Where others saw conflicts of interest – such as those between the needs of drug companies to satisfy the stock market and the needs of the public for better, cheaper, and more accessible drugs – Briner assured his audience that they simply didn't exist. "It is an insult to our industry, an insult to our ethics as health-care professionals, and an expression of utter contempt for the numerous legal obligations by which we are bound by our ethical practice."

Bernard Lemoine was also fed up.

As director-general of France's National Pharmaceutical Industry Association, he had a real problem with anyone who refused to understand that the pharmaceutical business was just that, a business. "I don't see why special effort should be demanded from the pharmaceutical industry. Nobody asks Renault to give cars to people who haven't got one."

That same year, Big Pharma – despite all its bragging about science and innovation – spent more money on marketing to sell its drugs than it did on research and development to find new drugs.

And so it has, ever since.

CHAPTER 2

THE THIRD WAVE

For most of our history, the best that the science of medicine could achieve was to make patients more comfortable. Pain could be relieved and some illnesses could be treated, but pain relief was temporary and most illnesses ran their course regardless, or led to more serious complications and eventually death.

It could be argued that the turning point came in 1928. Until then, the greatest single contribution to the well-being of humankind – the one innovation that actually extended our lifespan – was neither medical nor particularly scientific. It was indoor plumbing – running water brought into homes and waste taken out.

At this point, a forty-seven-year-old Scottish bacteriologist working at St. Mary's Hospital in Paddington, London, changed the world.

Alexander Fleming had been studying the antibacterial qualities of nasal mucus, trying to determine how it affected Staphylococcus bacteria. In September 1928, Fleming went on holiday, leaving a bacteria-smeared culture plate on a table that, somehow, while he was away, became contaminated. By the time he returned, the plate was covered with a yellow-green mould surrounded by a clear halo. The mould, he expected. But the clear halo excited him, because it meant that some sort of substance from the contaminating spore had stopped the bacteria's growth.

That was penicillin.

Fleming published a few papers on his discovery but within three years had turned his attention to other matters. Those papers remained relatively obscure until 1939, when a pair of Oxford University researchers – Australian-born physiologist Howard Florey and German refugee chemist Ernst Boris Chain – took a fresh look at them. With a grant from the Rockefeller Foundation, they were able to isolate and purify penicillin. By 1941, the drug was being widely used in an injectable form. By the end of the Second World War, it was universally considered one of the greatest discoveries of all time.

Work on biosynthetic penicillins, formed through mould fermentation, led to work on semi-synthetic penicillins, which led to the science of antibiotics, which altered the way the medical profession dealt with illness. And as science changed, the nature of the pharmaceutical business changed too.

For much of the first half of the twentieth century, the industry was a by-product of the big German and Swiss chemical corporations. The companies supplied bulk chemicals to pharmacists, who then compounded those chemicals – mixed them right there on a bench in front of the customer – into finished drugs. But the war destroyed the German factories and, at the same time, required so many drugs, especially penicillin, that the American government backed American companies to assure production for the army. Once the war was over, those American companies, and a host of European companies too, filled the vacuum left by the destruction of German industry and moved gradually away from bulk chemical supply to become manufacturers and distributors of finished drugs.

This set the stage for the second wave, somewhere around the end of the 1960s, which saw science shift from chemical-based research towards what would be called biopharmaceutical research.

By learning how to clone proteins that can kill bacteria and otherwise reinforce the body's natural ability to fight disease, and by learning how to produce what are called monoclonal antibodies – which prevent bacteria from releasing poisons into the body – the industry opened the door for doctors to treat conditions that had once been considered untreatable and to prevent illness that had once been considered inevitable killers.

Superimposed over this were the earth-shattering social and economic ramifications of jet travel, satellite communications, and, before long, the Internet.

Within a quarter-century, the world would shrink into two distinct markets: the industrialized online First World, of which no corner is any farther away than the price of a local phone call; and the so-called developing markets, or Third World, which is the fragmented have-nots in the midst of being left behind.

Computers became faster, more powerful, and were better able to complete enormously complicated tasks in nanoseconds. Libraries of molecules were now easily stored, analyzed, and referenced. Databases were moved between laboratories with the click of a mouse. Disease models that once took years to create in test tubes or in living organisms were efficiently recreated on a desktop. Chemistry by robotics, and other microprocessor-controlled approaches, vastly increased the number of compounds that could be tested each year.

Out of these developments emerged the biotech sector, companies whose only assets were, often, whatever money shareholders poured into them. In a modern version of the California Gold Rush, suddenly every punter in tech stocks was betting that five scientists crammed into an office in Cambridge – England or Massachusetts – was on the verge of a breakthrough molecule that some drug company would pay handsomely for.

In the midst of this frenzy, the human genome was being mapped.

James Watson's and Francis Crick's discovery of the structure of DNA in 1953 galvanized the most dramatic transformation the pharmaceutical industry might ever see. Even though it would take nearly half a century before the final pieces in the map of the molecule of life could be put into place – it was officially declared complete in spring 2000 – the excitement and the promise generated by the project rivals any in science.

Even as recently as the early 1990s, the quest for new drugs saw the same companies chasing the same molecule because that was the limit of science and medicine at the time. Genomics dramatically changed that by expanding exponentially the number of molecular targets available. By understanding the basic mechanisms of disease, scientists had the keys to unlock the cures to human disease. Whatever blockbuster gene-based therapies that followed would guarantee Big Pharma's prosperity for decades.

⊂▭

Research and development, which is the heart of the pharmaceutical business, is an obstacle course.

It begins with the synthesis and extraction of a new molecule that scientists hope might produce a desired change in a biological system. They may be looking to arouse or to repress an enzyme, to somehow alter a metabolic pathway, or to create a physical change in a cellular structure.

Once those chemical compounds are identified, they are subjected to biological screening and pharmacological testing in the hopes of pinpointing any therapeutic potential. This goes from test tubes and isolated cell cultures to computer models and animals. As long as the compound continues to meet the therapeutic potential test, then structural modifications are made and every related compound is tested. The idea is to see which version of the molecule produces the most therapeutic promise while, at the same time, is the least potentially harmful.

Next, decisions must be made about dosage and stability. This is when the active compound is converted into a liquid, a tablet, a capsule, or any other delivery system. This is when strength dictates dosage – 50 mg twice a day, 100 mg before sleep, 500 mg once a week, etc. This is also when additional substances, called excipients, are added to the active ingredient – flavours to improve the taste, chemicals that bond the active ingredient into stable tablets, and chemicals that determine the drug's absorption in the body.

Further tests are now done on tissue cultures and animals to determine just how safe this new drug will be when finally administered to humans.

Drug trials are divided into three obligatory and well-defined stages:

Phase I is to determine how well the human body tolerates the drug at various doses, and studies the drug's rate of absorption, distribution, metabolism, and excretion. The testing is normally done on a small sampling of healthy volunteers.

Phase II uses a group of a few hundred patients suffering from the condition the drug is intended to treat. The idea is to look for efficacy and short-term side effects.

Phase III is the big study. The drug is administered to the largest sample group – which can range from hundreds to several thousand patients – to determine how it performs over an extended period of time. This is also the most expensive aspect of testing and can cost tens of thousands of dollars per patient.

More and more these days there is also a Phase IV, which is after-approval testing. This process can look for adverse events associated with the drug – most of them don't appear for the first year and, by law, must be reported to the regulatory agency – or can be turned into a cleverly disguised marketing device to interest doctors in the drug.

It can also be used by the marketing department to find its elusive USP – unique selling point.

Merck had been heavily promoting Mevacor and seizing a very large niche in the cholesterol-lowering market. It also had Zocor in the pipeline, a second anti-cholesterol drug that would one day replace Mevacor. Making the market even more crowded was Parke-Davis' Lipitor.

So Bristol-Myers Squibb decided to come at the competition from the blind side. After having spent nearly $150 million in clinical tests to win Federal Drug Administration (FDA) approval for its cholesterol-lowering Pravachol, the company committed another $50 million for a Phase IV trial to prove that the drug didn't just lower cholesterol but could also reduce the risk of heart attacks in otherwise healthy people with high cholesterol.

A sample group of nearly seven thousand people received either the drug or a placebo for six years. When the results were in, four years after Pravachol was already being marketed, the group taking the drug had 31 per cent fewer heart attacks and deaths than the group taking the placebo. It was an investment worth the time and money. Having proved that to the FDA's satisfaction, Bristol-Myers was then legally permitted to advertise Pravachol as a heart-attack prevention drug. And sales skyrocketed.

From synthesis and extraction of the molecule through to the end of Phase III can be a decade's work. To ensure that the end result is a safe and efficient drug, the industry is, at least in theory, very tightly regulated. But the regulations governing pharmaceutical products come from two distinct reservoirs of interest: public despair and corporate expediency.

There was once something called the 1906 Food and Drug Act in the United States, which did little more than require manufacturers to believe their drug worked. Companies could promise that their latest miracle drug would grow hair, cure cancer, and alter the tides, but as long as they mainly told the truth on the labels about what was inside the bottle, there was little the government could do about it.

In 1937, the S. E. Massengill Pharmaceutical Company of Bristol, Tennessee, changed that.

It developed a liquid form of Sulfanilamide, which was a popular concoction in those days to treat children's sore throats. Basically, the company took the powdered form of the drug and mixed it with diethylene glycol to make a drink. The company was not required to do any testing or otherwise prove that the drug was safe.

As anyone who drives a car in winter knows, diethylene glycol is antifreeze.

Children started getting very sick, and the fledgling FDA – created six years before – issued warnings to physicians that this drug was not to be used. Then children started dying. Massengill denied any responsibility. But after its chief chemist committed suicide and more than one hundred deaths were attributed to the drug, S. E. Massengill Pharmaceuticals Company was fined $26,000 for mislabelling – the only sanction the law would allow the government to place.

A year later, Congress acted to make certain that any company repeating an incident like that could be criminally responsible for producing an unsafe pharmaceutical. The Federal Food, Drug, and Cosmetic Act required drug companies to prove to the FDA that their product was safe and to include on labels such information as ingredients, recommended dosage, and side effects.

Whenever the need for primary regulation of the pharmaceutical industry is questioned, the Thalidomide story is dragged out.

Developed as a sedative by Chemie Grünenthal in Germany in 1957, Thalidomide's brand name was Contergan and it was billed as "completely non-poisonous." Although the drug was never manufactured in Canada, it was available as medical samples from late 1959, imported by the American company holding the rights, Richardson-Merrell.

By that time, reports were already circulating that patients who had taken Thalidomide in tablet form were showing symptoms of peripheral neuritis. An illness that can cause severe muscular cramps and a lack of coordination in the limbs, the damage is often irreversible. As Chemie Grünenthal was about to move the patient population away from a tablet to a liquid, nothing was done. Years later it would be reported that the company's pharmacologists had discovered, sometime in 1959, that liquid Thalidomide could be fatal under certain conditions. That report, if it ever existed, doesn't now, and all these years later, there's no way of being sure what the company knew.

The drug was extremely popular, sold in nearly fifty countries – at one point it was the third best-selling drug in Europe – and, at least in some of those countries, considered so safe that it was retailed as an over-the-counter remedy for morning sickness.

But not everybody was convinced that Thalidomide was harmless. Dr. Frances Kelsey was the medical officer at the FDA who was handling the Thalidomide approval dossier. Sometime in 1960, she heard of the peripheral neuritis side effect and was dissatisfied with the way Chemie Grünenthal had handled some routine pharmacologic tests. Kelsey's misgivings delayed the drug's approval for more than a year.

By that time, stories of horrific birth defects were sweeping across Europe, Australia, and Canada.

In the autumn of 1961, an Australian physician writing in the British medical journal, *The Lancet*, suggested there was a connection between Thalidomide and this sudden wave of babies being born with malformed arms and legs. A few months later, a physician in Hamburg published a study that directly linked those birth defects to Thalidomide. He was roundly accused of incompetence by Chemie Grünenthal and vilified by drug company experts who insisted he didn't have any scientific basis for his wild accusations. Two days later, Chemie Grünenthal conceded defeat and withdrew the drug.

Thalidomide stayed on the market in several countries for up to a year afterwards. It wasn't removed from the market in Canada until March 1962.

No one knows for certain, but it has been estimated that eight thousand to twelve thousand Thalidomide babies were born in Europe, Australia, and Japan. It's estimated that two hundred Thalidomide babies were born in Canada. Fewer than thirty were reported in the States. In those cases, the drug had either been obtained in Canada or was dispensed in Europe to the wives of American servicemen.

Kelsey received a medal from President John F. Kennedy for having saved the nation from this catastrophe, and, largely as a result of Thalidomide, Congress passed the Food, Drug, and Cosmetic Act of 1962, increasing the FDA's powers. Until Thalidomide, drugs were approved for safety only. Senator Estes Kefauver had been trying for years to include the concept of "efficacy" to drug licensing, and that's what was done. Post-Thalidomide drug approval in the United States – the Kefauver-Harris Amendments to the Food, Drug, and Cosmetic Act – now required that drugs had to be proven both safe and efficient.

Coinciding with the arrival of second-generation Thalidomide victims in Germany, Japan, Bolivia, and Britain – the deformed children of the original Thalidomide babies – the drug is seeing something of a resurgence. An Israeli doctor, having prescribed it as a sedative for leprosy patients, noticed that it healed some of their sores. He reported his findings and serious testing began in the early 1990s. The FDA approved the use of Thalidomide in 1998. It is being used today as a treatment in certain cancers, and also for mouth and throat ulcers that accompany AIDS. Needless to say, at the same time, the FDA imposed unprecedented restrictions on its distribution.

It is available in Canada, also highly restricted, through the Emergency Drug Release Program, used in trials for several illnesses, including leprosy.

Health Canada, as administrators of the Food and Drugs Act, is responsible for approving new drugs. The system is much like the FDA's in that manufacturers are required to prove that their drug is safe, pure, potent, stable, and effective.

There is a general impression that Health Canada approves or disapproves on the basis of what other countries do. And there may well be an influence. But the Health Protection Branch, which carries out the reviews, goes through all the paces itself.

"We sometimes do arrive at different decisions," notes Dr. Michele Brill-Edwards, a former senior regulator. "Even if a drug has gone to market in the U.S., we will hold it up if we have to, and vice versa. In general, an FDA decision can have a strong influence on a Canadian reviewer. After all, how important is the Pope to the Catholic Church? But an FDA decision is not a red light or a green light in Canada. You can't just say it's cleared in the States, so I'll just sign my name. A good reviewer, someone who is competent scientifically and medically, would see it as a challenge, to look at a drug already cleared by the FDA and try to find something they might have missed."

One area where the two agencies are exactly alike is in what they're looking at: scientific evaluations and clinical tests that have been designed and paid for by drug companies looking for specific results.

"The pharmaceutical industry," Brill-Edwards continues, "is highly skilled at controlling the world in which they operate. They tend to be able to suppress a lot of the information that would normally have the public up in arms. The stories are never heard. The impression is that this is a wonderful industry, highly principled and ethical, but really it's an industry like any other."

The power of the industry is very visible to someone working at a regulatory agency.

"The interest of citizens is obscured by the power of corporate money in the political system. As a senior physician at the Health Protection Branch, I would say, 'We're going to lose lives here,' but it would have little weight because no one was worried about losing lives as long as they don't get blamed. What people were worried about was the continuance of power. The dilemma of those in power is not 'Do you serve citizens versus do you serve corporations?' That's a no-brainer. People in power serve the corporations because they have the money. The dilemma is 'How do you serve all of them or most of them in any given decision?' If Merck wants drug policy to go one way and Glaxo wants it to go another way, then there's a real dilemma. But as long as the industry is consistent in its demands, they hold sway. On the issue of individual drugs, what you often find is that the companies curry favour with the people at the top, and the people at the top then signal the people in the lower echelons."

Brill-Edwards witnessed that first-hand.

Since she was the senior physician responsible for drug approvals, one of her staff informed her one day that he'd just had a telephone call from a senior administrator asking why a certain dossier was still on his desk. He wanted to know why the drug wasn't yet marketed in Canada when it was marketed in England.

The staff member found this call quite unsettling because he had perhaps a dozen dossiers he was working on, but only one this administrator was interested in.

"The call he'd received was totally inappropriate," says Brill-Edwards. "I told him to forget about it and to keep asking questions about the drug." She says she then rang the administrator and said, "It's my understanding that you're concerned about such-and-such a drug. It is not yet on the market in Canada, whereas it is marketed in England, because this is not a safe drug and we have unanswered deaths we need to investigate." The administrator said thank you and that was the end of that. "The minute he knew that his bullying was not going to work," says Brill-Edwards, "he stepped back. He didn't want any record that would show he'd been trying to push this fellow around."

Michele Brill-Edwards resigned from the Health Protection Branch in 1996 after making allegations about corruption and safety abuses.

The drug went to market and is commonly used.

Without research and development, there would be no pharmaceutical industry.

Without patents, there would be no research and development.

The Oxford English Dictionary defines a patent as "an open letter or document, usually from a sovereign or person in authority, issued for various purposes, e.g., to put on record some agreement or contract, to authorize or command something to be done, to confer some right, privilege, title, or office; now especially, to grant for a statutory term to a person or persons the sole right to make, use or sell some invention."

Historians trace the origins of modern patents back to the Venetians, who, around 1470 or so, found themselves losing trade to Florence and the other city states. They needed to stimulate local industry with new products. At the same time, they recognized two important facts of medieval business life: inventing a new product or a process to make a new product was expensive and risky; and no inventor could be expected to take such risks unless he had a reasonable chance to recoup his costs and make a profit.

Needing some sort of mechanism to shorten the odds for the inventor, the Venetians came up with a pact: If an inventor could prove that the "fruits of his genius" were novel (a product or process the world had never seen before); and if his invention accomplished a task (it solved some sort of problem); and if his invention worked (he had to build it or demonstrate it); and if a committee appointed by the state could understand how it worked (so that, eventually, other people could duplicate the product or process); then the state would award, guarantee, and protect a time-limited monopoly during which the innovator was free to exploit the process or product for commercial gain.

The idea quickly spread from Venice through the rest of Europe, encouraged by trade guilds seeking protection on the manufacture and design of their products. More than half a millennium later, almost all nations maintain comparable deals with inventors.

Interestingly enough, patent law – along with the English language – is one of the more substantial vestiges of the British colonization of North America. First established in the Massachusetts Colony in 1641, patents were set in stone in the United States – alongside copyright – by being included in the constitution. The founding fathers assigned Congress the power "to promote the progress of science and useful arts, by securing for limited times to authors and inventors the exclusive right to their respective writings and discoveries."

Arguably, the pharmaceutical industry's global might derives directly from those twenty-seven words.

When Jonas Salk invented the polio vaccine, back in the 1950s, researchers and pharmaceutical companies didn't rush to the Patent Office. Salk was even asked one day who owned the patent on his vaccine. He answered, "No one," then asked, "Why? Could you patent the sun?"

The world is not the same place today.

Pharmaceutical patents fall into four basic categories. First, there are patents that protect the chemical compound. Second, there are patents that protect the compositional use of the compound as a drug. Third, there are patents that protect the specific way the drug is to be used. And fourth, there are patents that protect the process the drug company uses to manufacture the drug.

By the time a drug reaches a pharmacist's shelf, there may be dozens of patents protecting the company's rights to it. That way, even though a drug may have only that twelve-year average of market protection under the first patent, it can still enjoy many more years under subsequent patents.

According to Stephen Schondelmeyer at the Prime Institute, a classic example of that was SmithKline's Tagamet. At one point it boasted twenty-six different patents.

"But that's not unusual," says Schondelmeyer. "You can get a patent on the chemical entity itself and on every process by which you can make that chemical entity. That way, when the entity's patent expires, you still have a patent on all the processes by which you make it, so you're not going to have any competition. Then you can have a patent on the dosage form that the product is placed in, such as a sustained-release tablet or a patch or whatever fancy delivery system can be developed for it. You can patent use, that is, a patent on the drug for arrhythmias, and another patent on the drug for AIDS. It's not unusual to have twenty to thirty patents on any given drug product because it keeps away the competition that much longer."

The haste to patent every possible aspect of a drug has reached such proportions that multinational corporations are claiming patents on human genes. That's the result of a 1980 U.S. Supreme Court decision. The court felt that by allowing scientists to patent more than just a process, it would open up a unique American industry. In that sense, it was right. What it didn't anticipate were the conflicts in intellectual property it was creating and the impact this would have on the rest of the world.

This colonization of the genome is similar to what happened when Europe sailed to the New World. They carved up whatever they found and marked their rights to it by sticking flags in the sand. That's essentially what's happening with the genome. Pharmaceutical companies feel they should be able to patent indigenous plants found in countries where the pharmaceutical company is not even necessarily open for business. It's happening, for example, all over Asia, where Asians don't have the sequencing technology and can't just declare these things their property. Big Pharma and an army of biotech firms are shoving flags onto the mountaintops, claiming patents on these genes, ostensibly so that they can develop drugs that will help humankind, but in practice, simply because some day they may be profitable. Anyway, it's only Big Pharma and western biotech that has the technology that allows them to say, "We can patent it."

Until 2000, the length of patent protection varied from country to country. The average was seventeen years starting from the date the patent was issued. But as a result of heavyweight political lobbying from special interest groups – including Big Pharma – America exerted enough influence over the World Trade Organization to change that. These days the norm is twenty years, although the clock starts ticking from the date the patent is filed.

The two industries most dependent on patent protection in the modern world are the chemical and pharmaceutical sectors. Pharmaceutical and related biotech industries file more patents each year than any other sector with chemical companies, many of which have pharmaceutical interests – including Bayer, Hoechst, BASF, ICI, and Roche – ranking second.

There's no set time to file for a patent, nor any connection between the development stage of a drug and the patent filing. It can happen at any time during the process, but typically it comes as soon as possible after the invention is discovered. The philosophy is "File now and worry how good it works later."

"As soon as they identify a compound family that they think will be valuable to them in their research," says Dr. Michael Ryan, who directs the Study on Innovation, Expression and Development at Georgetown University in Washington and is the author of *Knowledge Diplomacy: Global Competition and the Politics of Intellectual Property*, "they file for the patent right away."

That gets into what Ryan calls "the appropriability problem" – how does a company appropriate its investment in a new product. As an example, he looks at an auto manufacturer such as BMW. "They are known to have extraordinary engineering capabilities, and they produce this awesome sports sedan that nobody can quite copy. Is it because BMW has patents? Yes. But that's not the source of their competitive advantage. It's much more dispersed than that. They have new technologies, the way they manufacture the car, their brand, their trademark. It's hard to actually appropriate what BMW puts into that car."

Comparing BMW to a pharmaceutical company, it's easy to see that the investment is the patent. "BMW's product is very difficult to copy. The product that a pharmaceutical company makes is very easy to copy," says Ryan. "At the end of the day it's just a little chemical compound. It may take them ten years to innovate it, but it doesn't take very long to copy. What then is the source of the competitive advantage of a pharmaceutical company? Manufacturing is important but manufacturing is easy. So, it's their marketing ability and the patent on the compound."

Drug companies always equate returns on R&D with patent length, although there are arguments to suggest that, in fact, extended patent length can inhibit innovation. Take the case of a drug well established in the marketplace. Unseating it from a prominent position can be excessively costly. Included in those costs are the risks of patent infringement. Instead of competing, many companies simply choose to take a different direction and invest their R&D budgets in areas where they can win a prominent position, or they elect to extend the line of their own block-buster drugs or they invest in me-toos.

Ironically, it is probably not the lure of a patent monopoly on just any drug as much as it is a pending patent expiration of a blockbuster that drives real ingenuity. The imminent loss of patent rights to Prozac moved Eli Lilly and Company to new heights in its quest to replace it. The company even acknowledged in its 1998 annual report, "The Prozac patent expiration is serving as a catalyst to bring greater intensity to everything we do."

It's much the same for AstraZeneca racing to replace the ulcer drug Losec, for Schering looking to replace Claritin, and for Merck needing to find a high-cholesterol medication to replace Zocor.

Back in the 1950s, U.S. Senator Estes Kefauver set out to examine the prescription drugs industry. His staff studied innovative, widely used drugs, looking at such areas as price and also at patents. What they found was that a large number of countries did not have patent protection. Either it wasn't written into law, or if it was, it wasn't enforced. In other countries, there was compulsory licensing, a system that permits a government to override a patent, legally permitting a company to produce under license a product – in this case a drug – in which a valid patent is held by another company.

It's not a system Big Pharma likes at all.

"The issue Kefauver looked at was what happens without patents," says Larry Sasich at the watchdog organization Public Citizen. "Our drug industry's argument has always been that without patents, innovation is stifled and nobody would bother developing new drugs. But Kefauver's argument, based on what had been developed and was widely used, suggests that may not be true. Certainly patent protection and exclusivity is a driving force for some companies who go to extraordinary lengths to protect the exclusivity of their products."

Some companies are less subtle than others when it comes to patents. Under American law, a drug company may be entitled to a six-month patent extension for every year the drug has spent in the regulatory approval process. Ever since the mid-1990s, Schering-Plough has been trying to convince Congress that because unnecessary delays and ineptitude by the FDA slowed the agency's approval of Claritin, the government owes it an extra three years' protection. Since the 1996 congressional elections, the company is said to have spent nearly $20 million lobbying Congress and donating money to campaigns. Public Citizen, which has been charting Schering's course through the political waters, estimates that for its investment, if it succeeds, the company can expect an added return of $7 billion over the next ten years. This on top of its usual $2.7 billion in annual sales. In the meantime, Schering-Plough swung an additional six months from the FDA under a law that grants extra patent protection for drugs tested on children. That alone is worth another $1.35 billion.

Actually, it almost succeeded getting its three-year increase during the summer of 2000 when nobody was looking. The company's extension legislation was snuck onto the bottom of a military construction appropriations bill. At the last minute someone spotted it, leaked the story to the press, and it was removed.

There's no disputing that FDA approval for Claritin took longer than for most drugs. A U.S. Government Audit Office (GAO) report issued in mid-2000 explains that the FDA studied Claritin for six years and five months, which is nearly three years longer than the average for a similar drug. Six years in the process could, indeed, qualify the company for that extra three years. Schering-Plough's version is that one of the reasons for the delay was an FDA reorganization. But a closer reading shows that the FDA reorganization played no part at all in the Claritin approval process. Instead, the GAO found, the company had supplied inadequate studies supporting the tablet form of the drug and the FDA was concerned about the potential significance of animal carcinogenicity data for humans. Schering-Plough had also submitted thirty-seven major amendments during the agency's consideration of the drug, almost four times more than most companies and most applications.

CHAPTER 3

MONEY, EGO, AND POWER

A drug manufacturer in Bombay, India, felt the pain of the people of Ghana – where nearly one-third of the population is HIV-positive – and decided to do something to help. So in mid-2000, Cipla Pharmaceuticals shipped to the Ministry of Health in Accra a drug called Duovir, which Cipla legally manufactures under Indian law.

For its effort, Cipla received this letter from Glaxo Wellcome:

"It has come to our attention that you have imported your product Duovir, which contains lamivudine and zidovudine, into Ghana. Glaxo Group Limited has exclusive rights under the following patents that cover lamivudine and zidovudine formulations in Ghana: AP11, AP136, AP162, AP3000. Importation of Duovir into Ghana by Cipla or any of its affiliates represents an infringement of our Company's exclusive patent rights."

G. G. Brereton, head of patents in the global intellectual property department at Glaxo, understood that the shipment was characterized as a donation, and therefore Glaxo would not on this occasion be seeking immediate redress. Still, Brereton made it perfectly clear that the company took patents and intellectual property very seriously – irrespective of those people who could not possibly afford to pay Glaxo for the drugs they needed to stay alive – and the company categorically reserved the right "to enforce our patent rights against any further acts of infringement."

⊂▶

By the mid-1980s, the pharmaceutical industry found itself a prisoner of the new technologies.

In many ways, drug companies were in the same position the automobile industry had found itself when Henry Ford invented the assembly line. There were a lot of other people making cars in those days, but this more efficient, cheaper way forced the automobile industry into massive consolidation until only three or four top players were left.

What began as a trickle of drug company mergers soon turned into a flood.

Wyeth and Ayerst combined and then became part of American Home Products; Bristol-Myers linked up with Squibb; and Smith Kline French merged with Beckman.

Marion Laboratories merged with Merrell Dow Pharmaceuticals; Hoechst purchased Roussel Uclaf, then acquired Marion Merrell Dow, and began to operate as HMR. Rhône-Poulenc took over Rorer; Rhône-Poulenc Rorer grabbed Fisons and then the two merged their life sciences business with Hoechst to form Aventis.

Sanofi merged with Winthrop, then took over Synthelabo; Pharmacia merged with Upjohn; Ciba-Geigy teamed up with Sandoz to create Novartis; Alliance Sante merged with Unichem; and the Swedish Astra joined forces with the British Zeneca to become AstraZeneca.

By now SmithKline Beckman was a major player in the American market. The Beecham Group had an important presence outside the United States. And rather than go head-to-head in Europe, it made much better sense to become SmithKline Beecham.

Glaxo took over Wellcome, largely driven by the fate of the ulcer drug Zantac. Representing more than 40 per cent of Glaxo's sales, Zantac was just two years away from losing patent protection. Wellcome's product line offered drugs selling strongly enough to soften the loss.

After several years of trying to work it all out, SmithKline Beecham and Glaxo Wellcome merged to become the industry's biggest company, Glaxo SmithKline.

Pharmacia & Upjohn went into talks with Monsanto, and Warner-Lambert tried to merge with American Home Products when Pfizer stepped in to grab Warner-Lambert. "We look at every merger to see if we should have done it or whether we should try to screw it up," Bill Steere, Pfizer's chairman and chief executive, said at the time.

For many observers, these mergers were a solid indication the companies could no longer expect organic growth.

Dr. P. Roy Vagelos, former chairman and CEO of the pharmaceutical giant Merck, is one of them. "This is often what happens when drugs are running out of patent protection and a company doesn't have adequate new products coming through its own pipeline. They merge to fill holes in pipelines. And, of course, to cut costs. One could work with much smaller manufacturing capacity, perhaps make R&D more efficient, and make sales and marketing organizations more efficient by putting more drugs in the hands of smaller numbers of people. All of that has driven the industry to consolidation."

So has, Vagelos acknowledges, the "biggest lion in the jungle" syndrome: the animal that doesn't eat gets eaten. "When I left Merck, we were number one in the world for prescription drugs with something like 5.5 per cent. The share we had of the U.S. market was something like 10.5 per cent. This, at a time when market leaders in other industries could enjoy shares ranging from 20 to 30 per cent. We were significantly larger than the number-two drug company but not very large in overall market share. Because it is such a very fragmented market, for many companies, consolidation was always likely to follow."

Investment analysts suggest that, in order to maintain "acceptable growth expectations," each of the top-twelve drug companies needs to come up with three major new drugs per year. Plainly, that's not going to happen. And once a board of directors accepts that the company will fall short – in so doing, possibly antagonizing the investment community – the company becomes susceptible to a deal aimed at keeping Wall Street happy.

Which brings into play the often overlooked role of the investment banks themselves. As a group, they make absolute fortunes by midwifing mergers. The carrot they dangle are huge payoffs for the board members who won't be in the new company and huge salaries and bonuses for the board members who stay on. While board members are not supposed to put their personal interests in front of the interests of the shareholders, with so much at stake, it's not all that difficult to find shareholder value somewhere.

One of those places is yet another force that seems to be propelling mergers: the reshaped markets.

Merged companies are always crowing that they now have more money to spend on R&D. But when *Business Week* looked at the Big Pharma mergers of the 1990s, the magazine was left to conclude that few of them had actually delivered on that promise. "Big budgets do allow companies to conduct cutting-edge research, but there is little evidence that massive research spending leads to a better record in developing hot new drugs."

None of the Big Pharma mergers since 1980 – for example, Glaxo plus Wellcome, and Ciba-Geigy plus Sandoz – produced the promised long-term growth. Nor were there any real increases in productivity. In fact, almost every merger since 1970 has led to a subsequent loss in market share. In the end, what many of these mergers become is a substitute for capital investment. The combined companies have more to spend on marketing and – critically – a clearer field in which to market. In 1995, twenty-five companies controlled more than half of the global drug market. Five years later, 53 per cent of the market is in the hands of fifteen companies. The top four alone account for just over 20 per cent.

Simply put, mergers are a lot better for the industry and for investors than they are for consumers because they make for diminished competition.

They also translate into increased political might.

"Big Pharma is too politicized and too politically powerful," says Dr. Sheldon Krimsky of Tufts University in Boston, one of the country's leading authorities on urban and environmental policy. "This is increasingly so, especially with the consolidations that are going on throughout the industry. Just look at the amount of capital now invested in these pharmaceutical companies. A lot of this happened because genetic engineering created even greater expectations on the industry. The tower of genetic engineering gave them that much more incentive to invest."

In 1980, there were approximately eighty major pharmaceutical houses in the world. Twenty years later, there were only thirty-five. By 2010, there may be as few as twelve global players. Between 1997 and 1999, more than half of the top-twenty-five drug companies were involved in some sort of merger. Seven of the top-ten largest companies in the year 2000 started the previous decade with a different name.

CD

During the earliest years of the Mulroney-Reagan era, it was increasingly evident to Big Pharma that patent protection had weakened since the General Agreement on Tariffs and Trade (GATT) was established in 1947. Pharmaceutical companies were especially worried by the prospect of losing their return on investment in developing countries where patent protection was either non-existent or totally disregarded. And while Big Pharma was hardly alone – the film and music industries had a stake in seeing intellectual property protection reinforced – the industry took it upon itself to call Washington to arms.

Helping to marshal the forces was Vice-President George Bush, an old friend Big Pharma knew it could count on.

After losing his job as director of the CIA when Gerald Ford lost the White House to Jimmy Carter in 1976, Bush made himself available for corporate directorships. He was soon invited onto the board of Eli Lilly in Indianapolis, where he remained active for two years until launching his own presidential bid. When he was beaten in the primaries by Ronald Reagan, Bush accepted the number-two spot on the Republican ticket. At the time, the largest single holding in Bush's personal portfolio was $145,000 worth of Lilly stock. Once he took office, he was legally obliged to place his shares in a blind trust. But he had the right, which he exercised, to appoint one of his oldest and closest friends to maintain the trust. In theory, Bush should have had no way of knowing whether, at any point during his tenure in office, the trust continued to hold those shares.

In March 1982, the vice-president took the unprecedented step of intervening in a rule change then making its way through the Treasury Department. At issue were substantial tax breaks afforded pharmaceutical companies operating in Puerto Rico. Treasury Secretary Donald Regan appeared to be ready to tighten the rules, which would result in America's pharmaceutical industry – including Lilly – paying higher taxes. Bush urged Regan to look at the rule changes with an eye towards making them more amenable to Big Pharma. When someone at Treasury leaked the story, Bush wrote Regan to ask that his original request be withdrawn because he felt "uncomfortable about the appearance of my active personal involvement in the details of a tax matter directly affecting a company with which I once had a close association."

Nothing quite so nakedly transparent was attempted, at least not until the 1988 Republican Convention. Once Bush had secured his party's nomination for president, he chose as his running mate Indiana's Senator Dan Quayle, a member of the Pulliam family, who were among Lilly's biggest and most influential shareholders. It had been Quayle's father who'd brought Bush onto the Lilly board eleven years before.

With friends in high places, Big Pharma's lobby persuaded Congress that U.S. trade negotiators had to safeguard American products from any and all violations under GATT, the North American Free Trade Agreement (NAFTA), and the Trade Related Aspects of Intellectual Property (TRIPS) agreement.

It's arguable whether governments should flex their muscle in private commercial disputes. But when Bristol-Myers Squibb complained to Washington that the Argentinians were violating patent rights to the cancer drug Taxol, the American government stared down Buenos Aires by threatening stiff trade sanctions.

On those occasions when the TRIPS argument doesn't work, trade representatives preach a gimmick cooked up by Big Pharma called TRIPS-PLUS. They warn governments and health ministries that it is illegal for generic manufacturers to develop drugs in a country when a valid patent is still in force (which is not true everywhere); that the practice of compulsory licensing, which allows poor countries to produce essential drugs in a national emergency, is flat-out illegal (untrue); and that no national health system is permitted to use only the generic product when the brand-name drug is available in the market (again untrue).

A few years ago, Thailand had only one drug available to treat cryptococcal meningitis, a fatal disease associated with AIDS. The drug fluconazole was manufactured locally by Pfizer under the name Triflucan. A month's treatment cost 15,000 bahts — more than $400 — which pretty much put it out of the reach of the average citizen. So two Thai companies came along and manufactured a bioequivalent version for less than a third of Pfizer's price. It was still too expensive for the bulk of the population, but it opened up the market to a lot of people.

Pfizer complained. And U.S. trade representatives threatened the Thai authorities that, under TRIPS-PLUS, if the two copycat patent violators weren't shut down, Washington had the right to tax Thai exports to the United States. In less than six months, Pfizer's monopoly had been restored.

The reason it's called TRIPS-PLUS is because it's what Big Pharma would like to add to TRIPS. But TRIPS-PLUS is nothing more than a figment of Big Pharma's imagination. It does not exist in law or treaty.

Then, too, sleight-of-hand is something it's pretty good at. When it came time for the U.S. Congress to ratify the Uruguay Round Agreements Act as part of GATT, the bill was put to a vote late one night when there was only just a quorum in the Senate. Big Pharma, whose strategy is simple – seek to extend patents wherever possible – had somehow lobbied an extra few lines into the bill that would grant an additional three-year patent extension to a number of top-selling drugs. No one noticed it was there, or understood the ramifications of it, until the treaty had long been ratified.

It was Big Pharma's lobby in Washington that also set the stage for major changes to come out of Ottawa.

Canada's Patent Act of 1923 had opened the door to compulsory licensing, which was designed to encourage competition and lower prices. But it didn't work. Because the act required that those drugs made under licence had to be manufactured in Canada, only forty-nine applications were filed in forty-six years for compulsory licences and a mere twenty-two were granted.

So until 1969, the situation for pharmaceuticals in Canada was pretty much the same as it was in the United States. There were very few generic drugs, and prices were, accordingly, high.

As Canada began to develop a more comprehensive system of medicare, the cost of drugs became a real concern. In response, there were three commissions of inquiry: the Restrictive Trade Practices Commission; the Royal Commission on Health Services; and the Special Committee of the House of Commons. The commissions generally agreed that drugs were too expensive – they were being priced at up to one thousand times cost – and that there was no rational justification for it other than the fact that the pharmaceutical companies could get away with it. At the same time, there were few pharmaceutical industry jobs in the country. Big Pharma's turnover in Canada was out of all proportion to the number of people the companies employed when compared to other industries.

It was clear that something was very wrong.

All three commissions singled out patent protection as the villain.

Prime Minister Pierre Elliott Trudeau's Liberal government set about trying to fix it with Bill C-102, which extended compulsory licensing and allowed the importation of drugs under licence. The royalty payment, which the licensee had to pay to the patent holder, was set at 4 per cent. The bill provided the necessary impetus to Canada's struggling generic industry and fostered the growth of provincial drug programs. They not only subsidized medication for the elderly and people on welfare, they also mandated that generics should be substituted for the more expensive branded versions. Generics, which by law must be the bioequivalent of the patented drug, now arrived on the market within five to seven years of the original. But the faster prices dropped, the faster Big Pharma stepped up its lobbying efforts to get the law changed.

Two years after C-102 was passed, the Economic Council of Canada issued *A Report on Intellectual and Industrial Property*. The council recommended a generalized system of compulsory licensing, which frightened the multinational drug companies so much they leapt into the arms of their new best friend, Quebec. The provincial government there offered concessions to the multinationals – all of which were foreign-owned subsidiaries – and, in return, looked to them for investment and employment. It was the start of a beautiful friendship that would see Big Pharma work its way into the very soul of Quebec, becoming such an economic and politically powerful force that it caused some people to wonder if the province had made a deal with the devil.

Interestingly enough, despite Big Pharma's warnings, there is very little evidence that compulsory licensing affected its profitability or, for that matter, its prices. According to a major study at the beginning of the 1980s, Canada was the world's second most profitable pharmaceutical market, behind the United States. In fact, since 1967, the multinationals had been growing at a better rate in Canada than they had in the States. The industry consistently ranked in the top-five most profitable industries in Canada and had only lost about 3.1 per cent of the market to the generic companies.

Still, Big Pharma pushed to get rid of compulsory licensing.

The federal government established the Eastman Commission, named for H. C. Eastman, the bureaucrat designated to investigate the effects of compulsory licensing for the minister of supply and services. His findings, published in 1984, were formally known as the *Report of the Commission of Inquiry into the Pharmaceutical Industry*. His conclusion was that the Canadian system was the best in the world. Not only was it making health care affordable in Canada, it was saving hundreds of millions of dollars a year.

But 1984 was an election year and Brian Mulroney was promising that if the Tories formed a government, he intended to do something about compulsory licensing. Once he came to power, he negotiated the Free Trade Agreement between Canada and the United States. With the Reagan administration's connections to Big Pharma, it's hardly surprising that the United States lobbied heavily on behalf of the drug companies.

But then, Mulroney didn't need much persuading.

His pal Ronny Reagan let it be known that there could be problems with the free trade agreement unless Mulroney got rid of compulsory licensing. That was just the excuse the prime minister needed. In 1987, the government passed Bill C-22. It was couched as a compromise, but what it did was hand the branded drug companies a monopoly by delaying licences for generics until the patented drug has been on the market for seven years.

For the generic industry, after so many years of feast, it was a major setback, albeit one they could live with. However, Mulroney didn't stop there. The branded companies kept up the pressure and so did George Bush when he took over at the White House. Mulroney cooked up Bill C-91, had to table it until he got re-elected, then dusted it off again and passed it in 1993.

He'd finally eliminated compulsory licensing altogether.

The Canadian generic drug company Apotex was intending to make enalapril, its version of Merck's Vasotec, then the best-selling drug in Canada. The American patent was issued in 1983, but the Canadian patent wasn't issued until 1990. Apotex was already making enalapril by then. As soon as Merck got its patent, Apotex went after the compulsory licence.

The government, needing to find a date after which no compulsory licences would be issued, made C-91 retroactive to December 20, 1991, stopping Apotex in its tracks.

It has been suggested that some of the lawyers hired to lobby for Merck were former associates of Brian Mulroney. Although Michael Wilson was the minister of industry at the time, insiders insist that the bill was driven directly out of the Prime Minister's Office.

Early in the new year, purportedly to bring Canada's drug patent laws in line with the Reagan-Bush-Mulroney North American Free Trade Agreement, a few extra clauses were added at the very last minute. Apotex filed a lawsuit to force the government to issue the compulsory licence for enalapril on the grounds that when the request was originally made, Apotex had satisfied all of the regulatory requirements. As part of the litigation, Apotex brought a motion for judgment that the court decided would be returnable on March 9, 1993.

In late February, upon the third reading of Bill C-91 in the House of Commons, the government stuck in another provision, this one allowing them to pass regulations to prevent patent infringement. The generic industry was up in arms. It was a clear ploy to cater to Big Pharma. The government promised to consult the generic companies before anything was put into place.

On March 9, counsel for the government went into court, where Apotex was expecting a judgment, and asked for an adjournment of the hearing. The judge granted it and asked the parties to reconvene March 16.

As soon as the postponement was given, the government rushed into law – effective March 12 (and without the promised advanced discussion) – the Patented Medicines Notice of Compliance Regulations.

Specific only to pharmaceuticals – some people claim they are therefore discriminatory – they are all the more outrageous in light of Mulroney's original justification for the elimination of compulsory licensing, which was so as not to discriminate against any single field of technology.

In the case of *Apotex v. Merck*, Mulroney had substantially moved the goalposts in favour of Big Pharma.

But Apotex had a rabbit up its sleeve. It had been developing the drug and had stockpiled some supply, awaiting the day when it could sell it. The court ruled that Apotex had a vested right to the compulsory licence because it was all done before Parliament said it couldn't do it. So the court went with Apotex. The government appealed, lost, and took it to the Supreme Court, where Apotex won again.

Yet the victory was Pyrrhic.

Apotex was only allowed to use up its non-infringing inventory, and once that was gone, it was out of the enalapril business.

Merck took back its cash cow.

When a generic company files a new drug submission, it has to notify the branded company that it's doing so. Mulroney's regulations specified that notification had to take place before the new drug submission was made. They also said that no generic drug firm would get an approval from Health Canada until after any claim of alleged patent infringement was litigated. In other words, Mulroney managed to impose an automatic injunction not when a patent was actually being infringed, but when Big Pharma said it might be.

Jean Chrétien came to power and changed things again. The law as it stands states that the new drug submission must come first, but it keeps the clause that allows the branded company to halt the submission by producing a list of patents it claims will be violated. The list can be as long as the branded company cares to make it, and the patents on it may or may not be applicable. The generic company then has to respond. Of course, the response will be, the patents are invalid or will not be infringed. At that point, the branded company files a lawsuit. The government is then prohibited from issuing a notice of compliance to the generic company until the claims are litigated. That can take a long time. Cases that run five years or more are not unheard of.

It effectively keeps the generic off the market until the case is settled.

Making the situation even more intolerable for the Canadian generic industry, there's no oversight of what the branded company has included on its patent list until everybody comes to court. Obviously, the longer the list, the more work and time it takes to whittle it down. There's only one other country in the world that has a similar provision, and that's the United States. But in the U.S., the branded company only gets up to thirty months to fight the infringement.

By changing the notification time to after the new drug submission is made, the government further tightened the screws on the generic companies. Now, for a generic firm to get on the market, it has to spend millions of dollars developing the drug to meet the new drug submission requirements, knowing that as soon as it notifies the branded company, its development work is guaranteed to be halted for an unspecified time. It then has to spend more millions of dollars in litigation with the real possibility that, at the end of it all, even if it wins, by the time it finally gets the drug onto the market, the market for it may no longer exist.

It's draconian, the generic manufacturers complain, and makes their part of the drug industry no longer viable.

Which is exactly why Big Pharma romances politicians.

CHAPTER 4

IN A PERFECT WORLD

Getting a drug to market is a process in which momentum builds so quickly – fuelled by political influence, the sheer weight of its legal muscle, and ingeniously sophisticated marketing techniques – it takes on a life of its own.

Companies that discover problems looming on the horizon automatically go into damage-control mode. They snuff out in-house fires while denying that anything is burning. The media pick up on the story and say, "There's something wrong." The company denies the story while rushing around to get rid of the evidence, just in case. The media now come up with proof that people are dying. The company rounds on the media for errors in reporting, castigating them for sensationalizing what is obviously a minor story and is, in any case, under control.

Eventually the politicians wake up, if for no other reason than to get their faces on the evening news. Now the company refuses to allow any employee to go on camera – that will teach the bastards in the media a lesson – and instead issues written statements that point to a deliberate conspiracy by competitors, left-leaning newspapers, and alien forces all plotting against loyal employees and their families. The politicians find themselves forced to embarrass the regulators into asking questions. When the company finally runs out of room, its lawyers hunt down loopholes through which the company can escape.

Built into the system is a fall guy. It's hard to generalize about how high up the ladder this goes – it's different in every case – but more often than not it's someone in the pharmaceutical division. A senior medical executive who's about ready to retire anyway. Perhaps the medical director himself. Someone who makes the go or no-go decisions on what to test and what trials to do. The company says, "We'll pay you off, but we're going to use you as the patsy here." Inside the industry, he's referred to as "the vice-president for going to jail." The only requirements for the job is that his prosecution must have very little corporate impact in the long run and that he's far enough away from the board of directors so as not to jeopardize them.

Once the company has someone's head firmly banged onto the stake, the board comes down from the mountain to make everything right to the dead patients' families by offering a settlement with a lot of zeroes on the end, but only, of course, with the proviso that, despite all this money, it must be understood that no one did anything wrong.

At least that's how it usually works when the regulators can be bothered to act, you know, in a perfect world.

The Fen part came from the compound fenfluramine, which was approved by the FDA as a treatment for obesity in 1973 and commercially called several names, among them Pondimin. It was a tablet manufactured, distributed, and marketed by A. H. Robins until 1987, when American Home Products acquired Robins and moved the drug onto its Wyeth-Ayerst product list. There it languished, unimpressively, for the next five years.

The Phen part came from the compound phentermine, another appetite suppressant, which had been around since 1959 and wasn't exactly setting the world on fire.

In separate approvals of the two drugs, the FDA stipulated that they be used alone and only for a few weeks at a time. The FDA had also listed some side effects, most notably that fenfluramine induced fatigue. But in 1988, the National Institutes of Health sponsored a study at the University of Rochester in New York that combined the two drugs. Four years later, the data showed that patients taking this combination over a six-month period rapidly lost weight, sustained their weight loss for several years, and did not suffer the drowsiness that had been seen with fenfluramine.

The combination was not approved by the FDA and therefore was considered an off-label use. Yet doctors prescribed it so often, creating a major sales boom, that for three years just about all fenfluramine sales went into the mixture. Weight clinics even advertised Fen-Phen as the fastest and easiest way to lose weight.

Then, in June 1996, Redux arrived.

This newer, supposedly better variation on fenfluramine, a compound called dexfenfluramine, was also not recommended for use in combination with any other drug. Originally patented in 1980 by a professor at the Massachusetts Institute of Technology, Redux was licensed first to a French pharmaceutical company, Laboratoires Servier, which sold it under various brand names throughout Europe, including Isomeride and Adifax. It was approved in more than seventy countries, and one estimate has it that more than 10 million people have used it.

A small drug development company called Interneuron obtained the American rights from Servier in 1990 and ran all the necessary trials to take it to the FDA. The first time the drug came up for approval, the agency's advisory committee voted no. It was concerned about side effects. When the group met a second time to discuss Redux in April 1996, the meeting was unusually hot-tempered. The FDA chain of command recommended against approval. That was signalled first by the medical officer with the dossier, then his immediate boss, who is called the team leader, and then the division director, the third person in the chain. The drug was approved over their recommendation by the next man up, the office director, Dr. James Bilstad.

It's been said that his thinking at the time was that obesity in the United States had reached epidemic levels and the benefits of Redux outweighed the risks.

⊂▬▶

Towards the end of July 1996, the Warner-Lambert company submitted to the FDA a new drug application for a compound generically known as troglitazone, but which it intended to call Rezulin.

Just six months before, the company had admitted to fraudulently withholding information from the FDA about manufacturing problems with Dilantin, a drug generically called phenytoin and used for treating seizure disorders. It cost the company $10 million in fines. A Warner-

Lambert vice-president was charged with conspiracy and causing the shipment of adulterated phenytoin. The FDA has since ruled that the sloppy manufacturing practices have been solved.

Rezulin, the first of a brand-new class of type II diabetes drugs, controlled the blood sugar of people who'd become immune to insulin and other therapies. When blood sugar is not controlled, the results can include blindness, strokes, heart disease, and kidney failure. The market for Rezulin was huge, matched only by its potential benefits.

The company was, of course, outwardly optimistic. But getting onto the market first was paramount to its strategy. Other companies had similar therapies in their pipelines — SmithKline was working on Avandia and Lilly was working on Actos — but it's the first drug that gets the lion's share of the business. The others are forced to play catch-up, usually at great expense and with diminished reward.

Rezulin was granted a priority review, which means the FDA took action in six months instead of ten months. Later there would be questions about this, suggesting that Warner-Lambert had pulled political strings. But all drug companies ask for priority review, it's unusual when they don't; and although most are turned down, Warner-Lambert wasn't. For a new chemical entity, the FDA says, it would not be unreasonable to review the drug in that time.

The FDA medical officer assigned to the Rezulin dossier was Dr. John Gueriguian, an eighteen-year veteran of the agency, who says he works in a very systematic way, staying in constant touch with the company before the approval application is made so that he knows what's happening, knows how the drug is being developed, and knows how the safety issues are being assessed.

"I did that for three years with Warner-Lambert," says Gueriguian. "But after three years of asking them about the development of Rezulin and urging them to do the development in a proper fashion, and after three years of them playing games with me and not responding, I got to the end of my review."

There seems to have been a lot he didn't like. Most studies for efficacy are "two-tailed," meaning they will show either effectiveness or ineffectiveness. He claims that the company did what is called a "one-tailed protocol," simply to show effectiveness, and then stacked the deck by using definitions that suited it, as opposed to definitions from unbiased experts.

He was also uneasy about some of the details the company was telling him and how the company kept changing its story. Finally, he claims to have told the company that he wanted them to delay its application for three months, to wait for the results of a larger study because he didn't like the toxicity numbers he was seeing.

Warner-Lambert refused.

"So they asked me, 'Well, what do you think of this drug?'" Gueriguian continues. "By that time they knew I was saying that the drug showed very low efficacy and a very high probability of toxicity to both the liver and the cardio-pulmonary system. They knew I was going to recommend non-approval. But they asked anyway and so I told them, 'The drug is shit.' That's the word I used. And they attacked me on that. They said it was intemperate language."

The company complained to the FDA – "They went behind my back, directly to the higher-ups, who conducted a kangaroo court without confronting me with the evidence" – which removed Gueriguian from the case. "That shows how powerful these companies can be."

The next man up the chain of command, Gueriguian's team leader, Dr. Alexander Fleming, wrote the primary review for Rezulin, recommending approval. From him, the review was signed off by the division director and then went to the office director for final approval.

The same Dr. James Bilstad who'd approved Redux.

In January 1997, a doctor named Robert Misbin was assigned the Rezulin dossier. As medical officer, his job was to look at adverse reactions and deal with supplemental applications. Rezulin had been approved initially for patients with diabetes that could not be controlled by insulin. Subsequent submissions were for more general use in diabetes.

Some people inside the agency still contend that the approval of Rezulin was correct. Although the manufacturer had been extremely aggressive in its representations to the FDA – so much so that the diabetes community was led to believe Rezulin was a miracle drug and added its political weight to the concerted campaign to get it approved – liver failures hadn't been seen yet.

Misbin explains, "The benefits of the drug were available to hundreds of thousands if not millions of people, whereas the adverse effects were limited to several dozen. That's not to understate the problem. One patient dying of liver failure unnecessarily is a tragedy and a failing. But one could not automatically assume that those patients offset the many more patients who should have benefited from Rezulin."

That said, several doctors at the FDA now claim they had doubts about the drug from the beginning. But their doubts weren't about the liver problems, they were related to cardiac matters. They now say there were reasons to believe that early clinical tests in animals had revealed difficulties related to fluid retention. But those were obviously not enough to keep the drug from being marketed.

Within two months, Warner-Lambert was promoting Rezulin at full steam. In its first year, it was one of the top-ten fastest-selling drugs on the market, hitting the $545 million mark. The following year, sales climbed to $748 million.

However, by the autumn of 1997, the first cases of liver failure were being reported. Then there were deaths. It turned out three people had already died during the clinical trials.

On October 28, 1997, at the behest of the FDA, Warner-Lambert issued a "Dear Healthcare Professional" letter to explain changes in prescribing information and some side effects. A week later, the FDA issued a "Talk Paper" on those prescribing changes.

Rezulin had never been approved in Canada. And the only regulator in Europe to certify it was the U.K. Medicines Control Agency (MCA). Glaxo had been selling it in Britain since July under the name Romozin. But the MCA saw the adverse events reports too, and 122 days after allowing the drug into the country, after reports of 4 deaths and 147 cases of liver damage associated with the drug, the MCA yanked it off the market.

That alarmed a lot of people at the FDA. After all, the Americans and the Brits had the exact same data. Some people at the FDA had convinced themselves the label change and letter was the appropriate response to the problem. Now there was a sense of panic.

Petitions poured into the FDA from concerned citizens and watchdog groups, urging the agency act for the same safety reasons the British had. But certain people in power at the FDA stood firm. As far as they were concerned, the British had made their determination and the FDA would make its own. It was hard for them to admit why, just because the British did something, the FDA had to act again.

Yet the agency did act again. It issued a second "Talk Paper," this one warning doctors that they needed to increase patient monitoring to look for signs of liver toxicity. That same day, Warner-Lambert issued a "Dear Healthcare Professional" letter that detailed the additional liver monitoring and was supposed to have mentioned three newly reported deaths associated with Rezulin.

The exact words in the company's letter were: "You will be reassured to know that the additional reports received since early November do not indicate a greater frequency of liver injury or potential for serious harm than had been previously estimated."

Some people at the agency argued that this was being downright deceitful, so the agency asked the company to send yet another letter. This time Warner-Lambert showed the FDA a draft, the agency approved it, and the letter was sent on December 15, 1997. Enclosed with it was a copy of the revised labelling and the FDA's previous "Talk Paper."

And more adverse events were reported.

In January 1998, the FDA demanded that a boldfaced warning be put on the label noting that the drug was dangerous. Four months later the *Los Angeles Times* revealed that Rezulin had been used in a $150-million NIH-sponsored diabetes prevention program since 1996 – before the drug had been approved by the FDA – and that a fifty-five-year-old high-school teacher from East St. Louis, Illinois, had just died of liver failure after taking it as a volunteer patient. Rezulin was eventually removed from that study. The newspaper then revealed that the government physician with overall responsibility for that study, Dr. Richard Eastman, head of the NIH's division of diabetes, endocrinology, and metabolic diseases, had been a contracted consultant to Warner-Lambert since 1995.

As adverse events and deaths mounted, the official FDA stance, as revealed in a letter to Congressman Henry Waxman, was, "At this time, after careful re-evaluation, we believe that the benefits of the drug outweigh the risks."

Waxman wrote back, asking, "Why was Dr. Gueriguian removed from the review of Rezulin?" and "Did Dr. Gueriguian recommend against the approval of Rezulin?"

The answer he received was from Diane Thompson, the FDA's associate commissioner for legislative affairs: "FDA is unable to provide responses to these questions based on the confidential nature of the information which is not releasable under the Freedom of Information Act (FOIA) (5 U.S.C. S552) and FDA's implementing regulations. The issues also involve personnel matters which are not subject to disclosure under the same Act and regulations."

Waxman followed up with two more questions. He wanted to know what had been the response of Gueriguian's superiors to his recommendations and about a September 1996 meeting between FDA staff and representatives of Warner-Lambert, in which Gueriguian voiced reservations regarding Rezulin.

The FDA responded, "Although the Agency is not able to provide specific responses to these questions for the reasons noted in the above response, we would like to provide general information concerning the review of Rezulin. Dr. Gueriguian did not complete his review of Rezulin and thus such review materials are not included in the new drug application file that is releasable to the public."

Interneuron sold an exclusive licence for Redux to American Cyanamid, and American Home Products (AHP) purchased American Cyanamid. It signed a co-promotion agreement with Interneuron and brought Redux to market on the Wyeth product list. Shortly thereafter, the FDA revised the labelling of Redux, requiring Wyeth to state that the drug brought with it a high expectancy of pulmonary hypertension.

Because Pondimin and Redux were so chemically similar, Interneuron and Wyeth had jointly accepted that any adverse medical experiences associated with one could affect the ongoing safety analysis of the other. And because monthly safety meetings were being held at Wyeth's offices to discuss Pondimin anyway, once Redux came to market, Interneuron officials were invited to those same monthly meetings.

But the cosy relationship wasn't destined to last.

Dr. Heidi Connolly, a cardiologist at the Mayo Clinic, had seen a young female patient with a heart valve problem, which was fairly rare, but not rare enough to think a lot about it. That is, not until a year or so later when the young woman returned to the Mayo Clinic with a second damaged heart valve.

A few months after that, Connolly saw another female patient with the same problem, and then learned of a physician out west who had also seen several women with damaged heart valves. Before long, Connolly had put together a file on two dozen women with this problem.

The only thing that she could find these women had in common was Fen-Phen.

Now, in early March 1997, Connolly began writing an article that would find its way into the *New England Journal of Medicine* (*NEJM*). As she was doing that, on March 5, she contacted AHP and voiced her concerns.

The call was an upsetting one for the company.

Under the laws of the U.S. Securities and Exchange Commission (SEC), information as significant as the problems Connolly was talking about – adverse medical events that could influence share prices and dealing – had to be disclosed. AHP's Pondimin label fenfluramine was far more successful than Redux, selling around 140,000 new prescriptions per week. It would be reasonable then that it had chosen to protect the better-selling product. But telling the SEC also meant telling Interneuron. And that company, which had no involvement at all with Fen-Phen, could be reasonably expected to do whatever it had to do to save Redux from any collateral damage. An AHP team agreed to meet Connolly at the clinic a week or so later.

At the regular monthly meeting with Interneuron on March 11, there was no discussion about Fen-Phen and heart valve problems. The AHP team flew to Minnesota. Connolly told them what she was seeing. And when the drug company executives left, their line was that more study was needed.

In April, Wyeth split the monthly meetings with Interneuron into two, claiming it was "due to operational requirements." It meant that Interneuron would now be invited to discuss only Redux's safety. Later, Interneuron would come to believe that this was done specifically to conceal the Mayo Clinic data and prevent – or, at best, postpone – disclosures that could derail Pondimin's substantial sales.

A summary of the minutes of the March 11 meeting was handed out but made no mention of Pondimin. This, despite the fact that Interneuron officials present in March insist that the drug was discussed. The summary was titled, "Redux AE Overview Meeting." A separate summary, "Pondimin AE Overview Meeting," later appeared, making no mention of the Mayo Clinic data. This, Interneuron insisted, proved that Wyeth knew about the problems with Pondimin and Fen-Phen and was deliberately keeping that information from becoming known outside the company. Given the similarity with Redux, Interneuron saw a threat to Pondimin and Fen-Phen as a threat to Redux. The company's lawyers would later claim, "To avoid any risk of commercial disadvantage from disclosure of the Mayo Clinic data, and to maximize sales Pondimin, AHP and Wyeth-Ayerst withheld that data from Interneuron."

Connolly's findings had originally been scheduled to run in the *NEJM* on August 28. But she managed to convince the editors that the matter was urgent. They agreed, exceptionally, to allow her to release her data before publication.

On July 1, an official at the FDA phoned Dr. Richard Gammans, vice-president for clinical research at Interneuron, to invite him to an emergency meeting the next day in Washington to discuss Fen-Phen and related cardiac problems. The FDA official explained that because of that chemical similarity between Redux and Pondimin and because the Mayo Clinic data assessed safety issues for Fen-Phen and also for Redux, he wanted both Interneuron and Wyeth to attend.

That was a real bombshell. Interneuron insists that this was the first time it heard about this.

The FDA announced at the meeting that the Mayo Clinic would hold a press conference on July 8 to reveal that twenty-four patients who had used Fen-Phen had been diagnosed with cardiac valvular disease and that this would be discussed in detail in a forthcoming issue of the *NEJM*.

Interneuron CEO Dr. Glenn Cooper confronted Dr. Marc Deitch, then Wyeth senior vice-president for medical affairs, asking why his company hadn't been advised of the Fen-Phen problem. Deitch allegedly answered that there was no legal obligation to have mentioned it. So now Cooper wrote to AHP's chairman and CEO, John Stafford, criticizing Wyeth for not keeping Interneuron informed. While Deitch is alleged to have claimed that he did in fact inform an Interneuron official of the Fen-Phen problem in a phone call, Interneuron insists that Stafford never bothered to respond to Cooper's letter.

Later, testifying under oath, Wyeth official Dr. Ian Ballard would claim that the order to separate the meetings came from Deitch. "He felt it was a matter of corporate intelligence," Ballard said. When asked if Deitch split the meetings so that Interneuron wouldn't find what was happening with Pondimin, Ballard answered, "That's correct."

In her press conference from the Mayo Clinic on July 8, Connolly told the world that there was a possible relationship between heart valve disease and Fen-Phen.

That same afternoon, the FDA notified 700,000 physicians of the potential dangers of Fen-Phen and Redux.

At Wyeth, they were still maintaining that Connolly's study was inconclusive and that more work needed to be done before these alleged dangers could be verified.

On July 11, 1997, Health Canada's Therapeutic Products Directorate (TPD) acknowledged that it had been informed of serious cardiac adverse reactions as reported to the FDA in connection with Fen-Phen. It issued a warning to physicians, reminding them that the use of the two drugs in combination was not approved in Canada. It also acknowledged that "one possibly two cases of adverse cardiac events" had been reported to the Bureau of Drug Surveillance.

The *NEJM* article was published in August.

Two weeks later, the FDA announced it had compiled information on 291 patients, most of whom had been taking Fen-Phen for up to twenty-four months, many of whom were suffering abnormal echocardiogram findings.

On September 15, Interneuron and Wyeth withdrew Redux from the market. The same day, Wyeth withdrew Pondimin. Coinciding with the action in the United States, the drugs were also pulled in Canada.

But that was only the beginning.

There is something nauseatingly cruel and soulless when the deaths of innocent people, who have put their trust in pharmaceutical companies and regulatory agencies, are considered "statistically acceptable."

And yet, as more deaths were linked to Rezulin in the press, Warner-Lambert announced it was "disappointed with the mischaracterization of its actions and intentions regarding the development and marketing of Rezulin."

Particular rage was levelled at the media for "coverage of the drug that seems to focus primarily on risks, but largely ignores the significant patient benefits that this medication provides."

For good measure, a corporate director of media relations added, "I am clueless as to why there has been so much focus on Rezulin."

Later, a senior executive in Warner-Lambert's pharmaceutical division would chastise the press because Rezulin sales had been hurt "by uninformed commentary in the media."

The FDA required one label change, which the company made, and then required a second label change, which the company complied with. Both were to warn patients that they needed to have their liver enzymes measured regularly.

By July 1998, when it was reported that twenty-one people were dead after taking Rezulin, Public Citizen petitioned the FDA to remove it from the market.

The agency said no.

Public Citizen would later allege that Warner-Lambert withheld evidence of liver toxicity from the FDA in twenty-one patients who'd contracted abnormalities while the drug was in clinical trials.

In fact, sentiment was slowly building at the ground level around the FDA that something needed to be done about Rezulin. If it was to happen, the decision would have to be made all the way up the chain of command, and then the FDA could only ask nicely that Warner-Lambert comply. Despite the fact that the FDA is one of the very rare regulatory agencies in the world that actually has its own investigative force, it is oddly one of the few that doesn't have the authority to summarily order a drug off the market. For the FDA to manage anything like it, there is a long-winded process that invariably ends up in court and takes years. The point of getting a drug off the market is that when the decision is made – because the drug presents a health risk – it must come off immediately. So the FDA "persuades" companies to remove the drug voluntarily. Because the United States is such a litigious society where class-action suits can take on mega-proportions, once the FDA determines a drug should go, any adverse events that subsequently occur represent a terrible liability risk to the company. Between 1972 and 1997, only fourteen drugs had ever been the object of the FDA's wrath and taken off the market. However, from September 1997 through June 1998, the FDA raised sufficient concerns about four more pharmaceutical products to have them also pulled from the market.

Still, by March 1999, the FDA had not spoken up about Rezulin.

Dr. Robert Misbin was coming around to the view that it was time to act. While he favoured waiting a few more months, at least until Avandia and Actos came on to the American market to safely replace Rezulin, it wasn't his call. Anyway, Misbin was hardly the agency's flavour of the month. He'd recently written a letter to the *Washington Post* complaining about how things were done at the FDA. He griped that the agency did not take ethical issues seriously, that patients were not being protected, and, as far as he could see after more than four years there, the higher-ups didn't seem to care.

When the agency held an advisory committee meeting about Rezulin in March, Misbin wasn't asked to speak. However, it would take more than that to silence him. He heard the FDA saying, "We don't have enough data yet," when he knew they had plenty of data all along. He found bureaucratic foot-dragging unacceptable. So, having failed to make his views understood by going up the chain of command, he decided to go to a greater authority.

He wrote a personal letter to several members of Congress, spelled out the problem – "I have been frustrated in my efforts to convince my superiors that the time has come to remove Rezulin from the market" – and enclosed documents that would make the case. He asked them to intervene. No one at the agency knew he'd taken this step until Senator John Ashcroft, a Republican from Missouri, wrote to the FDA's commissioner, Dr. Jane Henney, voicing his concerns.

The FDA responded immediately not by asking Warner-Lambert to take the drug off the market but by opening an Internal Affairs investigation into Misbin for "the possible inappropriate release of information."

The press got wind of that by mid-March.

A meeting took place a week later, at which time the director of the Center for Drug Evaluation and Research (CDER), Dr. Janet Woodcock, personally made the decision to invite Warner-Lambert to remove the drug. The company complied immediately.

CBS News now reported that sixty-three liver deaths had been linked to Rezulin. Warner-Lambert's own press release claimed it was repeated media reports that had sensationalized the risks to the point that patients and physicians were unable to make well-informed decisions.

In that regard, the company was half right.

The final blow to Rezulin was not liver toxicity but the publicity surrounding the FDA investigation of Robert Misbin.

It took lawyers acting for Rezulin patients less than four weeks from the day the drug was pulled to file the first federal class-action lawsuit against Warner-Lambert. It took lawyers representing the victims of Fen-Phen less than three weeks to go after American Home Products.

Since then, suits have rained down on those companies like Noah's deluge. And to the utmost exasperation of the entire pharmaceutical industry, when these cases happen, the advantage is with the plaintiff.

"Spreading the cases out widely, forcing the company to defend itself in multiple forums, makes it harder for them to hide documents," affirms Mike Williams, an attorney in Portland, Oregon, who regularly represents plaintiffs in personal and class-action lawsuits against big corporations. "When you've got thirty or forty different lawyers with thirty to forty different judges all issuing orders for the company to answer questions and produce documents, it's a lot easier to get to the truth with these things."

It's easier too, says Williams, to find smoking guns.

"As soon as one judge orders some document to be produced, it's available everywhere. So when you suspect that a document exists, you really only have to get one judge to order it produced. This is especially effective when you've got a document that the defendant claims is covered by attorney-client privilege. When executives in a company start getting into trouble, they send copies of everything to their in-house lawyers, who then claim they don't have to produce the documents because they're privileged. Well, different states have different interpretations to that so all you need to do is find one judge who'll let it out, and it's out."

Among the smoking guns to emerge in the Fen-Phen case was a little yellow Post-it Note. Written in the handwriting of medical director Deitch, all it said was, "I need to discuss implications re dexfenfluramine before proceeding."

In the context of the case, Williams contends, it was very damaging. "What he was saying was, 'Let's hold up making this warning change.'"

Without that kind of evidence, the plaintiffs have to work their way through the maze of games that companies have gotten very good at playing.

"One of their tricks," Williams points out, "is to rely on a committee, especially when something needs to be signed off by different departments before it's communicated to the regulators. If all the department representatives say okay, then they tell. If one says maybe we shouldn't, then it doesn't get told. It's rare to see argument within the company. But then, they're very crafty about the way they couch things in their own internal memos."

Another well-worn strategy is for a company to get a drug approved on the narrowest possible application where it has solid evidence of efficacy and safety. "Once they've got it approved, they encourage doctors to use it for any damn thing they want, including in combinations, including in higher doses, including for other indications. The industry recently got Congress to relax the rules so it can better promote off-label uses. It's made the business much more of a free-for-all than it ever used to be."

At the start of any big corporate lawsuit, Williams is willing to concede, it's likely that the company's own lawyers don't know the truth. "They're so busy looking for defences, or legal technicalities so they can get the company off the hook, that it's hard for them to appreciate the truth. A lot of time the company succeeds in hiding the truth from their own lawyers, at least for a while."

But they're confronted with the truth eventually. "In Fen-Phen, the company produced, maybe, a million pages of documents. Now, no single attorney on the defence team could read all of them. They're given to lower-level attorneys who have the time to read those documents. But because they're not very experienced, they miss stuff. It's only when you get the experienced plaintiffs' lawyers digging through this thing and you start to put the pieces together that the liability picture begins to emerge. By the time you're well into the litigation and you've hired experts on both sides, either to defend or condemn the company's conduct, that's when the lawyers know everything."

The bigger the company, Williams says, "the harder it is for them to hide any major perfidy. You'll eventually come across it by just sorting through the multiple copies of documents and figuring out who reported to who when, and what the critical days were when they were making bad decisions."

Williams had run up against AHP and Wyeth before. In 1994, they'd been warned by the Canadians that the drug Cordarone could cause blindness, and that Health Canada required the company to label that as a possible side effect. In the United States, the FDA warned the company to add that side effect. But the Canadian wording must have lost something in the translation heading south because the American label warned of inflammation of the optic nerve, noting that it occurred in less than 1 per cent of the patient population. There was no mention of sight loss.

That same year, a fifty-six-year-old man named Douglas Axen was diagnosed with life-threatening cardiac arrhythmia and prescribed Cordarone. What Axen didn't know was that in 1988, the year after the FDA licensed Cordarone, studies had begun to show a link between the drug and optic neuropathy, which causes blindness.

Within a month or so, Axen complained about vision problems and his doctor immediately took him off the drug. But it was too late; Axen's vision deteriorated and he was eventually ruled legally blind.

In his suit against AHP, Axen claimed that the company had intentionally failed to warn that Cordarone could cause permanent blindness. A jury awarded him $207,000 in "economic damages," $1.5 million in "noneconomic damages," and $20 million in punitive damages.

AHP called the award "irrational, ill-considered and excessive," and appealed on those grounds.

It turned out that the FDA had in fact been highly critical in 1989 of the way the company had promoted Cordarone. What's more, the Oregon Appeals Court ruled there was clear and convincing evidence that AHP "had acted with extraordinary disregard of, or indifference to, known or highly probable risks to others."

Williams notes, "We won that case. They appealed. And only after they exhausted every possible appeal did they pay up. My guess is they made more than $20 million while they appealed."

He's been left to conclude that some companies are more prone than others to lie to the regulatory agencies, to the public, or both.

"Some companies do this sort of stuff all the time. There is a spectrum of evil. Some companies are not as good as others at being honest. Often the employees don't conceive that what they're doing is evil. It's the culture in some companies to conceal, to interpret the regulations in such a way as to require the minimum possible disclosure, and to look at everything as a bottom-line rate-of-return issue. What I saw in the Cordarone case was a pattern. AHP did the same thing there that they did with Fen-Phen. Exactly. Some of the same people too."

Like Williams, Dan Sigelman is also a lawyer who saw the Fen-Phen case up close. Then out of Atlanta, now out of Washington, he took the deposition of a medical officer accused of being responsible for the Fen-Phen cover-up.

"What never ceases to amaze me about the pharmaceutical industry is how people accept responsibility when something goes wrong, but then deny they're responsible," says Sigelman. "When I probed [the medical officer], he was willing to take responsibility for his decisions but wrote them off by saying that these decisions didn't matter. He acknowledged that responsibility, but then wanted us to believe that he was only responsible for doing what he was supposed to do and that the fuck-up was somewhere else. In other words, 'I'm responsible, but we really didn't do anything wrong.'"

This sort of thing is nothing new to Sigelman, who served in the 1980s as the principal investigator on a congressional committee with oversight of the FDA.

"I became very jaundiced about the drug industry. And I don't believe they've gotten any better. Frankly, I think it's worse. There's no oversight of this industry any more. You have to wonder what's going on. Obviously Big Pharma has a lot of clout."

That clout, says Sigelman, was clearly demonstrated in the case of Rezulin. "The drug was pulled in the U.K. in 1997. It's disgraceful that the FDA allowed it to remain on the market in the United States. An absolute disgrace."

The day after Rezulin was yanked off the American market, and for the next several weeks, full-page ads appeared in newspapers, barking headlines such as "ATTENTION REZULIN USERS." SmithKline wanted Rezulin users to switch to Avandia. Eli Lilly wanted Rezulin users to switch to Actos.

Largely ignored, that same week, Johnson & Johnson pulled its billion-dollar seller, Prepulsid, off the market over FDA concerns about irregular heartbeats and death in some users. And SmithKline won an appeal at the European Agency for the Evaluation of Medicinal Products for approval of Avandia, originally rejected by the agency, marking the first time it had ever reversed one of its own decisions.

At last count, there were more than nine thousand suits filed in the Fen-Phen case.

A federal grand jury was convened in New York in May 2000 to investigate the way AHP reported to the FDA – or failed to report to the FDA – adverse events in relation to Fen-Phen.

Another federal grand jury has been looking into Rezulin.

In June 1999, Interneuron set aside $70 million to pay for all Redux-related claims against the company. In August 2000, a federal judge in Philadelphia cleared the way for AHP to settle claims made against it in the Fen-Phen matter for $3.75 billion. Included in more than 9,000 suits against American Home Products and Wyeth are 45,000 people who have refused the settlement and 266,000 others in class actions.

In one of those lawsuits, a plaintiff in Texas alleged that Wyeth hid health risks associated with the drugs and outlined the way the company supposedly went about this. According to documents filed in court, Wyeth hired a media consultant to write ten articles that were to be submitted to various medical journals that just so happened to have been owned by the media consultant's parent company, Reed Elsevier Plc.

Only two of the articles were published before the company pulled the drugs. According to editors at the journals, both articles were scrutinized for fairness by independent editorial boards. Whatever plans there were to publish the remaining eight were abandoned.

Despite the fact that the researchers who signed the articles now claim to have been unaware of Wyeth's financial or editorial interest in the articles, a Wyeth spokesperson defended his company to the Associated Press. "This is a common practice in the industry. It's not particular to us. The companies have some input, it seems, in the initial development of the piece, but the proposed author has the last say."

Throughout the course of these tragedies, the FDA attracted its share of criticism. In response, Commissioner Jane Henney wrote an op-ed piece for *USA Today* in which she claimed that the FDA had revised its policies towards clinical testing by establishing safeguards to protect participants in drug trials and rules that require fully informed written consent.

Misbin believed that wasn't the case. If there had been a revision of the FDA's rules, the changes had never filtered down to him. So he further endeared himself to his superiors by writing a letter to *USA Today* refuting his boss. He explained how, when he'd complained that written informed consent had not been properly obtained from approximately three hundred patients in SmithKline's Avandia trials, he was instructed to keep quiet. He suggested, "The FDA could have sent a message to the pharmaceutical industry that it took informed consent seriously."

To that he added, "Although Henney states that her obligation to protect patients' rights is 'deeply felt,' her method of implementing that obligation seems designed to be ineffective. Why did she write to *USA Today*, but not to her own staff?"

CHAPTER 5

SECRET SCIENCE

A woman in her late sixties had gone to see her physician for an annual check-up and, in the course of what was normal routine for a patient her age, the doctor recommended she have a colonoscopy. She was sent to a specialist, who conducted the exam, and when the results were in, he phoned asking to see her again. Believing that if everything was okay he would have said so, she nervously returned to his office. He assured her there was nothing to worry about, but added that he wanted to treat her with a new drug.

She asked why.

He said he wasn't going to bring up the subject of colon cancer . . .

She panicked.

No, he said, colon cancer was not the problem.

But every time she asked what the problem was, he was evasive: it was as if he didn't want to tell her. All he would say was that he wanted her to take a series of drugs and to return for another examination in a few months.

Instead, she raced back to her own doctor and related the story to him.

Her GP looked into the matter and when he discovered what was happening, he ripped up her prescription, persuaded her that she did not have colon cancer or, in fact, any problem at all, and swore he would never again refer a patient to that specialist.

It turned out that the specialist had been hired by a drug company to run trials on a new treatment and was being paid on a per patient basis for recruiting people to take part in that trial. His behaviour was totally unethical and his failure to inform his patient that he was working for a drug company was in direct violation of the drug company's own rules.

This is said to be the cardinal sin of medical research. But the patient has not reported him to any regulatory authority, nor has her GP. And he is still recruiting patients for the drug company.

Conflicts of interest and secrets permeate Big Pharma's relationship with medical research. Some are less dangerous than others, but when patient health is involved, even those less dangerous conflicts and secrets can have serious ramifications.

Full disclosure is not the norm. Because drug companies are paying for the tests to exhibit the efficacy of their drug, they are hands-on when it comes to the design of the tests. Knowing the results that will suit them best, it's easy then for a clever designer to stack the deck.

Testing a drug in a young patient population may result in fewer side effects. That's what a company developing a nonsteroidal anti-inflammatory drug (NSAID) – to treat osteoarthritis – found when it tested a young patient population, despite the fact that the drug would be used most often by elderly patients.

Comparing the drug being tested with a placebo does not always produce better results, but it's sometimes a better bet than comparing it with a competing drug already on the market. Unless, of course, dosages are different. Again, that company testing the NSAID found that when its drug at full dose was compared with a competitor at less than recommended dose, the results came in on the desired side of the equation.

Another trick is to mix delivery systems. Orally administered drugs cannot usually be compared with drugs administered intravenously, except when the company sponsoring the drug needs to find a better result.

On those occasions when results haven't gone the company's way, results are buried. If there is any sort of confusion about what the tests have shown, it's easy to find people with serious credentials to interpret those results in a favourable way.

A few years ago some academics looked at 151 published studies of NSAIDs. In 149 of them, they found the drug being tested was compared to equally or more expensive NSAIDs. Only two studies bothered to compare their drug with a much less expensive and otherwise risk-free analgesic, such as Aspirin. The point was to demonstrate that the drug being tested was more effective than a competing NSAID, which would give the company a selling point. If it had turned out to be no better than Aspirin, nobody would bother paying for it.

"I always talk about the gold standard and we're nowhere near it," says Dr. Sheldon Krimsky of Tufts University. "For the pharmaceutical industry, it would be something like the following. A company wants to have a drug tested for efficacy and safety. They would be required to put a certain amount of money down to pay for these tests at some sort of national institute of drug testing. The tests would be assigned a crew in the institute and the results would be available to anyone in the scientific community. The company could use the results to get the drug through the FDA or to promote it, whatever they want. But there would be a distant relationship between the company paying for the test and the data. It would all be carried out independently. No one who works at this institute could have any direct equity in any of these companies. That would be the gold standard. Anyone I've suggested this to says it's ridiculous, they don't want the government involved in this."

Or, for that matter, any organization that would be totally independent.

A second study of clinical trials on NSAIDs looked at fifty-six tests in which the sponsoring company's drug was compared directly to a competing NSAID. In every single case – that's fifty-six out of fifty-six – the sponsoring company's drug came out equal to or better than the drug used in the comparison.

Larry Sasich at Public Citizen says that such results are not unusual. "It starts with clinical trials designed, conducted, and contracted to get drugs approved. And we're seeing fewer and fewer published articles before a new drug is approved. What we think is happening is, because the companies control the publication of these trials, they are selectively only publishing the most favourable trials. You can influence a clinician's interpretation of the therapeutic value of a drug that way."

The example he cites is the story behind a popular flu drug.

"There were three trials submitted to the FDA and only one of them was published. That was done in the southern hemisphere. It was small and came out positive, and the researcher said there's more research that needs to be done. But the largest of the three trials, which was almost as large as the other two combined, conducted in the United States and Canada, found no statistical difference between Relenza and the placebo. That one was never published."

The dangers to the public are evident.

"You can talk about *caveat emptor*, buyer beware," wrote Dr. Drummond Rennie, West Coast editor of the *Journal of the American Medical Association* and one of the most prestigiously vocal people in the profession when it comes to identifying and condemning conflicts of interest and secrecy, "but patients are *emptors* that can't *caveat* because they don't know how. When you are a patient, it's not like buying a Toyota. Patients don't know how to choose their own anesthetic."

We all, therefore, depend on our doctors and other people with scientific degrees to protect us from what could easily turn into a personal disaster. After all, we put our health in their hands. And yet there is no shortage of people willing to take drug company money and, in some cases, do so at the expense of our health.

In 1984, the *New England Journal of Medicine* became the first of the major professional publications to formulate a workable policy towards conflicts of interest and secrecy between authors of original research and the private sector. Financial agreements were nothing new, but the *NEJM* felt they were becoming sufficiently widespread that readers needed to know who was paying whom. So it ruled that authors must disclose any arrangements they might have with the products or companies they were writing about. The journal next decided that anyone writing in an editorial capacity, such as a peer review, should have no direct financial ties with anyone, any product, or any company named in the article.

It worked in theory. But in reality, it required everyone to be honest enough to always disclose interests that, in many cases, they necessarily wanted to keep secret. When the *Los Angeles Times* decided to put the policy to the test, it looked at thirty-six drug therapy articles published in the *NEJM* between 1997 and 1999. It found eight that had been written by researchers who had not disclosed their financial links to drug companies.

Within a year, the *NEJM* was embarrassed again, forced to admit that it had violated its own conflict-of-interest policy by publishing nineteen drug reviews written by researchers who did not disclose financial links with the companies making those same drugs.

It was almost as if full disclosure never stood a chance, not just at the *NEJM* but throughout the scientific community. Industry links have grown more and more important to research, so much so that by the time the *NEJM* published its May 2000 issue, the financial ties between the authors and the companies discussed in one article were so extensive, the *Journal* simply had to amend its own policy for the sake of space and merely summarize those connections. Full disclosure was only made on its Web site.

Without even suggesting there is anything untoward or unethical about these authors and their associations, the sheer weight of the list is worth noting. Financial associations included support from Bristol-Myers Squibb, consultancy work, research grants, and/or honorariums from Pfizer, Bristol-Myers Squibb, Forest Laboratories/Parke-Davis, Wyeth-Ayerst, Merck, Janssen, Eli Lilly, Pharmacia & Upjohn, Smith-Kline Beecham, Glaxo Wellcome, Abbott, AstraZeneca, Neurocrine Biosciences, Organon, Otsuka, Lipha Pharmaceuticals, Johnson & Johnson, Mead Johnson, Hoechst Marion Roussel, Shire, Sanofi Research, Scios, Biovail, TAPPharma, Mitsubishi Pharmaceuticals, Scirex, Solvay, and Quintiles. Some authors also held advisory board appointments with Wyeth-Ayerst, Pfizer, Bristol-Myers Squibb, Eli Lilly, Parke-Davis, Organon, SmithKline Beecham, Merck, Janssen, Mitsubishi Pharmaceuticals, Zeneca, Scirex, and Otsuka. Others revealed shareholdings in Pfizer, Forest Laboratories, Warner-Lambert, and Eli Lilly.

When Dr. Allan Detsky of the University of Toronto tried to establish who'd been saying what about calcium-channel blockers – a class of drugs used by millions of people for angina and hypertension – he looked at seventy articles published between March 1995 and September 1996. He divided the judgments made on calcium-channel blockers into three categories: critical, neutral, or supportive. He and his staff then sent a questionnaire to eighty authors listed on those papers asking what sort of financial support they may or may not have received from the drug industry. Detsky also queried forty drug companies to ask what their support had been. It turned out that a startling 96 per cent of the authors who wrote favourably about calcium-channel blockers had some sort of financial relationship with the drug company manufacturing the specific calcium-channel blocker being discussed, and that in only two of the articles did the authors divulge their financial ties to drug companies.

Detsky was careful to say that the results of his study did not necessarily mean the views of those researchers had been in any way altered by their relationship with the industry. But he did add, "That doesn't mean that there couldn't be an unconscious bias."

When the *British Medical Journal* (*BMJ*) carried an article stating that antidepressants such as Prozac are not addictive, it turned out that the doctors who'd written the article had once been flown to Arizona as the guests of Eli Lilly, the company manufacturing Prozac. This is not to say there was actual bias, but it is hardly the most suitable of relationships.

And when the U.K. Committee on Publication Ethics (COPE), a group funded by several medical journals, decided to look at medical research in Britain, it concluded that "research fraud" was more prevalent than anyone had previously recognized. The reasons for it, COPE suggested, were increased pressures on scientists to publish and financial incentives for research.

Arguably, there are perhaps half-a-dozen internationally important journals of general medicine: the *NEJM, JAMA*, the *Lancet*, the *British Medical Journal*, the *Annals of Internal Medicine*, and the *Canadian Medical Association Journal*. For the most part, they all have a similar policy in that they want to know the financial interests of authors. The *BMJ* is slightly different in that it also asks authors to declare non-financial interests – personal, academic, religious, moral, political, whatever – but doesn't necessarily publish those interests.

Most medical journals receive anywhere from five thousand to eight thousand articles a year for possible publication and only accept a small percentage of them. The basic criteria are simple: the work must be original, must be important, the methods described must be sound, and the subjects must be relevant to the readers. When a paper meets those four requirements, it's considered. If it's accepted, it is then sent out for peer review. If the peer reviewer thinks it's important and correct, the article goes in front of another committee, where further decisions are made.

In 1996, Dr. Sheldon Krimsky at Tufts wondered how many journal article authors had a personal financial interest in the outcome of the study they were writing about. It took him two years to sort through fourteen of the leading biomedical journals, to choose nearly eight hundred articles, and to query some eleven hundred lead authors.

He discovered that in 34 per cent of the articles − 267 in total − the authors held a patent related to the inventions they were writing about, or were employees or stockholders of a biotech company exploiting the research, or were members of scientific advisory boards of a drug company involved with the research, or held some other financial interest in the outcome. And not one of those 267 papers mentioned authors' financial interests.

"You'd be surprised," Krimsky says, "how many doctors don't know how to make a critical judgment when journal articles look respectable. You'd be amazed at how many of them don't even know the difference between a peer-reviewed and non-peer-reviewed journal. Or where to go to find the difference. There are tens of thousands of journals out there. We had one expert come in recently on a case, a leading expert in his field, and when we showed him citations from journals that claimed to be authorities in his field, he'd never heard of five of them. These things can be very easily masqueraded."

Krimsky wrote *Hormonal Chaos*, a book about how a small group of scientists came to link some synthetic chemicals to more than a dozen human and animal abnormalities and how, when public safety is involved, industry rushes to defend its turf. In his book he quotes a scientist whom he describes as "very credible" about an incident in which the Dow Chemical Company sent a toxicologist to the scientist's laboratory asking him not to publish a result, and hinting that if he obliged, it might be mutually beneficial. True to industry form, Krimsky soon received a letter from Dow objecting to the story. Krimsky was appalled and fired a letter back to Dow standing by his version of the event. A few weeks later, he received a journal in the mail dedicated to the very chemical that the scientist in Krimsky's story had questioned.

"An industry group published it. It looks like a journal and has articles in it, abstracts, literature, and nice drawings. But they invented it. They created their own science to talk about how safe this compound is."

It's so very dangerous, Krimsky notes, because people fall for it, and the reason they fall for it is because the companies themselves purposely make it hard to tell what's real and what isn't.

"Non-peer-reviewed journals and industry-supported journals are everywhere," says Krimsky. "You also find peer-reviewed journals that are industry supported. That makes it even more complicated. The industry goes out and gets their own peers. The independence of science is at stake here. It's about who you trust. In pharmaceutical studies, that's increasingly a problem. We're looking at direct-marketing people, at more and more industry conglomerates that have more and more money, and at academic departments that are more beholden to companies than ever before. We're looking at for-profit clinical trials, which changes the whole nature of the game."

Contract research organizations (CROs), which are commercial businesses set up specifically to handle clinical testing for drug companies, have sprung up everywhere. Many of them are qualified to do whatever it is they're asked to do. But critics are fast to point out that some of them take on work they're not qualified to do – after all, these are commercial enterprises – while others are perhaps too willing to give the drug companies the results they're looking for because in business you keep customers by satisfying them.

Here, the possibility of conflicts of interest is not even couched in polite terms. What happens, critics ask, when one of these research companies for hire finds something wrong with the drug it's testing? Are they being paid by Big Pharma to tell the truth, or are they being paid to get results? Big Pharma would say, right away, we need to be told the truth, but the anecdotal evidence suggests that they may not always get it or, for that matter, sincerely want it.

Doctors working research for profit and seeing an experimental drug failing may be tempted to take their patients off the drug and put them on something they know that works, thus distorting the testing process. Or they may be tempted to leave their patients on the drug, regardless of the risk. Or they may think, "We'll tell the drug company what's happening and then it's up to the drug company to tell the regulators," meaning it's no longer the doctor's problem. Or they may do whatever they have to do to give the drug company the results they're hoping to get, which might ensure that the for-profit research company will get a contract to test the next drug.

Academic institutions generally have review boards that, at least in principle, operate at arm's length to ensure patient safety. Most CROs also

have oversight procedures, but many do not have sufficient independence. According to a White House advisory commission on national
bioethics, "significant revision" is called for.

Not that everything is perfect in the world of academic research,
either. Pharmaceutical companies speak of universities as "partners." But
not all partners are created equal. The partner with the chequebook gets
to talk the loudest.

A researcher in the United States writes a proposal and begins hunting
for grant money. He goes to the government or some public body and,
for the sake of argument, the grant is a small one, $100,000. The university
where the researcher works has "an institutional overhead rate" that can
be as much as 50 per cent. That means, in this case, the university gets
$50,000 for keeping the lights on, paying the janitor, that sort of thing.

Now, suppose the same researcher goes to Big Pharma and is paid on a
per-patient basis. Say that figure is $3,500 per, although the more impor-
tant the study, the higher the capitation fee. In this case, the researcher's
costs may be $1,500, meaning that he's going to clear $2,000 per patient.
Out of that, instead of an overhead rate, he pays the university a small
piece of the fee, usually 15 per cent.

It's a typical example of how public funds can subsidize industry research.
However, the extent to which industry can bias research is hotly debated.

Many researchers with financial ties to industry adamantly insist that
those associations could not and do not affect their work. They insist that,
as scientists, they can and do remain objective. Undoubtedly, many try.
How well they succeed over the course of time and in the face of constant attempts to influence them is another matter. If they do succeed,
then what's the chance of landing the next industry contract? After all,
it's Big Pharma that hires the researchers and there is a growing body of
evidence to suggest that drug companies know what they're getting for
their money.

Or, at least, what they can expect for their money.

Commercial research is a business. Academic research is not supposed
to be.

"Researchers with ties to drug companies are indeed more likely to
report results that are favourable to the products of those companies than
researchers without such ties," wrote *NEJM* editor Dr. Marcia Angell.
"That does not conclusively prove that researchers are influenced by their

financial ties to industry. Conceivably, drug companies seek out researchers who happen to be getting positive results. But I believe bias is the most likely explanation, and in either case, it is clear that the more enthusiastic researchers are, the more assured they can be of industry funding."

At the same time, physicians are freelancing.

The American College of Physicians and the American Society of Internal Medicine jointly reported that the number of private doctors conducting clinical trials nearly tripled during the 1990s. Clinical research has become a multibillion-dollar industry, and doctors have been lining up to get their share of it. With drug companies offering $1,000 to $5,000 for each patient enrolled in a trial, there's no shortage of physicians willing to enrol patients.

Problems arise, the two professional bodies agree, when these stipends entice physicians to influence unduly their patients to enlist. In some cases, patients agreeing with their doctor's request to sign on to a trial don't have the medical conditions being studied. Occasionally, the doctors aren't right either. One recently reported case was of psychiatrists asked by a drug company to partake in a study on hormone replacement, diabetes, and to do Pap smears. Another was asthma specialists dispensing experimental psychiatric drugs.

According to the *New York Times*, doctors who know the ins and outs of recruiting patients can earn as much as $500,000 to $1 million a year from drug companies for their efforts.

"Patients expect you to be a dispassionate advocate for them," notes Dr. David Shimm, a member of the ethics committee at Porter Adventist Hospital in Denver and someone who has not been afraid to speak out loudly about the conflicts doctors face doing clinical research. "Patients assume that you're making decisions in their best interest. They have no idea that if a doctor puts them on a clinical trial, he may be making money for doing that. They don't even know to ask the question. The problem that I've often seen is patients run through a series of clinical trials that really have very little chance of bringing them any benefit. One short-term study for an antidepressant that I saw at the University of Arizona had a capitation payment of $42,000 per patient."

Shimm is among those doctors who feel that some colleagues doing drug company research for hire can sometimes forget that their primary responsibility must always be to their patient.

"The most egregious problems I've seen in terms of patient care are people who came to me in terrible pain with metastatic cancer. I asked, 'How long have you been hurting this bad?' They said perhaps six months. I asked, 'Why didn't you come in sooner?' They told me they came in when the pain started and their doctor put them on a bunch of experimental drugs. In other words, these people were being used in clinical trials until they ran out of options and only at that point was their primary problem being addressed."

It is a prime example of how drug company money can distort a doctor's loyalty. Shimm recalls an American College of Clinical Oncology study some years ago that looked at the probability of a patient obtaining a complete response during a Phase I trial for a cancer drug. He says it was in the region of 1 in 1,700. "Typically, partial responses are four or five times as common, so you figure the probability of a complete or partial response is perhaps 1 in 300 to 400. It's fine to try drugs on patients, but only if you level with them. If you have somebody in a lot of pain and say to that person, 'There's a chance this might help you,' what they're probably hearing is that there's a 50 per cent chance. Or maybe even a 10 per cent chance. But unless you tell them, they're not going to know it's less than a 1 in 100 chance."

Patients must be told that they're taking part in a trial, and they must sign consent forms. That's required. What patients are not generally told is who's paying for the study, if the doctor has an equity position in that company, if the doctor is on the board of directors or an advisory board of that company, if the doctor is a paid consultant, if the doctor is receiving a capitation payment, and, if so, how much that capitation payment is. The reason for not giving patients that information, Big Pharma knows, is because a lot of them will then have second thoughts about signing the consent forms.

Of course, trials have to take place in order for a drug to get regulatory approval. But Shimm insists it is the indisputable responsibility of everybody involved with the trial – physician and drug company alike – to make certain that the patient knows everything that's happening.

"It's a hard circle to square, to make sure that physicians' loyalties aren't going to be torn between the drug company and the patient. If a doctor tells a patient, 'I'm putting you on a Phase I study,' he may say, 'You'll be contributing something in developing a new drug,' but he's also got to say,

'This is basically a toxicity study and your chances of benefit are minimal.' Unfortunately, all too often, patients hear what they want to hear. When you tell somebody who's in a lot of pain there's a chance they will be helped, they say that's great, there's a chance. Well, yeah, there's a chance if I flap my arms I can fly to the moon. But it's not a very big chance."

There is the corporate sector dishing out the funds and the academic sector taking them. Researchers receive grants, serve as consultants, are brought onto advisory boards, and are included in company-sponsored speakers' bureaus. Academics share patent and royalty arrangements with drug companies and are hired to put their names on articles ghostwritten by the companies. Academics are invited to promote products and receive fees for attending company-sponsored symposia.

Most schools have rules about these things, but they are particularly difficult to enforce, especially when the schools themselves maintain financial relationships with industry and are, often, dependent on corporate funding for major projects. Colleges and universities regularly enter into partnerships of all kinds with drug companies and not only allow but actively encourage the private sector to establish research facilities and programs.

That process was greatly distorted in 1980 when the U.S. Senate passed the Bayh–Dole Act, allowing American institutions supported by federal grants to patent and license products developed in their labs and to allow those researchers to share in royalty payments.

The ramifications for institutions outside the United States has been momentous. As a result of Bayh–Dole, the biotech sector was born. As a result of Bayh–Dole, drug companies have been able to turn academia into subsidiaries. Prior to the act, American universities were issued with around two hundred and fifty patents a year. These days there are more than two hundred colleges and universities at work developing products, with patent awards now averaging fifteen hundred a year. One estimate suggests this has become a $33.5 billion industry.

There is so much money in the pot, it hardly matters that the act doesn't cover anyone working at Oxford in England or McGill in Canada or the Pasteur Institute in Paris. The lure of sharing the bounty is such a magnet to researchers all over the world that it forces everyone else to compete. In this regard, American universities are way ahead of their Canadian and European counterparts. They have tapped into a vein of funding and are exploiting it mercilessly. For example, the entire plant pathology department at one of America's most prestigious universities is now under contract to a biotech company. Everyone in that department has signed on.

Traditionally, there's supposed to be some distance between corporations and researchers. But traditions change and if universities outside the United States expect to compete, their options will come down to a simple either-or: either they too seek closer corporate bonds or they risk losing big-name researchers to the much wealthier American campuses.

"Universities are eager to share in the profits," comments Dr. Sheldon Krimsky at Tufts. "There's so much competition for corporate money that they're forgetting the traditional values of the university. They're willing to give up on things like openness and the sharing of information. Institutional conflicts of interest are not being addressed."

He refers to it as "the colonization of academia" and feels it is getting close to the point where the next step is the outright sponsorship of a university.

"I think we have really crossed some very important boundaries and the next stage is for an American corporation, a large corporation, simply to buy a private university. Imagine a large American corporation that wants to have as one of its sub-units a university. Would that be an outrage? Well, we're getting close."

No institution is immune, not even the often praised, ethically backboned Harvard.

For years Harvard has maintained the strictest of conflict-of-interest policies. It was usually described as the model other universities should aspire to. Faculty members must disclose their financial interests in any business that has a relationship with the university and/or their job there. They are barred from spending more than 20 per cent of their time on outside work. They are not permitted to hold more than $20,000 worth of stock in any company funding research that involves them or their lab. And they are restricted in the fees and royalties they are permitted to receive from corporate benefactors.

But over the past couple of years, some administrators at the university began to think that perhaps the rules were too strict and that, to compete for entrepreneurial researchers with other top schools, it might be prudent to allow staff and faculty a little more leeway in their financial dealings with the private sector.

A meeting was proposed to discuss changes to the rules. The instant the proposal became public, academic outrage ensued.

"It's unthinkable," commented one professor, "that while university and industry ties are creating more and more conflicts of interest in the sciences, here's Harvard deciding rather than raise the bar to lower it."

The clamour of "Harvard sells out" became so earsplitting and so shook the administrators that the meeting was cancelled and the plan has, at least for the time being, been abandoned.

"The whole reason we have ethics is not to allow profits to dictate everything," argues Krimsky. "They should dictate some things, and maybe a lot of things, but they should not dictate everything. That's why we have ethics and try to define ethical behaviour and put restraints on conflicts of interest."

While the desire to maintain secrecy in science is understandable, many academics agree, it is rarely, if ever, justifiable. Corporations defend secrecy by claiming that misuse or leaking of proprietary information presents a real financial danger. What those corporations really mean is that where the choice is truth or profits, coming down on the side of truth is not a given.

Dr. Andrew Millar, who made headlines as a whistleblower when he was head of clinical trials at British Biotech, has seen the problem from two different viewpoints.

"When you're a relatively junior manager in a country operation of a large pharmaceutical company, you're very isolated from the board of directors," Millar explains. "You don't actually realize why they're trying to suppress what are clearly problematic factors. All you can see is what the company is doing. And you think to yourself, 'It's not all that clever long term to cover things up or to plaster things over, because these problems are real.' These problems are there all the time that the drug is being administered to patients."

The conflict is easier to see, he claims, in a biotech company. "You're in the same building as the board of directors. You're much more on top of the different factors. You start off with the same sense of puzzlement about what the company appears to be doing and what you see as the best thing to do. Then you start realizing they're doing what they're doing because the guys making those decisions are thinking about the share price. They're worried about what the city thinks, and about their own stock options."

British Biotech was once a darling of the London Stock Exchange. There had even been talk of the company one day becoming the next Glaxo. Although the shares had been slipping for nearly a year, there were a few drugs in the pipeline in the mid-1990s that seemed to hold out some hope. That is, until Millar told the truth about some of those drugs.

In a series of meetings with a pharmaceutical analyst at Goldman Sachs, Millar admitted that he did not believe in the prospects of two key pipeline drugs: Marimastat, which was a cancer treatment, and Zacutex, which was a treatment for acute pancreatitis.

The reason he spoke up, he says, is because he had to. "Share prices have nothing to do with doctors treating patients for their diseases. I felt we were in the business of treating diseases."

At Goldman Sachs they're in the business of valuing expectations, and based on what Millar had told them, their assessment of British Biotech sent the shares into a free fall. Millar was fired and sued by British Biotech for what it considered gross imprudence. He fought back and eventually won. And despite the trouble and stress that came from telling the truth, he says he did not see this as an ethical dilemma.

"If patients are going to be misled or harmed, it's not a dilemma at all. It's very clear-cut what your responsibility is. I was forever telling the board that we need to remember our product, that doctors use drugs to treat patients, and that's what our market is. All boards of directors, I think, finish up being at significant risk of viewing their main market as the city and the shareholders."

As academia becomes more savvy about such gagging clauses, and institutions vet contracts to make sure they don't contain any, Big Pharma gets smarter too. Contracts are written to hide those clauses, clearly stating that the researcher indeed has the right to publish, but somewhere much further on, noting that the company owns all the data in the study.

It means you're welcome to publish, but it's not going to be this study.

Big Pharma has even become more creative about the reasons why.

At a recent meeting of the American Association for the Advancement of Science's Committee on Scientific Freedom and Responsibility, one of the featured speakers was a representative of the research industry. When he was asked about secrecy in science, he said there were several reasons why information had to be suppressed, and listed as his top answer, "to sabotage the competition."

After all, he explained, when a company is spending millions of dollars looking for a solution to a problem, and the solution they're researching turns out to be ineffective, it's important to make sure that competitors also waste money heading down the same dead end.

When money isn't being used to sabotage the competition, it has the power to turn pharmaceutical companies into bullies and universities into cowards. Few people understand that better than Dr. David Kern and Dr. Betty Dong.

Kern is the former head of occupational medicine at Brown University in Providence, Rhode Island, and of the occupational and environmental health service at Memorial Hospital in Pawtucket, Rhode Island.

In 1994, an employee of Microfibers Inc., a textile manufacturer in Pawtucket, came down with symptomatic interstitial lung disease (ILD), a condition considered rare in young men. It was brought to Kern's attention and he asked the company if he could bring some students of occupational medicine on a tour of the factory. The company agreed, but insisted that everyone in his group sign a confidentiality agreement ostensibly to protect the company from industrial espionage and to safe-guard trade secrets. Everyone in the group agreed. After all, this was a one-time visit under the auspices of medical student education.

Two years later, and completely unrelated to that visit, another Micro-fibers employee was referred to Kern as a patient at Memorial Hospital, also suffering from ILD. Kern was now brought in as a consultant by the company to investigate the cause of the problem. He quickly uncovered ILD at other Microfibers plants. The hospital had provided a formal con-sulting contract, which Microfibers never signed, although the company paid the hospital more than $100,000 for Kern's consultation.

Kern now decided to present his findings at the spring 1997 conference of the American Thoracic Society. Microfibers heard that and threatened to sue him and Memorial Hospital if he did. The company claimed that Kern's publication would be a violation of the confidentiality agreement he'd signed in 1994. Insisting that he had never signed a nondisclosure agreement relevant to the study, Kern published. One week later, the hospital announced it would not renew his contract. Because his university appointment was contingent on the hospital, the university also announced his contract would not be renewed.

A claim that the family owning Microfibers is a substantial contributor to and maintains connections with the hospital corporation was met with the company's published response, "This is insulting."

Support for Kern poured in from around the world. In a face-saving exercise, the dean of medicine at the university assembled a committee of inquiry. Its conclusion was "The company's attempt to have the abstract withdrawn is not considered by the Committee to be an attempt to compromise the health of its employees but rather an effort to avoid bad publicity and to protect its economic position."

Kern noted that when he was invited by the company to consult on the illnesses, he handed Microfibers a copy of the operating principles that would govern his consultancy. Included was a clause saying, if necessary, he reserved the right to report his findings to the appropriate scientific and public health communities. In other words, if he found something that was a matter of public health, he would take the necessary steps to protect public health. Since then, Kern has claimed that a dozen lawyers and legal scholars have checked the company's confidentiality agreement and unanimously concluded that it is irrelevant, unenforceable, and contrary to the public good.

For Microfibers, the Kern affair has been a selfmade public relations disaster. Brown University and Memorial Hospital have suffered greatly as well. But then, that's the nature of these disputes. They don't go away. They don't get better. They can't be whitewashed for very long. And while everyone loses something, it is generally the institutions that not only have the most to lose but usually lose the most.

It was that way, as well, with Betty Dong.

A highly respected professor of clinical pharmacology at the University of California in San Francisco (UCSF), Dong had published a small study in 1988 suggesting that the leading thyroid medication in the United States – a drug called Synthroid – might prove more effective than its competitors in a randomized trial.

Some 8 million Americans were then taking the drug and the company making it, Flint Pharmaceuticals, was eager for yet another selling point to justify the high prices it was charging. Flint decided Dong was on to something and paid her $250,000 to compare Synthroid with its three leading generic competitors. Its own scientists designed the protocols.

By the time Dong finished the trial, in 1990, Flint had been acquired by Boots Pharmaceuticals. Unfortunately for Boots, the study it inherited concluded that Synthroid was no better than the three less expensive generic versions.

Dong's contract contained a clause that gave the company exclusive access to her data and the ultimate right to veto anything she wanted to publish. So Boots spent the next five years attacking Dong's study at every turn, discrediting her science, and preventing her from publishing the damning results.

Believing that she had every right to publish her findings, Dong sent an article to the *Journal of the American Medical Association* in April 1994. It referred her manuscript for peer review to five independent experts, accepted it for publication in November, and tentatively scheduled it for an issue ten weeks later. But on January 13, 1995, Dong received an injunction prohibiting her from publishing and was forced to withdraw the article.

Two months later, Boots was taken over for $1.4 billion by Knoll Pharmaceuticals, a division of the German chemical group BASF. With it, Knoll inherited the right to manufacture and sell Synthroid, and to continue the fight against Betty Dong.

Clearly, it had been in Boots' interest to keep the Synthroid story out of the papers, especially while the deal with Knoll was being put together. If consumers knew there were three cheaper generics proven to be just as good, the Synthroid market might collapse and that would have a bearing on the deal. Accordingly, Knoll now needed to protect its investment. So, the medical services director of Knoll published a sixteen-page re-analysis of Dong's data in a new publication called the *American Journal of Therapeutics*. It just so happens that he was also one of the editors.

By this time, the FDA was onto the case. It queried the company's claim that Synthroid was both unique and superior to the competing products, decided the company was misleading the public, and eventually accused Knoll of misbranding Synthroid. In the face of mounting criticism and particularly good investigative reporting by the *Wall Street Journal*, Knoll had little choice but to allow Dong to publish her work. The article appeared in *JAMA* in April 1997. Along with it was a letter from Knoll apologizing for having delayed publication for so long, a statement from Knoll challenging Dong's conclusions, and a rebuttal from Dong defending her conclusion.

As soon as the report came out, an $8.5-billion class-action suit followed, alleging that Knoll had defrauded Synthroid users by overcharging them for the drug.

The attorneys general of thirty-seven states also stepped in. Among other things, they didn't like the marketing of Synthroid and the company's communications with the FDA, particularly a 1990, unpublished, in-house study that showed Synthroid's potency to be more consistent than the competitors'. Ignoring the Dong study, the company had claimed that this report was credible, objective, and contained new information.

Boots and Knoll both insisted they'd really been saying all along that the Dong study was neither an adequate nor well-controlled study. This despite the fact that their own scientists had designed it.

Facing lawsuits, Knoll now added that it had been willing right from the beginning to publish her work as long as the errors of fact and interpretation were corrected.

That might well have been the end of this episode had Boots not systematically complained about Dong to her chancellor, all her vice-chancellors, and several department heads at UCSF. The university investigated the controversy twice but never uncovered anything that would significantly support Boots' accusations. The problem it saw was that the university specifically prohibits secrecy clauses and any contractual restrictions on the right to publish. Dong had signed the contract with the clause mistakenly believing that it was routine. She'd even been assured by the university lawyers that such clauses had not in the past prevented anyone from publishing. But by going to the university, Boots had inadvertently thrown the administration into a quandary. To the administrators, it looked as though Betty Dong and her Synthroid report might somehow become embroiled in the Knoll takeover of Boots. They worried that the university could find itself party to lawsuits stemming from the sale of Boots to Knoll.

There was also the sentiment by some at the university that Dong was at fault for signing the confidentiality clause and that the ensuing controversy somehow jeopardized their own research grants. Although the university had, at first, encouraged Dong to publish, it quickly and firmly backed down. It warned Dong that she and her fellow researchers might be putting themselves in personal danger by publishing because the university would not defend them. In other words, it not only refused to stand up to a drug company, but it was also willing to sacrifice Dong.

Knoll maintained its tough stance right up to the end. Yet the more it tried to defend the indefensible, the worse it got. In August 1997, looking at years of litigation in the class-action suit, the company announced that the prudent thing would be to settle. They paid $135 million to sixty Synthroid users who were claiming that because the company had suppressed research relevant to their condition, they otherwise would have been unaware of effective, cheap alternatives.

At the end of July 1999, Knoll and the attorneys general reached an agreement that included – as the company is fast to point out – no finding of wrongdoing. Knoll maintains it settled to avoid the burden and expense of lengthy litigation. Included in this agreement was a payment by Knoll to the states of $41.8 million and assurances that its marketing of Synthroid would be "fair and accurate."

The class–action settlement and the agreement with the states may sound like a lot of money, but at $400 million a year, seven years' worth of manoeuvring to suppress Dong's report earned back $2.45 billion.

CHAPTER 6

JUST TAKING CARE
OF BUSINESS

They say, *It's all about research and development.*

They say, *Everyone agrees that the innovative work of our scientists has been extraordinarily successful.*

The spiel never changes. *Our dedicated scientists are devoted to their work and want to continue developing new treatments for Alzheimer's, cancer, heart disease, Parkinson's, and many other diseases.*

They even make promises. *We're closer than ever to finding new medicines, and hopefully to coming up with cures, and we want to go full-speed ahead.*

What Big Pharma really means is, *Be grateful for all the wonderful things we do and don't be so rude as to ask why we charge so much for it.*

⊂▭⊃

Where scientists in the pharmaceutical industry see lives at risk and hope to save them, the marketing people quantify disease in terms of a business. Which is why, for example, almost all of black Africa is systematically being denied certain drugs. The governments simply cannot afford to pay whatever Big Pharma demands.

In July 2000, the 13th International AIDS Conference met in Durban, South Africa. And for the first time, collective anger shook the very roots of Big Pharma's foundations. This was when Pretoria waved the sticks of compulsory licensing and parallel imports if drug companies didn't come to the rescue voluntarily.

Three years before, Nelson Mandela's government had passed the Medicines Act, a law granting authority for compulsory licensing. Big Pharma had gone screaming all the way to Washington, where Congress and the U.S. trade representatives promised to help. At the same time, a pharmaceutical industry lobby went to court in South Africa and won an injunction blocking the law.

One year later, a New Jersey Republican, Congressman Rodney Frelinghuysen, managed to stick a clause into the 1998 federal budget that obliged the State Department to tell Congress what it was doing to keep compulsory licensing from being enforced in South Africa. The effect of Frelinghuysen's handiwork meant that no American foreign aid could be sent to South Africa until Congress was satisfied that Big Pharma's interests were protected.

In February 1999, the State Department reported to Congress that it was "making use of the full panoply of leverage in our arsenal" to take on the South Africans. That included, the report said, the vice-president's office, with Al Gore himself putting the problem at the top of his agenda in his meeting with the man who would become South Africa's president, Thabo Mbeki.

At that point, the industry lobby, PhRMA, admitted it was pushing the administration to label South Africa a "priority foreign country" in order to establish a deadline, after which trade sanctions would come into effect.

Towards the end of 1999, having decided to become a full-fledged candidate for the presidency, Gore was softening his stance. He wanted a solution in South Africa that would help those people who needed medicine, and promised to get affordable drugs to developing countries. He said he opposed legislation to extend the patent life of Claritin, labelling Schering-Plough's efforts a typical example of a drug company protecting profits at the expense of consumers. And he commented that some drug companies "are trying to pull the wool over the eyes of Congress and tag the American people with more of these absurdly high pharmaceutical prices."

By then, President Bill Clinton had already shifted American policy by ordering the trade representative to stop trying to bully South Africa on the Medicines Act. The White House exempted South Africa from U.S. trade laws on the compulsory licensing and parallel importation of AIDS drugs. South Africa softened its stance just enough to appear as if there had been a real agreement and the drug companies there suspended their court action, leaving the Medicines Act in limbo.

The crisis didn't go away.

Pressure continued to mount on Big Pharma. In spring 2000, UN Secretary General Kofi Annan made a personal appeal to the drug companies. Their first response was to fend it off by discussing patents and intellectual property rights and how prices equated to innovation.

The South Africans didn't give a damn.

Next the drug companies tried blaming the Africans for their own plight. They said that these countries needed to better educate the population and to create an infrastructure through which drug donations would efficiently be distributed.

No one bought that one.

President Clinton then issued an executive order exempting the rest of Africa from those provisions of U.S. trade law – just as he'd already done with South Africa – saying that the United States would not interfere with African countries that happened to violate American patent law in obtaining cheaper AIDS drugs.

Opening the door to both parallel imports and compulsory licensing would be a help to Africa. And it wouldn't really hurt Big Pharma all that much. They'd always feared that they might inadvertently create a black market, that corruption in many of these countries would see their drugs sent abroad instead of given to the people, which would in turn undermine Big Pharma's own pricing structures in the rest of the world. Eastern Europe, for example, is becoming a very lucrative market for western pharmaceuticals. But it is still a fragile market. Flooding it with drugs that had been destined for Africa could easily ruin it. Compulsory licensing and parallel imports lessened the chances of that happening. So now, having held out as long as they dared, five pharmaceutical companies – Boehringer, Bristol-Myers Squibb, Merck, Glaxo, and Hoffmann-La Roche – announced they'd always been anxious to help and agreed to negotiate steep price cuts for AIDS drugs. This was when Glaxo offered Combivir, a blend of AZT and 3TC that normally sells at $16, for $2.

The other four only spoke vaguely of cuts up to 80 per cent off American retail prices. That would take the price of a common triple-therapy cocktail of AIDS drugs costing an American $15,000 a year down to $3,000. In countries where health-care spending was as little as C$15 per year per person, that would help fewer than a couple of hundred people. And then, only on the condition that the others went without any health care that year.

PhRMA came up with its expected criticism, saying that by encouraging compulsory licensing and parallel imports, the White House was setting "an undesirable and inappropriate precedent, adopting a discriminatory approach to intellectual property laws, and focusing exclusively on pharmaceuticals."

Leave it to PhRMA to miss the point – that all those people in Africa who are still dying are also focused exclusively on pharmaceuticals.

⬤▬

Prescription drugs rarely compete on price for the very simple reason they don't have to.

For most patients, priority number one is getting well. Price only comes into the equation when it is so high that the patient cannot afford to pay for the drug – or a health service refuses to pay for it – and therefore hinders treatment.

One of the rare instances where price reductions come into play is when a drug company wants to get its products listed on a hospital formulary. They treat it like a loss-leader. Hospitals in many jurisdictions have turned themselves into businesses, or they've begun applying cost-containment measures to supply purchases. As a result, drug companies make some of their more expensive drugs so cheap to hospital purchasing departments that the hospitals can afford to put patients on them. Then, because we all feel more comfortable with continuity, when the patient leaves the hospital, the company can charge real money for the drug.

The price of branded drugs has nothing to do with supply and demand. Well, at least not supply. The cost of supply includes the investment in research, an allotment to cover the costs when R&D fails to deliver a drug, the costs of meeting all of the various regulatory requirements, and the marketing of the product to doctors, hospitals, and patients.

Since 1985, Big Pharma claims, development costs have more than doubled. It throws around figures such as $500 million to come up with a new drug. But when you press Big Pharma, it ducks and weaves and mostly asks you to take it on faith. Looking closely at its claims – and it doesn't make it easy because it won't release the real numbers – you find it's based on drugs developed entirely in-house by American-owned companies and does not factor in pharmaceuticals developed outside the United States that are licensed in, which accounts for around 40 per cent of drugs introduced by Big Pharma in the United States.

Same thing in Canada. It's much cheaper to bring a drug in from the States, but the cost they usually cite is the highest price they have to pay in country. Nor does their arithmetic factor in drugs researched and developed in government labs, universities, or hospitals. It neglects to consider me-toos, line extensions, and tax write-offs for research.

As for the demand side of the equation, that's much less complex. As long as the marketing department can convince doctors that the drug is the best in the field – and that it's safe – they will prescribe it for their patients, without considering cost.

Therefore, drugs can be priced pretty much at whatever the company chooses. The risk of pricing too low is the wrath of the shareholders when dividends are announced. The risk of pricing too high is the wrath of some legislative body complaining that the companies are gouging the public. But only rarely does mispricing affect sales. Accordingly, they err on the side of shareholders and price higher rather than lower.

According to Dr. Stephen Schondelmeyer at the Prime Institute, the best indicator of what it really costs to make a drug is what happens to prices of the branded product when a generic version enters the market.

"As soon as the first generic comes in, they set the price at 75 to 80 per cent of the brand name," Schondelmeyer explains. "As other generics enter the market, the price comes down until it's somewhere around 25 to 30 per cent of what the original brand name was. So the actual cost of production and distribution of the drug, with a reasonable level of profit to keep a firm in business, is about 25 to 30 per cent of what the selling price actually is. Promotion costs get added onto that, ranging from 25 to 40 per cent."

Granted, R&D must be factored in on top of that. But Schondelmeyer raises another point.

"Are the companies who spend the most on R&D finding the most new drugs? That's not always the case. A number of years ago, one of the Wall Street firms did a comparison of the amount spent on R&D with the number of innovative products that companies brought to the market. They found clear differences in efficiency. Some produced a lot more for the money than others. And yet the market doesn't discipline this. In other industries if one company is more innovative than another, they will grow and develop and prosper more than others. But in pharmaceuticals, even the ones who aren't particularly productive with their R&D expenditures seem to continue and prosper. That's because they can simply raise their prices to cover their expenditures."

He concludes, "People in the pharmaceutical industry must live in a kind of a fairy world. They isolate themselves, talk to people who think like they do, and lose their sense of reality. They justify their prices by arguing that the rest of us don't know what the real world of business is like. I argue, they're so isolated doing business they don't know what the rest of the world is like. They make policy based on their own experience with health care, and with a $100,000 a year job, and with a health insurance policy that covers everything. They say, 'I don't have trouble with my drug costs, so why is everybody else complaining?'"

With busloads of American tourists heading to Canada to buy prescription drugs for around half of what they'd have to pay in the United States, politicians such as Congressman Bernard Sanders, an independent from Vermont – who was on the first bus to make a drug run a few years ago – finds the pharmaceutical industry's pricing methods disgraceful. "Taxpayers get hit twice. Once when their tax dollars go to develop these drugs at government labs and again when they have to buy the medication."

The example he frequently cites is a drug called Levamisole. Originally marketed in the United States by Johnson & Johnson as an anti-worm treatment for sheep, the company was charging veterinarians a mere 6 cents a pill. Then it learned that Levamisole could be used to treat colon cancer. The price shot up to around $6.

It's not the only example. A one-month supply of Medrol cost $3.90 as an anti-inflammatory for dogs, but when it was priced as a treatment for human asthma, it cost $20.10.

"I represent one of the poorest districts in the United States," declares Congressman Marion Berry from Arkansas, and the only pharmacist currently in the House. "I come from a rural part of the state where there are about eight hundred people. Now, we don't lock our doors. And I can tell you that if someone came into our homes and started stealing from us, we'd have our own way of dealing with those folks. But that's exactly what the pharmaceutical companies are doing. They're coming into our homes with their outrageous prices and they're literally stealing money, especially from people who can't afford it."

They get away with that in America, Berry continues, because the United States is the only free pharmaceutical market in the world. "The drug companies reckon that Americans have more money than anyone else and can afford to pay the highest prices."

Bruce Downey, chairman and CEO of the generic manufacturer Barr Laboratories, emphatically agrees that Big Pharma's pricing policy has nothing to do with cost.

"They're not related at all. They price on what is called the marginal-revenue curve. As long as they're obtaining marginal-revenue, which they do because their mark-ups are so great, they continue to increase the price. Prices go as high as they can until the product becomes so prohibitively expensive that they start losing revenues."

Rationalizing all of this, claims Barry Sherman, chairman and CEO of Apotex in Toronto, is Big Pharma's assertion that because its product is 20 per cent more effective than some other product, it should be allowed to charge 20 per cent more for it.

"It's absurd. It means that progress drives prices up. It's like saying that our airplane can get you somewhere in an hour while a horse and buggy will take a week, so the airfare should be 168 times more than the cost of the horse and buggy. The salvation of the economy in a competitive market is that if someone charges too much, someone else will come along and undercut that price. But with pharmaceuticals, where there is no real competition, the natural desire of the brand-name drug company is to get whatever it can, regardless of cost."

It makes the pharmaceutical industry unique, Sherman continues, despite the fact that it's not the only business relying on patents.

"Compare the drug industry to the computer industry. They have patents. What do you see? The rate of progress is phenomenal and prices come down. Computer memory doubles every so many months and the prices halve. That's with patents. What happens with drugs? They don't get cheaper. Every time there's a new drug it's more expensive than the last one. And that's not to say it's necessarily better. The rate of real progress has slowed because no one is in any hurry to increase the rate of replacement. They've got twenty years of monopoly to exploit this one. In other industries patents don't stop progress. In other industries, if you don't want to pay for something, you buy something else. But here you can't do that. The patient has to buy what the doctor prescribes, and the doctor doesn't care about the price."

Dr. Sheldon Krimsky at Tufts agrees that prices depend on a company's view of market conditions and what it can get. But he suggests there are exceptions, and they're usually political. "They have to have people working inside the company who understand the politics of disease. Some diseases are politically more important than other diseases, therefore governments will pay for those diseases even if the costs are very high."

In September 1999, Congressman Sherrod Brown – as ranking member of the Commerce Health and Environment Subcommittee – introduced the Affordable Prescription Drugs Act, declaring at the time that Big Pharma had finally outdone itself.

"When a majority of Americans believe Congress should establish a prescription drug benefit for Medicare beneficiaries and buy your products," Brown wrote, "you protest because you're afraid you wouldn't be paid enough. When some members of Congress propose that senior citizens get the same price discounts that large, profitable HMOs enjoy, you buy very expensive television advertisements and accuse government of meddling in your medicine cabinet. And when a few members of Congress suggest we bring some good old-fashioned American competition into the monopoly drug-pricing system, you spend millions lobbying Congress and threatening to stifle the development of new drugs if we take that step."

Troubled that Americans pay significantly higher prices for drugs than anyone else in the world, he can't understand how the companies get away with it. "Taxpayers fund much of the basic research that produces new drugs. You are granted generous tax subsidies for your own research. You charge outrageous prices to taxpayers to buy your drugs. You tell taxpayers you can't do any more research if your prices drop to the same levels as citizens in every other country in the world pay. You devote huge amounts to promote lifestyle drugs. And you earn windfall profits."

He also went after the CEO's salaries. "A woman in Elyria, Ohio, told me she spends $350 on prescription drugs every month out of her social security check of $808. It takes 5,134 senior citizens like her to pay your typical CEO salary every year."

It's becoming increasingly difficult, Brown believes, for Big Pharma to convince anyone that prices can't come down to more reasonable levels without bankrupting the industry. "Despite your well-oiled lobbying machine, despite your scare tactics, something will be done to bring down the cost of prescription drugs. It's just a matter of what."

His bill called for the compulsory licensing of patented medicines deemed to be unreasonably priced. It would, he promised, finally open the market to real competition. Under the act, other companies would be given the right to manufacture and sell patent-protected drugs by paying a royalty to the patent holder. Drug companies would also be required to disclose audited financial information justifying the prices they charged.

"If drug prices are where they need to be, prove it." Brown said he wanted Big Pharma to explain why royalties would not be enough to fund the percentage of R&D that the companies themselves actually paid for. To explain why direct-to-consumer advertising for a product that consumers didn't choose was more important than research and development. To explain why prescription drug prices in the United States were one-third higher than in Canada.

An average dosage of Zocor for high cholesterol was priced at $102 in the United States and only $44 in Canada. One month's supply of Tamoxifen for breast cancer sells for $156 in the United States but a mere $12 in Canada.

He concedes that Big Pharma was never going to like his bill. And he was dead right. It used its heavyweight lobbying muscle to make certain it never became law.

With many drugs it would perhaps be unfair to compare prices in different parts of the world. But some drugs are so out of line that they make the point. The price of one hundred units of Nevirapine, a medication that prevents transmission of the AIDS virus from mother to child, costs $430 in Norway, where the market for the drug is small, and $874 in Kenya, where AIDS has reached epidemic levels and where the health-care system is, for all intents and purposes, broke. Glaxo sells Betnasol, a drug used in ophthalmology to help prevent blindness, especially among the elderly, for around C$.05 in India and nearly C$3 in Sri Lanka.

Sometime after Glaxo promised the Africans that it would cut the price of Combivir – but didn't say how long the company would keep the price way down or how much Combivir it would sell at that price – Pfizer took a different approach. It announced it would donate its anti-fungal drug Diflucan to South Africa. It was better than nothing, but the problem with donations is that they're never a long-term solution.

Nobody knows that better than Richard Walden.

A health lawyer by training, Walden is also the son of a pharmacist. "In the fifty-five years that my dad was a pharmacist, the shelf life of pharma-ceuticals, including antibiotics, never significantly increased. With all of the fancy new coatings for capsules, time-release capsules, it's amazing to me that they're so short. What they won't do for profit. The drug compa-nies don't want to change the dates."

He'd specialized in what he describes as "civil rights kinds of cases in the health field," and wound up annoying California Governor Jerry Brown so much that in 1979 Brown challenged Walden to put his talents where his mouth was. Brown appointed him commissioner of hospitals for California.

It was at about that time when Walden and a friend dreamt up a one-time-only relief flight to help Vietnamese boat people washed up in a refugee camp in Malaysia.

They got an airplane from McDonnell Douglas for free – "We told the head of McDonnell Douglas that we were calling from the governor's office, which was almost true" – and because they knew a lot of people in the pharmaceutical industry, and knew that they often donated outdated drugs, they started making the rounds with a begging bowl.

Walden also knew that a lot of charities often supplied needy areas with drugs that weren't of any use, so he asked the drug companies what they were prepared to give him. He drew up a list and sent it off to Malaysia to see where it matched what was needed.

"We did it all without any money, and twenty-nine days later we were airborne with a load of stuff."

A ton of publicity gave them a ton of access to other drug companies with pharmaceuticals to give away, and Walden got so into it he gave up his law practice, gave up his appointment as commissioner of hospitals, and went into this charity business full-time. He called the charity Operation California, but changed in the mid-1980s to Operation USA, although he admits that sometimes sounds a little too governmental. When the name turns off people in foreign countries, he reverts to Operation California.

Walden quickly realized that the problem with donating drugs to the Third World was that not just any drugs work, that the people receiving the drugs need to understand the contraindications and read the labels, that it takes a lot of coordination.

Crazy things happen. "Three hundred airplanes landed in Armenia filled with broken kidney dialysis machines but no chemical agents or manuals to operate them, good stuff, bad stuff, and silly stuff, which the Armenian government, then still part of the Soviet Union, sold to the ministries of health of other Soviet republics for hard currency."

Even with half-decent coordination, things can still go wrong. "Some well-minded people sent Bosnia seventeen thousand tons of useless medical supplies."

Visiting a UN refugee camp in Split, Walden discovered that "drug supplies were coming in from England and Germany. Half-empty bottles, seven years' out of date from someone's medicine chest. And wildly out-of-date stuff in bulk from Germany. I told the UN camp director he had to shut that down because people were going to get killed with these medicines. This camp barely had any English- or German-language capability. How were they supposed to read the labels? A lot of the medications should never have been accepted in the first place."

What makes Operation USA different is that Walden always matches what he gets with what people in the field tell him they need, and then he makes certain that it goes out quickly and properly, so that those people in the field can have what they need in time to make the most use out of it. He's worked in eighty countries and has always matched in-kind donations – drugs from the pharmaceutical industry – with needs.

But he turns out to be the exception. "Some of the high-visibility groups are really awful. Big Pharma supports them for all sorts of reasons, mainly because they get the press that makes Big Pharma look good. In one case, a group shipped ten thousand cases of oral rehydration medication to Zaire for the Rwanda refugees, which turned out to be Gatorade.

They also sent $2 million worth of medical aid to St. Petersburg, which was really just two million candy bars. These groups are shills for the pharmaceutical industry. They don't smell like a charity. They may be non-profit, but they're not a charity."

The reason they get away with it is because the pharmaceutical industry doesn't discriminate enough when it comes to who they deal with.

"There are some complete wackos out there, bogus groups who seduce drug company executives with evaluations of what they were giving away, moving outdated stuff that couldn't be sold, and sending these drugs to the Third World by sea, in hot container ships so that the gelatin capsules melt. The groups don't care and the companies got their tax write-offs."

What Big Pharma used to do, back in the days when nobody was looking, was send its surplus production to some country and wildly exaggerate its value. Or it would send goods that had passed their sell-by date. It was cheaper, it found, to give drugs away than go through the expense of properly destroying them. But the charity business has grown up and the old tricks are harder to pull off. Walden says he recently looked at the top-seven pharmaceutical companies that supply surplus to charities, and then looked at the top-five non-governmental organizations (NGOs) that take donations from pharmaceutical companies, and saw that the drug companies were honestly valuing what they gave away – it totalled something like $50 million – but that the NGOs had valued those same donations at over $1 billion.

Walden tells drug companies that because Operation USA needs to ship these drugs out to faraway places in a timely manner, it needs a minimum of a year's dating left on the drugs and prefers it when there's more. If they want to seduce him with some very expensive, vitally needed antibiotics that have only six months left on the sell-by date, he'll take them and fly them out to where the drugs are going to be used. But he doesn't want too great a quantity because he knows they're only going to sit somewhere and rot.

"The problem is," he insists, "other groups don't give a shit about that sort of thing."

Further complicating matters, he says, drug companies that wildly overproduce see charity as a way of compensating for their mistakes. That's especially true when it comes to analgesics.

"They spend a ton of money on advertising and the product falls flat, so they wind up with 10 million extra doses with two years of shelf life. They give that away. That's great. One year we sent Tylenol, Aspirin, and Dristan in 8 million doses to the Ministry of Health in the Philippines, which allowed them to divert $1.2 million they would have spent on those medicines to buy more expensive stuff for malaria and to buy antibiotics."

But it doesn't always work so well. At the end of 1998, during the Hurricane Mitch disaster, Walden went to the Nicaraguan Ministry of Health to ask what they needed. He was told they were seeing an out-break of leptospirosis, a horrible rat-borne fever. They said they needed doxicycline. So Walden's people went to a Nicaraguan pharmaceutical wholesaler who gets his stuff from Panama or Costa Rica and tried to buy some. A bottle of one thousand pills normally costs $20 in the United States. The wholesaler in Nicaragua said he wanted $95. Walden found it in Amsterdam for $12.

"We could have gone directly to the drug companies to ask for it, and we did that in the old days when there were only two or three charities asking. Now there are thousands of groups asking and it's just caused so much confusion."

With hundreds of groups begging for anything and everything, there's no telling what the pharmaceutical companies might be willing to unload. That's when you hear about planes landing in some disaster area and dumping stuff on the Tarmac.

"Some companies are better than others," Walden suggests. "I have to say that as a class, the cancer companies are the stingiest. One of the reasons is, and they say it with some justification, that every cancer case is a compassionate case. So if you call them for Little Joe in Vietnam who's got some sort of cancer, they're getting 150 requests from all over the place and prefer to sell the drugs. They don't have a ton of surplus."

But with the rest of Big Pharma, there's a great deal of confusion about who's giving what and how.

"For the most part, the pharmaceutical companies give everything away for free. We get a fax from, say, Glaxo saying here's what we've got, do you want it? We'll say sure, send it to us, and then we'll see it gets sent to some place that needs that drug and distributed for free, just like the drug company intended. But some charities resell the stuff they get for free, supposedly to cover their own costs. And that sometimes looks as though the drug companies themselves are selling it."

It turns out they don't have to sell any drugs they give away, because if the drug companies have their inventory management right, they can give away drugs that they can't otherwise sell, which saves the costs of destroying those drugs, and also take a tax deduction, which can be manipulated by average accountants to bring in more than they would have made selling the stuff.

Tax law is supposed to limit drug companies to the amount they can deduct for a donation. Theoretically, there is a tax advantage. But then, the pharmaceutical industry is among the lowest taxpaying industries. They take R&D expenses. They take unsold inventory expenses. They move money around the world to declare what profits they declare in the lowest taxed jurisdiction.

"Technically, they shouldn't get any tax deductions for worthless products. If it expires on the shelf, it gets written off, and that's all. But I can tell you that in twenty-one years of being an in-kind distributor, we've never been asked by the IRS whether we've received a product from any company, or what it was worth or what it was valued at or what we thought it should be valued at. They can write off whatever they want. There seems to be no oversight by the IRS."

A study done by Professor Michael Reich of Harvard's School of Public Health, called "The Global Drug Gap," looked at 16,566 charitable drug shipments between 1994 and 1997, going to 129 countries. He found that drug companies combine their donations' program with inventory management. Because disposal of unwanted, unusable, expired, or otherwise unsuitable drugs can be an expensive process – they must be destroyed in specific ways – the industry has found that drug donations kill several birds with one stone. It helps them reduce both storage and disposal costs, and allows them to take hefty tax breaks while all the time appearing as if they are indeed trying to do some good for a disaster-struck population or the Third World in general.

Further confusing the issue, some charities that take drugs from companies fool around with the valuations they assign to those drugs.

"There really should be some initiative by the pharmaceutical companies," Walden continues, "to keep abreast of what's happening with the drugs they donate. If I have any gripe with the pharmaceutical companies, it's that they should be better educated about the groups they're giving stuff to. They should know enough to tell these groups, 'You're putting us in a bad light by taking ten times the value of what we give you. Maybe the pill we give you costs us five cents and maybe we sell it for five bucks, but you should only declare the donation at five cents!'"

Walden says that a drug company got in touch with him one day to announce that it had twenty thousand vials of an influenza flu vaccine it wanted to donate. This was good stuff. With a long-enough sell-by date, it would be enough medication for two hundred thousand injections. Walden was interested but asked if there were any restrictions. Sometimes there are because drug companies have offices all over the world and they don't want these free drugs going into a market where they've got an active sales force. In this case, there weren't.

At the time, Walden was putting together a shipment for the Philippines. He mentioned this to the drug company executive offering the vaccine, the executive said it was okay, and Walden agreed to include the vaccine in the shipment and the drug company's name on his press release.

He then asked for a faxed copy of the specs on the vaccine. That arrived in a few hours and he refaxed it to the World Health Organization (WHO). The next morning, the WHO came back to Walden to say, "Don't bother, it's the wrong strain for the Philippines."

So he put in a call to the drug company, got that executive on the line, said thanks but no thanks and please keep us in mind.

"The next I heard was that another charity took the vaccine and sent it through a partner agency to . . . guess where . . . the Philippines. The drug company never bothered to tell them what we'd told them about it being the wrong strain. So it wound up in the Philippines getting injected into the arms of all these people to absolutely no effect. The drug company didn't care who got the drug, or what happened to it."

It is, Walden says sadly, a typical story.

CHAPTER 7

A TALE OF TWO MORE DRUGS

It was 1949.

Louis St. Laurent was prime minister, Chiang Kai-shek fled China, leaving it to Mao, Gussie Moran shocked Wimbledon with her lace panties, and Carol Reed directed *The Third Man*.

Richard Strauss died, Israel was admitted to the United Nations, and the United States Department of Agriculture (USDA) embarked on the first large-scale collection of plants ever undertaken specifically for scientific study. Over the next ten years, USDA botanists would collect some seven thousand samples. When the initial research showed that certain plants could produce anti-tumour activity, a small but determined group of scientists at the National Cancer Institute (NCI) petitioned the USDA to send more teams out to look for even more plants.

Arthur Miller won the Pulitzer Prize for *Death of a Salesman*, William Faulkner won the Nobel Prize for Literature, and the Toronto Maple Leafs won the Stanley Cup for the third consecutive year.

South Pacific came to Broadway, the Berlin blockade was lifted, and a young, first-generation Greek-American was a senior at the University of Pennsylvania. That campus in west Philadelphia was a wonderful place to be young, and fifty years later he'd recall those days with enormous fondness when he returned to dedicate a research laboratory that would bear his name. But now, in the winter of 1949, it was time to plan his future.

"I want to be a doctor," Roy Vagelos told his family, "to understand the nature of human disease and to make a difference."

He was accepted at Columbia University's Medical School in New York, earned his MD there in 1954, and did his internship and residency at Massachusetts General Hospital in Boston. Years later, one of his supervisors at Mass General would recall, "Roy was probably the most brilliant and impressive young doctor any of us had ever seen."

After Boston, he moved to Washington, giving up patients for a research post at the National Institutes of Health. For Vagelos, who would spend the next ten years of his life immersed in cellular physiology and biochemistry, the plains of West Africa were very far away.

It was 1963.

A botanist and three college students spent that summer traipsing through northern California and up into Oregon, gathering bark and leaves because someone at the USDA had actually listened to the researchers at the National Cancer Institute and, even though it took fourteen years, funding did come through to send more teams out looking for more plants. When the summer was over, the botanist and the three college students had collected samples from 450 species.

Back in Washington, the samples were sorted and catalogued and then sent to various contract laboratories around the country for analysis. One of those labs was the Research Triangle Institute in North Carolina, where two scientists – Dr. Monroe Wall and his associate, Dr. M. D. Wani – set out on what would become an eight-year quest.

Included in their batch of samples was the bark of the *Taxus brevifolia*, otherwise known as the Pacific yew tree. Although the scientists didn't yet know it, Native American tribes had ascribed healing powers to the tree and ethnobotanical records dating back several centuries referred to its medicinal properties. Until the bark arrived in North Carolina, however, no western scientist had ever done any serious work on it.

"Our job was to do a bioassay," says Wall, now in his eighties and officially retired but still working in his lab every day. "We were to take extracts from these plant samples and look for biological activity. When there was none, we abandoned it and moved on to the next extract. When there was some, we continued to purify the extract until we could isolate the molecule that killed the cells. Then we determined the structure."

The two researchers conducted a bioassay on the bark and, to their surprise, found that it killed in vitro cancer cells. But purifying it down and establishing the structure of the compound – which is called paclitaxel – was a very laborious process.

Wall explains, "To begin with, the compound had an extremely complicated structure. In addition, the purification instrumentation that we were using then was very primitive compared with what we have nowadays. I think we finally had the compound isolated and the structure of it by 1970. It took that long. We published our paper on it in 1971. I decided to name it Taxol."

After ten years at the National Institutes of Health – some of which were spent working at the National Cancer Institute – Roy Vagelos moved to St. Louis, Missouri, to join the medical school faculty at Washington University, where he eventually became chairman of the department of biological chemistry.

"I was doing there what I had always been doing, basic biochemical research. And I was very happy to keep doing that."

But in 1975 an offer came to him that he simply couldn't refuse. One of the premier pharmaceutical companies in the world invited him to head up its research group.

"I accepted going to work for a pharmaceutical company because I wanted to use what I thought was a new way to discover drugs. That was the challenge."

Merck & Co. in Whitehouse Station, New Jersey, had been suffering a decade-long dry spell. Drug development had slowed to a critical point. Vagelos' reputation as a scientist was indisputably established, as was his reputation as an original thinker. But, in those days, his new way of discovering drugs – known these days as "rational drug development" – was considered radical.

Instead of randomly screening compounds in the hopes that a molecule might someday become a drug – the way the NCI was doing with Taxol – Vagelos had come to believe the process should start from the other end of the equation. He wanted to prioritize diseases he was familiar with and for which no effective therapies were available, and to create specific molecules to attack those specific targets.

"In the life of each drug-development project," reads his often-quoted remark from those days, "there is always a crisis, a moment when it looked like years of research will go down the drain and the drug will never come to market. There are a million ways to fail in this business."

The backwards approach sounded like one of them to the marketing people at Merck, especially since no other drug company ran its R&D this way. Today, they all do.

Because he was personally interested in finding treatments for glaucoma and high levels of cholesterol in blood, he committed company resources to the development of Timoptic for glaucoma and Mevacor and Zocor for high cholesterol. All three became blockbusters and are listed among the most successful products in the history of the company.

He also encouraged the marketing people to take risks they were not used to taking. Merck broke the mould for advertising with Mevacor – including TV spots to warn the public about the dangers of high cholesterol – and for a time it was the most promoted drug in the world. Mevacor captured a one-third market share for cholesterol-reducing drugs and racked up some of the highest sales ever of any prescription medicine.

While other companies grew through mergers and acquisitions, Merck stayed ahead of them by growing organically, by developing new and important drugs through research. Still, Vagelos' victories did not come easily. He stressed science, but the marketing people did not share his enthusiasm for some of the diseases he was targeting. In fact, he says, they found many of his targets totally unimportant.

"Marketing people have marketing backgrounds. They work on surveys. They went into the market to see what important drugs were used for the control of high blood cholesterol and because the drugs out there then weren't very effective and had a lot of side effects, because at the time there were no good drugs for the control of high blood cholesterol, they decided there wasn't much of a market for that. Unless there's an obvious leader out there, marketing people don't recognize what's important. They don't have the scientific background to realize it. Of course, you try to educate them, but in the end you go about doing what's important. You follow your own instincts."

His instincts told him to make certain that the marketing people stayed out of his hair. "I never paid a lot of attention to marketing people. Early on, they opposed some of the things I wanted to work on, but they couldn't stop me because I was head of research. I reported to the CEO, who had great confidence in me for whatever reason. So I was left alone."

Besides coming up with a whole series of blockbuster drugs for the western world where patients and health-care services had the money to afford them, Vagelos helped to develop a vaccine for control of hepatitis B.

A serious enough problem in the developed world, it is an ever-greater problem in Asia. The infection is carried in about 13 per cent of the Chinese population, can lead to liver cancer, and is one of the leading causes of death in China. Merck, under Vagelos, developed a vaccine to prevent the infection. Beijing complained that it couldn't afford it. The marketing people haggled with the Chinese government for a couple of years trying to come up with a fair price, and when it didn't happen, there was a real risk that Merck would walk away.

Without Vagelos, it might have.

Certainly Big Pharma has never been shy about doing that. But Vagelos saw another way. He committed the company to help the Chinese build two manufacturing plants so they could make their own vaccine. Beijing paid a very low price for the licence, which Merck then spent on the technology transfer.

"It took over a year to get them ready. We had Chinese people working with us to learn how to do it. We built the process in one of our manufacturing plants, took it apart, shipped it to China, and rebuilt it there. Today those two plants in China have the capacity to immunize 20 million infants per year, which is essentially the birth cohort there. Eventually that disease will disappear in China."

Vagelos also swam against the tide on drug pricing. In 1985, the year he became chairman and CEO of Merck, the industry was in the midst of steeply rising prices, trying to catch up with steeply rising inflation rates.

"I don't like to see people not getting drugs or feeling that pharmaceutical prices are too high, so I asked the financial people to show me how much we had lost to inflation and what we'd made back by the increases in our prices. When we extrapolated, we found a point where we'd have caught up. I said, 'Once we've done that and once we've established a fair price for our products, we should not raise our prices faster than the increase in the consumer price index for the inflation rate.' We made that Merck policy. And it had a remarkable effect on the industry. Although, I must confess, there was a fair amount of grumbling because we were the market leader and we clearly enunciated our policy."

The rest of the industry was slow to follow – annual hikes were in the 10 to 12 per cent range – and for a while it looked as if the government might step in with price controls. By 1991, Vagelos was openly criticizing his competitors. "I detest regulation," he said at the time, "but it may be brought about by my colleagues. Drug prices are such an obvious target."

The Clinton administration took aim at drug prices, and even questioned Merck's figures. Whereas aggregate price rises had been low, the price increase of certain popular drugs was much steeper. In response, Vagelos instituted even more stringent voluntary controls.

His plan was to limit increases on any single product to 1 per cent above the inflation rate, to allow independent auditors to monitor this, and to impose penalties for violations. The fines would go into a government fund to improve health care. He calculated that if every company in the industry signed onto the program, consumers would save $7 billion to $9 billion over a three-year period.

Big Pharma responded publicly with every reason under the sun why this should never happen, and privately called for Vagelos' scalp. It was only under pressure from the Clinton administration that other companies reluctantly, but eventually, agreed to join.

Unfortunately, but to the great relief of most other Big Pharma CEOs, the Merck plan fizzled out. Which brings Vagelos to admit, "Prices have gotten out of hand again."

But then, the independence he brought to his job at Merck and all the battles he won there pale by comparison to what happened one day in 1981 when a physician walked into his office and told him about the blackfly.

⊂▯⊃

Neither Dr. Monroe Wall nor Dr. M. D. Wani understood how paclitaxel worked. At the time, no one did. But it was obvious to them that this was something very special and needed to be studied further. Unfortunately, several problems arose, not the least of which was the scarcity of the substance. Paclitaxel is so scarce that, years later when the major pharmaceutical companies would consider using it to make a drug, they'd find out it required an entire tree simply to supply one patient with one dose.

Still, Wall was determined. He'd seen the structure of it and was so firmly convinced of its promise that he spent the next four years trying to persuade the NCI to make a large-scale collection.

"I desperately wanted them to do more work in the lab and then go into clinical testing," says Wall. "But they chose not to do so at the time. They gave me every excuse in the book. They said it was expensive. They said the yield would be low. No matter what I said, they had more excuses. I tried desperately hard to get them to move faster, but I was unsuccessful."

At least it looked that way, until 1978.

The government had, by then, spent $270,000 on paclitaxel, for which it had the structure of the molecule but little else. Whether it was to protect that initial investment, which is not usually the way the government thinks, or because the people who believed in Wall were now senior enough to do something about it – and that is the more likely of the possibilities – the NCI picked up the project again and funded it for the next step.

Dr. Susan Horwitz is a biochemist at Albert Einstein Medical College in New York. Her expert work on small molecules had attracted the NCI's attention and it now wondered if she would be interested in taking a look at this one. After seeing the structure of the molecule as Wall had described it, she agreed to do a detailed study. Horwitz was the one who discovered the particular mechanism in Taxol that prevents a cell from dividing.

That mechanism binds itself to microtubules, which are fibrelike structures, sort of like cables inside cells that pull them apart when they divide. As the process begins, these microtubules build up. At the end of the process, they normally break down. What this mechanism did was prevent the microtubules from breaking down, in turn clogging cells with microtubules, stopping them from growing, and, in turn, preventing them from dividing.

This was something never before seen in any other anti-tumour drug, which meant that science suddenly had a new class of chemotherapeutic agent to work with.

Based on Horwitz's results, the NCI's interest was sufficiently renewed to ask for a larger sample and to begin the tests that Wall had always hoped for. Phase I clinical testing with paclitaxel began in 1983. Some of the initial results showed promise, but not all of them did and the picture became confused. When allergic reactions to the solvent in the formula stopped some trials and delayed others, questions were raised about the rationale for further funding. But the doubters were in the minority and more money was put into the project.

The NIH contracted with the Hauser Chemicals Company to collect yew tree bark and manufacture Taxol so that there would be enough for Phase II trials.

In November 1988, with Taxol now being used in experiments on refractory ovarian cancers, the head of the cancer therapy evaluation program at the National Cancer Institute left the government to become senior vice-president for cancer research at Bristol-Myers.

Three months later, heartening clinical results were reported by Johns Hopkins University. Researchers there claimed paclitaxel had produced a 30 per cent response rate in patients with advanced ovarian cancer.

Encouraged by that, in August 1989 – with the American taxpayer having now funded over $9 million worth of research on Taxol – the NIH decided to shop around for a company that could take this drug to market. Accordingly, a notice was published in the U.S. Federal Register giving any interested concern a month to respond.

Mohammad Aziz was born in Pakistan and spent several years working for the World Health Organization (WHO) as an infectious disease specialist in West Africa before coming to Merck. At the time, Merck had a drug that was very potent in the control of certain parasites but unfortunately didn't work on the two most important human parasitic diseases: tapeworm and hookworm. Instead, the drug was marketed to treat parasites in animals, especially heartworm in dogs.

It was popular with veterinarians, worked well, and Roy Vagelos had never given it a second thought. At least not until Aziz came to see him about the blackfly.

"Mohammad told me it was possible that this drug could work for river blindness. And I had to say to him, 'What's river blindness?'"

Medically known as onchocerciasis, it's a disease caused by a parasitic worm that can live and reproduce for up to fourteen years in the human body. Victims suffer constant itching, loss of skin colour, sores, premature aging, and eventual blindness.

The worm is transmitted to humans by the bite of the blackfly, which breeds in fast-flowing rivers. Very prevalent in west Africa, especially along the basin of the Volta River, blackflies spread the disease as much as 250 to 300 miles from where they breed, threatening approximately 80 million Africans a year.

Vagelos admits that when you're running the research department of a major pharmaceutical company in New Jersey – whose paramount market is the developed world – river blindness is not the sort of disease most Big Pharma executives can spend a lot of time worrying about. But Vagelos was not like most Big Pharma executives.

"Mohammad explained what had been done to try to eradicate the blackfly and told me how many people were at risk. He asked if he could take some of this drug we had and go to Africa. I said sure. Well, he went and he tried the drug on a very small number of patients and sure enough, it had a remarkable effect. Six months later, after a single initial dose, the worms were gone."

Without any hesitation, Vagelos ordered more testing. "I saw no problem with that. It was the right thing to do." And in so doing, he committed the company to a multimillion-dollar investment. Six years later, when the studies were complete, Merck had a drug called Mectizan that successfully treated the disease.

But Mectizan's success created additional headaches for Vagelos.

The marketing people and the corporate accountants wanted to know how much the company would charge for it. They weren't exactly overjoyed when Vagelos reminded them that the people who so desperately needed this drug lived in mud huts and couldn't possibly pay for it.

The word "donation" was not one that certain factions inside the company wanted to hear. Philanthropy might make for good short-term public relations, but like the adage says, No good deed goes unpunished.

Vagelos heard from the legal staff that they had apprehensions about corporate exposure to liability if the drug caused unexpected adverse reactions. He heard from the people dealing with Wall Street and shareholders that this might upset the investment community who expected the company to be in the business of profits, not charity. He heard from his finance people, who felt this could set a precedent that would make

Merck look terrible if it didn't give away other drugs to people who needed them. And he heard from other Big Pharma CEOs, who complained that if Merck made a habit of this, they might be expected to follow suit – to give away for free the products of their research into diseases of the developing world – which they really didn't want to do. They warned that one alternative, if Merck continued to put them in such an awkward position, was simply to stop doing any research into diseases of the developing world.

By now Vagelos was running Merck and, as chairman and CEO, he was not going to be challenged on this.

"Everyone knew where the disease was and that there was no money. So yeah, a lot of people worried about it. I knew going in that there was no way those people in Africa could ever pay for this drug. But this was something so incredibly important to do that there was no way Merck was not going to do it."

Needing around $20 million to help cover costs and distribution of the drug for the first year, his initial plan was to convince the WHO to join forces with Merck. But WHO didn't want to know – a bizarre attitude, considering that many people believed this project was exactly what WHO was supposed to be doing and, moreover, now does.

He then went to some of the African governments where the illness was rampant, but they couldn't raise the money.

Next stop was Washington. Hat in hand, Vagelos easily lined up plenty of congressional support and found loads of people in the government who said they were behind the project all the way. But when those people said, "All the way," it didn't mean what Vagelos hoped it meant, which was all the way to the bank.

"We weren't asking for a lot of money. Everyone kept telling me, 'This is good and we need to do it.' I met with Don Regan at the White House, he was Ronald Reagan's chief of staff, who said this was something we ought to do and that he wanted to do it. But as soon as we walked out of his office, the fellow I'd been in there with from the Agency for International Development said they'd love to do it, but they had no money. I also went to the State Department and had exactly the same experience. The deputy secretary of state said he wanted to do it, but as soon as I stepped out of his office, his guy said, 'Yes, we'd love to do it, but we're broke.' Can you imagine that?"

All these years later, he still finds it pitiful.

"The trouble with these bureaucrats is that they have their own priorities, their own agendas, their own opinions of what's important. Parasites in Africa was simply not very high on their list. But here was a chance to affect lives in a positive way and to plant the American flag for very little money. I tried to put that idea into their heads. I tried very hard. But they just didn't get it."

CD

Government laboratories and publicly funded institutions throughout the world are always turning out ideas that could qualify as being "for the advancement of the public good."

Transcending all the various disciplines, they can be especially potent when they touch on new technologies. And Big Pharma is always keeping an ear to the ground, just in case one of these ideas can be exploited as a blockbuster drug. Believing that ideas "for the advancement of the public good" should indeed be exploited, Congress passed the 1986 Federal Technology Transfer Act, which created Cooperative Research and Development Agreements (CRADAs).

The thinking behind the agreements was sound. Here's a product that taxpayer money has researched and helped to develop, and because the government has decided it is for the advancement of the public good, the public will turn over its rights to the idea to some private company to market it so that, in return, the public will benefit.

As for any strings attached – basically, there aren't any.

The company has to pay for the manufacturing and marketing of the idea, and there may well be some additional development costs. But the bulk of the research and development has been paid for by the taxpayer and handed to the company as a gift. The only clause in the agreements that protects the public is the company's promise to "price it reasonably."

No one in Congress seemed to think at the time that the taxpayer might be entitled to a royalty on sales of the item – some reasonable percentage that could be funnelled back through the government's coffers to fund future research – or that any company exploiting an idea could somehow confuse "price it reasonably" with a licence to gouge the public.

Dr. Sheldon Krimsky, an expert on corporate ethics at Tufts University in Boston, labels the process "reverse capitalism."

"The pharmaceutical companies justify themselves by saying that the public good is served by the very expensive product they produce," says Krimsky. "We say, 'What is your public value?' We say, 'You not only used the research that is publicly funded, but you also get all kinds of benefits from government subsidies, etc. What do we get in return?' They say, 'You get a very expensive drug.' The way capitalism is supposed to work is that private risks generate private profits or private losses, and public risks should generate public profits, or public losses. In this case we have public risks generating private profits. That is, we take risks with public funds by putting money into research, and when the scientists get results, the company gets the intellectual property rights."

It took the very first CRADA to demonstrate just how naïve Congress had been. Whereas the pharmaceutical industry often reminds critics that it funds 60 per cent of all health-care R&D, it's not terribly pleased when that statistic is turned around the other way. To wit: The government funds 40 per cent of all health-care R&D. At the same time, when it comes to government largesse, every drug company on the planet sings off the same hymn sheet. To wit: Public money is vitally important and must be encouraged because it is the essential groundwork on which the development of new drugs is built.

They argue, collectively, that information derived from government funding is indispensable and that anything that might somehow discourage governments from this partnership, or otherwise restrict Big Pharma's access to publicly funded R&D, is incontestably detrimental to science.

Leading the chorus to have it both ways is the Pharmaceutical Research and Manufacturers of America (PhRMA). The industry's Rottweiler lobby, it never hesitates to take aim at anyone daring to suggest that anything with Big Pharma is wrong, unethical, shady, greedy, or otherwise questionable. If you suggest that drug prices are too high, it snaps back, "We are a research-based industry and the costs of developing new drugs are very great." If you suggest that Big Pharma might somehow be made more accountable when taxpayers' money is used, it hits you with, "It would be harmful to erect deterrents to this public/private collaboration."

In both cases, what it really means is government funding is money in the bank for the industry, but don't ask us to pay any of it back because once the government stops writing cheques for research, we have to foot the rest of the bill, which makes us entitled to whatever profits we can reap on these drugs.

That taxpayers' money ought to earn money and that companies with successful products should reimburse the government is not what it wants to hear.

"We act strictly within the law," PhRMA reminds anyone who dares to insinuate that the industry might not always act in the public's best interest. "We play by the rules."

Which is not to say that acting within the law or playing by the rules is synonymous with ethical behaviour.

A team of investigative reporters from the *Boston Globe* found that forty-five out of the fifty top-selling drugs in the world were discovered, developed, and/or tested with the taxpayers' money. One example they cited was the $46 million spent by the taxpayer on the cancer drug Proleukin. Treatments with the drug reportedly cost up to $20,000. Another example is Abbott Laboratories use of $3.2 million of government monies in the design and development of Norvir, a protease inhibitor used to slow the progression of AIDS. In the first six months of 1997, Abbott's Norvir sales topped $41 million.

Through clever management, even foreign companies take advantage of Uncle Sam's benevolence. The multiple sclerosis drug Copaxone was developed by researchers in Israel, who, with the help of collaborators in the United States, had received a grant of around $5 million from the NIH. When they licensed the drug to Teva Pharmaceutical Industries, an Israeli company, Teva turned to the FDA. Under the Orphan Drug Program – which further subsidizes the development of treatments for rare diseases – Teva picked up $300,000 in grants and tax breaks plus a seven-year marketing monopoly. A year's treatment can cost up to $10,000. The company's first-year return in the United States alone was reported to be $50 million. A Teva executive has been quoted as saying that the company might be willing to reimburse the government for grants in the future, but this time the money had no strings attached.

In some of these deals there are royalty schedules attached to government funding, but they are not aggressively administered. It's almost as if no one really wants to upset the industry by asking for the rent because the industry has got everyone believing that, metaphorically, if you press them for the rent they'll pick up and move.

The *Boston Globe*'s reporters estimated that for every $1 billion spent by the government, royalty returns amounted to a paltry $27 million.

But the government really surpassed itself – and set a precedent – with that first CRADA, which was the marketing agreement for Taxol.

When the NCI invited pharmaceutical companies to develop the drug, twenty firms were interested enough to look into the possibility. Only four applied. When three of the four dropped out – their common complaint was that the minuscule supply of the compound severely hindered development of the drug – the winner by default was Bristol-Myers Squibb.

In subsequent statements, BMS has claimed that it was really taking a huge gamble to join the CRADA. It insists that success was never guaranteed and that the supply and purity problems might have been insurmountable. Yet within two years of signing the agreement, BMS had solved those problems, obtained initial marketing clearance from the FDA, and was producing enough Taxol to supply patients in the United States.

It got around the supply problem when it discovered that some of the compound could be isolated from the leaves. When BMS found the same tree growing in India, it further assured supply. While this was going on, the NIH had been funding a project at Florida State University to semi-synthetically reproduce the molecule. Over a twelve-year period, Dr. Robert Holton, a professor of organic chemistry, received a total of $2.3 million from the government for the work. The university licensed the method to BMS, who pays FSU a fee every year. Royalties have now surpassed $125 million. Holton personally receives a 40 per cent share.

Once the FDA approval came through in 1992, BMS announced that the wholesale price of Taxol would be $4.87 per milligram, which was ten times the price the NIH was paying Hauser Chemicals for Taxol and twenty times the amount BMS was paying Hauser for bulk Taxol. Today, the price of bulk Taxol is half what it was then – about $0.125 per milligram – while the cost of packaging and final preparation for distribution to doctors has been estimated to cost BMS about $0.15 per milligram. That leaves an inexplicably large margin, considering that the cost to the patient runs around $8.61 per milligram.

When a Dutch firm began conducting its own paclitaxel trials in the European Union, BMS decided that litigation would cost too much to keep it out of the market, so it bought the company.

When Congress wouldn't accede to a BMS request to block generic competition in 1997 by extending from five to ten years the company's exclusive rights to the taxpayer-funded data on Taxol — despite offering to pay the government a 3 per cent royalty for the privilege — BMS blocked generic competition first by claiming that it would infringe one of the patents taken out to protect the methods of administering the drug, then by returning to the public feedbox and getting Taxol declared an orphan drug for the treatment of AIDS-related Kaposi's sarcoma. That special status gave it extra funding, tax breaks, and the additional exclusivity it had asked for. This, despite an apparent earlier promise not to use orphan drug status for Taxol.

Since then, BMS has used its political pull in Washington to fight generic Taxol coming onto markets in the European Union, Canada, Australia, New Zealand, Indonesia, Pakistan, Taiwan, China, Thailand, South Africa, Argentina, and Turkey. The basis of those objections are the World Trade Organization provisions on intellectual property, which protects undisclosed data — the very same taxpayer-funded data — that BMS claims is exclusively its own.

The company continues to defend its pricing of Taxol by asserting that it has had to commit huge sums to secure future supplies of the drug. On closer inspection, a watchdog agency in Washington revealed that this commitment consists primarily of long-term contracts with companies such as Hauser and has nothing to do with the research and development of the drug.

It is true that, early on, BMS supplied the NIH with seventeen tons of Taxol — bought from Hauser for around $5 million — and eventually negotiated a deal with the government to extend the monopoly on the drug in exchange for a $3.4 million payment to the NIH.

Also, to give the company its due, it now offers the drug for free to women who can't afford it or are otherwise uninsured. Although "free Taxol" isn't listed in the Yellow Pages, many people who can't afford it, or don't know how to get it from BMS for free, still wind up going without.

Faced with the predicament that if Merck didn't donate Mectizan to the people of Africa, it wasn't going to be used, Roy Vagelos made the decision that Merck would make the drug available to anyone who needed it and for as long as it was needed.

As far as Vagelos can see, Merck is still dedicated to doing that. "Once the decision was made, we did what we had to do. A year later, one hundred thousand people were treated."

Just before he retired, Vagelos went to see how the drug was working. In early 1994, he and his wife visited Africa with former U. S. president Jimmy Carter and his wife, Rosalynn.

"We went in by big plane, then farther in by little plane, then farther in still by Land Rover, and finally we walked until we got to a village. These people are dirt poor, they live in mud huts, they have barely enough to eat. And in a population like that, 20 per cent of the adults might be blind. It's devastating. I saw young people, seventeen, eighteen years old, completely blind."

Although Mectizan hasn't yet eradicated the disease, Vagelos thinks it will. "If you go into a region and give one tablet to all the population, then the blackflies no longer have a source of the infectious parasite, so that whole area becomes free until flies come in from elsewhere. Once the whole population in the endemic area is treated by drugs, the flies will have no source and the disease will disappear. That's on track, but it might take another ten years of treatment."

The key to that are the partners, who, as it became more obvious the project was going to be a success, happily jumped on the bandwagon. The World Health Organization came along to deliver the drug to the bush and to administer it. The World Bank came along to commit over $100 million in funding. Merck's success even shamed a few other companies into programs of their own. Dupont developed a fabric that's used in Africa and Latin America to filter water to stop guinea worm; SmithKline Beecham contributed a drug, albeit on a small scale, to control elephantiasis; Glaxo is providing some parts of the Third World with a new anti-malaria drug; and Pfizer put together a program to control trachoma, another eye disease.

"They've all referenced Merck's program," Vagelos says with unabashed pride. "But they'd never say they patterned their actions on ours. They wouldn't want to admit that. When, in fact, they did."

It was 1999.

Depending on whose accounting you use, American taxpayers had shelled out somewhere between $12 million to $35 million – funding biological cell screening, chemical purification, isolation and identification of the molecule, dosage formulation, toxicology, filing the Investigational New Drug application, and sponsoring clinical studies – so that Bristol-Myers Squibb could commercially exploit Taxol "for the advancement of the public good."

At the University of Pennsylvania, the senior who dreamed of being a doctor fifty years before now returned to dedicate the Roy and Diana Vagelos Laboratories of the Institute for Advanced Science and Technology.

The fair-pricing clause in the CRADA that Bristol-Myers Squibb signed reads: "NCI has a concern that there be a reasonable relationship between the pricing of Taxol, the public investment in Taxol research and development, and the health and safety needs of the public. Bristol-Myers Squibb acknowledges that concern, and agrees that these factors will be taken into account in establishing a fair market price for Taxol."

In Africa, the total number of people who have now received Mectizan from Merck, and been saved from river blindness, has surpassed 25 million.

And Bristol-Myers Squibb sells $4.5 million worth of Taxol every day.

CHAPTER 8

NANCY O TALKS FAST

Nancy O talks fast.

"I published the paper in the *New England Journal of Medicine* on August 13, 1998, and this was when the hospital was expecting a huge donation from Apotex to the tune of $10 million, and the university was expecting one to the tune of $25 million from Apotex, so unknown to us when we raised this, the hospital was nervous as a kitten."

With a backpack instead of a purse, jeans, track shoes, and curly blonde hair off-setting her college-girl looks, it's still not easy to mistake Nancy Olivieri for what she really is: a force of nature.

"Apotex went after me with a ten-foot pole and said, 'You'll be sued,' which was very lucky, I've never been luckier, because if they had been subtle, I mean, they said, 'You're going to be sued if you tell anyone, and it's tape-recorded.'"

Trying to keep up with her is a neat trick because she talks at the same speed she thinks.

"So Leslie Stahl at *60 Minutes* says, 'Well, but there's a transcript, and there's Barry Sherman on camera,' right, and then they showed it and everyone who's watching with us starts cheering. I mean, come on, it's hard to beat a tape-recording."

Nancy Olivieri was born and raised in Hamilton, Ontario, where her father was a pediatrician. A straight-A high-school student for whom med school seemed an obvious option, she graduated from the University of Toronto in 1975, got her MD at McMaster, and did postgraduate clinical and research training in hematology and oncology at Toronto and Harvard. She was, by all accounts, a brilliant and dedicated doctor. In fewer than ten years, she worked her way up to a full professorship in pediatrics and medicine at Toronto, was awarded a Career Scientist prize from the Ontario Ministry of Health, and was directing the Hemoglobinopathies Program at both Toronto Hospital and the Hospital for Sick Children, affectionately known as Sick Kids.

In the meantime, she also established herself as an internationally recognized expert on thalassemia, a rare group of blood disorders characterized by insufficient hemoglobin, the protein that carries oxygen through the body. It used to be called "Mediterranean Anemia" because there was a very significant patient population clustered around Cyprus, Turkey, Italy, and what was once Macedonia: northern Greece, southern Yugoslavia, and southwest Bulgaria. It is also prevalent on the Indian subcontinent and in Sri Lanka, in the Philippines, Indonesia, Thailand, Burma, Malaysia, and China. Some variations of thalassemia are relatively minor. A few, slightly more serious variations resemble anemia. The most brutal forms, however, show up in infancy, stunt growth, and almost always bring about premature death.

Treatment of the severest variation is equally brutal. Regular blood transfusions must be given to keep iron levels from becoming dangerously low. The transfusions are given overnight and, especially when children are involved, are a horrible nightmare for both the child and the parents, who often administer it.

Understandably, for thalassemia sufferers, for their families, and for the medical staff who treat them, the Holy Grail is a pill that will do the same thing as the transfusion. And in 1987, when Nancy Olivieri first read in the *British Journal of Hematology* about a drug scientifically known as deferiprone, but referred to as L1, she quickly became its biggest champion.

The drug had been discovered in a research laboratory in London, England, and had shown some early promise but turned out to have had a checkered history. Ciba-Geigy – now Novartis – thought enough of L1 after preliminary tests to patent it. But when Ciba did some testing on animals, it concluded that L1 was too toxic to develop further. Because the thalassemia community was desperate for anything that would eliminate those harrowing transfusions, other researchers continued to look at the drug. Olivieri phoned the doctor in Britain who did the research for the article, but found him to be extremely dismissive. Unable to get the information she wanted from him, she decided, in typical Nancy O fashion, "I'll just do it myself."

She easily obtained the molecule's structure, showed that to Robert McClelland – a highly respected professor of chemistry at the University of Toronto – and asked if he could replicate it. He said it was easy, and he did. And for the next four years, Olivieri ran trials with her consenting patients at Toronto and Sick Kids, funded by the Medical Research Council of Canada.

"It was an experimental drug in Britain," she says. "We needed an alternative to the standard infusion and this looked exactly like what we needed. An oral alternative would be a godsend. So we made the first pills at the University of Toronto and a huge Canadian generic drug company called Novapharm agreed to encapsulate them for us for free. The Health Protection Branch gave us approval, and we started using it."

Along with Dr. Gary Brittenham – then at Case Western Reserve University in Cleveland and now at Columbia University in New York – the two decided that the next step should be to find out what they needed to get approval for this drug in the United States.

The FDA has a service it provides to drug developers, one that other agencies around the world don't offer. The agency will actually sit down with an investigator or a company and go through the knowledge that's available about a drug, examine the proposed package of trials that are likely to be done in the future, and tell the investigator or the company what the agency would likely find wanting if that development plan goes forward. In essence, it helps you do your homework.

"The FDA told us we needed four things," Olivieri explains. "We needed to continue the long-term trial. We needed a comparison trial between standard therapy and this experimental drug. We needed a large toxicity trial. And we needed a commercial source of the drug to make it under good laboratory practice."

The long-term trial wasn't going to be a problem because she'd been following the same patients for four years. A comparison between therapies wasn't a problem either. There was plenty of data to relate L1 to the drug used in the transfusion, deferoxamine. The toxicity trial did, however, present a worry because the patient population in Canada is small. She and Brittenham decided they could get around that by going to Europe and the Far East, where there were plenty of patients.

"In Sardinia where I've worked," she mentions, "there's an entire hospital where all three floors are just for thalassemia."

As for a commercial source of the drug, Olivieri didn't have to look far. Her connection was right down the hall at Sick Kids.

Gideon Koren was a physician from Tel Aviv who'd been on the Toronto and Sick Kids staffs since 1986. He too was a full professor in pediatrics and medicine but had added pharmacology to his studies and had established his own international reputation in clinical pharmacology and toxicology. He was highly successful at bringing in funding and was described by one university colleague as "our poster boy." He was head of the pharmacology/toxicology division and ran extensive programs through the Research Institute at Sick Kids with support from, among other sources, the pharmaceutical industry.

Enter here, Koren's friend and sometime benefactor, Dr. Michael Spino. A former full-time member of the university's faculty of pharmacy, Spino had also held an appointment in the department of pediatrics. In 1979, he'd established a laboratory at Sick Kids where he conducted research and supervised graduate students. In 1992, he resigned from the university to take a job at Apotex, Canada's leading generic drug company, where he was now vice-president for scientific affairs. But uniquely, he was awarded a full professor "status-only" position by the university, allowing him to keep office space there and at Sick Kids, and also to maintain his lab at Sick Kids. Spino continued doing research at the hospital and supervising graduate students who were assigned to work with him and alongside Koren.

It is this relationship that lies at the heart of the matter.

"There are many people who would say this is unacceptable," claims Dr. Michele Brill-Edwards, a former senior physician responsible for prescription drug regulation at Canada's Health Protection Branch, who watched the drama unfold with growing disgust. She argues that it is unacceptable behaviour for Michael Spino to hold a post with a pharmaceutical firm and to retain his post in the clinical pharmacology division at the hospital. "That," she says, "clearly mixes the work of the pharmaceutical firm with the work of the clinical pharmacology division. Most people would say, 'Wait a second, there is too much opportunity here for his role as the vice-president of Apotex to colour his thinking about the products they make and then to colour the thinking of the unit at the hospital.'"

But at the time that didn't concern Nancy Olivieri. Koren was a prestigious colleague and also the route to Spino. And Spino offered the possibility of money from Apotex.

The company had flown high for many years, driven by its chairman, Bernard "Barry" Sherman, one of Canada's twelve richest men. Sherman started Apotex in the 1960s, at a time when the generic drug business was a buccaneering exercise in freewheeling capitalism. The market for copycat drugs was wide open, the government had been encouraging generic companies – in those days Ottawa believed it needed to keep drug prices down and this was the best way to do it – and by selling Big Pharma's drugs cheaper than Big Pharma, fortunes could be made. But the politics of drugs in Canada had changed over the years and Sherman's business had slowed down considerably. Still, when he heard about L1, he insists, he didn't hesitate to say that Apotex would get involved.

"The regime that thalassemia patients have to go through is so terrible that many patients just refuse to do it and die as a result. Or they don't do it regularly and die. Or the reactions to it are so bad that they can't take it. What's needed is a tablet. That's deferiprone. Mike Spino came to me and said, 'We could take this over. We have the chemical plants and the know-how. We would have to fund all these studies to get it approved. It will cost us $20 million to $30 million, and by the way, we won't make money on it, but we're going to save a lot of lives.' He asked, 'Will we do it?' And I said, 'Yes, we'll do it.'"

So, in 1993, Olivieri signed a contract with Apotex Research Inc. to evaluate the use of deferiprone in the treatment of iron overload in patients with thalassemia major. Gideon Koren was also brought on board, signing a contract with Apotex as Olivieri's co-investigator, despite the fact that Koren was not an expert in thalassemia and would not be an active participant in the trials.

Apotex did not come up with C$20 million to C$30 million. At this point, the company's commitment was only around C$120,000. Still, in those days, Mike Spino and Barry Sherman liked Olivieri's credentials. And, in those days, she appreciated the money they were putting into the studies that she would design for 180 patients in Toronto, Montreal, Philadelphia, and Italy. But included in her contract was a clause to protect trade secrets – just like the gag clauses that were meant to shut up David Kern and Betty Dong – designed, the company said, to prevent any researcher from disclosing proprietary information. For Spino and Sherman, L1 was their first expedition into international clinical trials and this sort of drug development. For them, the gag clause was perfectly normal. For Olivieri, this was her first contract with a pharmaceutical company. She naïvely believed that the gag clause was standard.

The drug trials finally began in January 1995.

In the meantime, Olivieri had been analyzing all the data she'd collected to the middle of 1994. She liked what she was seeing, and wrote a paper saying as much. The *New England Journal of Medicine* published it in April 1995.

To thalassemia suffers, it looked as though the Holy Grail might well be at hand.

Three months later, Nancy O's life started to come undone.

By summer 1995, Nancy Olivieri was seeing a different picture.

While the data she'd used for the *NEJM* article had demonstrated a steady decline in iron levels in her study group of twenty-one patients, liver biopsies in some of those same patients now indicated seriously increasing iron levels.

Shaken by this development, Olivieri spent a good part of the summer going over the data with Brittenham and trying to convince Spino and Apotex that they needed to change the protocols of the trials to find out what this problem was. She also told Apotex that the Research Ethics Board (REB) at Sick Kids would need to be informed about any change of protocols. In August, she sent Spino a draft of the report she intended to present to the REB, dealing with L1's "loss of efficacy."

Spino objected. He said Apotex needed more data and time to study her claims. He wrote her that unless the company was shown all the raw data and was able to carry out its own analysis, Apotex would not be able to form its own opinion and would, consequently, have to terminate her study.

The Olivieri–Apotex relationship deteriorated from there.

She was looking at data obtained through serial biopsies, liver samples taken over a long period of time and, in fact, was the only one doing these serial biopsies. They weren't being done in any of the other trial centres. She'd also been doing these tests long enough to understand the changes she was seeing. "We told Apotex what we were seeing and they basically said they didn't believe us."

In the middle of September, Olivieri sent Spino a brand-new protocol for the trial, specifically designed to investigate the irregularities that concerned her. She desperately wanted to continue the trial, and if Apotex had agreed to these new studies, she feels, everyone would have had a clear answer as to whether her concerns were justified. But Spino and Apotex refused. As far as the company was concerned, her findings were wrong.

To support the company's views, Spino and Apotex summoned a panel of twelve scientists, who decided that Olivieri was mistaken. Many of those scientists had direct financial ties to Apotex. Joining the bandwagon was Koren. Put on the spot, and possibly fearing that if he turned his back on Apotex his own funding would be jeopardized, Koren reinforced the company's line by stating that he too didn't think the data showed any danger.

Olivieri now produced her own list of supporters.

The line drawn in the sand got very deep.

Spino contended, "She's highly opinionated, and if you don't see things the way she wants, then you're wrong."

Olivieri was equally terse. "I am not going to be bullied. Apotex thought, 'We'll just railroad this dumb-looking little blonde.' Bloody hell."

By February 1996, both sides had so firmly dug in their heels that the trials were now doomed.

Olivieri was characterizing Spino and Apotex as unwilling to recognize and respond appropriately to an evident decrease in the drug's efficacy. She urged the company to reconsider what she'd been telling them. Apotex responded that at no time had it denied some patients showed a decreased response to deferiprone. And it even acknowledged that some patients are responding less than desirably. But it objected to her interpretation that there was a change in responsiveness beyond which could be expected. Apotex said the decision to present her information to the REB rested with her, and urged her to do that if she felt it was warranted, but it wanted her to include its side of the story.

So she went to the REB and told them about the nineteen patients she'd been following in Toronto. She explained how twelve of them had shown increased liver iron, some to levels dangerous enough to risk iron-induced complications and even death. Spino submitted a rebuttal, explaining the Apotex view and stating that none of the other trial centres were seeing this and none of the various experts they'd consulted agreed with Olivieri.

A second meeting was held, during which Olivieri rebutted the Apotex view. At the end of that, Dr. Stanley Zlotkin, who chaired the REB, confirmed that Olivieri had to change the patient consent forms and further got her to report her findings to the Drug Directorate, which is the Canadian government's drug approval office.

Zlotkin's answer to Spino was "The Research Ethics Board does not act as an intermediary between the investigator and the sponsoring company when different opinions arise. Consequently your correspondence should be directed to Dr. Olivieri for resolution."

While this was going on, the hospital's contract to conduct the study for Apotex expired.

On May 20, 1996, Olivieri submitted her revised information and consent forms to the REB and to Apotex. Four days later, Apotex announced it was not renewing her contract and, effectively, terminating the trials.

Now she could never obtain enough data to prove her point.

After announcing that the other three trials would continue, Spino warned Olivieri that Apotex would take all possible steps to ensure that her obligations of confidentiality were met and that the company would vigorously pursue all legal remedies in the event that there was any breach of those obligations.

The secrecy clause had come back to bite her.

The usual excuse, the same one used against David Kern and Betty Dong, was brought out this time too: confidentiality is vital to keep trade secrets. But Olivieri points out, "The drug had already been written about at length in dozens of publications. The drug was there. It was being used in thalassemia and the molecular structure was published. I mean, come on, I'd been making it for four years. What was Apotex trying to protect?"

Incensed, Olivieri consulted a lawyer, who recommended that she contact the Canadian Medical Protective Association because the matter had serious ethical implications for the safety of her patients. A letter to that effect was sent to Dr. Arnold Aberman, dean of the faculty of medicine of the university. At Olivieri's request, he met with Apotex, looking for a way to settle this so that the clinical trials could continue. He also told Apotex that he hoped it would not proceed with its threat of legal action against Olivieri.

Apotex agreed to continue the supply of L1 to the hospital, but would not reinstate the trials. Nor would it withdraw the threat of legal action.

In June 1996, Spino wrote to Brittenham, "Since we do not concur with her assessment of the drug's effectiveness, we could not allow such information to be transmitted to patients, thus misinforming them. In addition we could not justify Nancy as the Principal Investigator in studies of a drug she does not believe works."

The following month, Spino convened a panel of experts to reinforce his view of the data. Although their conclusion disagreed with Olivieri's, the data they looked at was not hers but rather an Apotex summary of her data. One of the experts Apotex called on was Dr. Beatrice Wonke of the Wittington and Royal Free Hospitals in Great Britain. She had a financial relationship with Apotex. The company was supporting some of her research, albeit in a minor way. In this case, Apotex says her opinion was that the drug was adequately effective for ensuring the safety of patients in the trials.

Ever defiant, Olivieri announced that she was intent on publishing her findings and planned to do so at the December 1996 meeting of the American Society of Hematology. Apotex again reminded her that if she published she would be in breach of her contract with the company. Allegedly, Spino personally petitioned the chairman of that conference session to refuse her this forum.

She managed it anyway.

At this point she was beginning to say that the data demonstrated L1 might itself cause liver fibrosis.

Apotex demanded to review her data, but Olivieri's lawyers insisted it had no entitlement to it. Her intention was to present her data at the International Conference on HIV and Iron in Bruges in March 1997, a second time at the International Conference on Thalassemia and the Hemoglobinopathies in Malta a month later, and a third time at Biomedicine '97 in Washington, D.C., a few weeks after Malta. Apotex successfully lobbied to get the presentations stopped, insisting that before the data could be shown, it needed to evaluate it.

To head her off at the conference in Malta, Koren furnished an abstract apparently co-authored with Apotex, making use of Olivieri's own data to refute her findings. Olivieri would later claim that he had not actively participated in the research, had no right to the data, and, anyway, misinterpreted it.

She wrote a second article for the *New England Journal of Medicine*, this one very critical of L1. Published in August 1998, the editors acknowledged there was disagreement about her results and that her conclusions were based on the limitations to the study. But the editors also determined, "It is important to make a concentrated effort to ascertain the safety and efficacy of this agent."

As the story gained momentum in the media, Olivieri became a lightning rod.

"A lot of people didn't want to publicly identify with me. I realized that no one wants to be on a whistleblower's side until the truth comes out. Even then, they won't agree with me, they'll just lean over and whisper, 'We were always with you.' But nobody wants to be publicly identified with a controversial figure when the controversy is raging."

Olivieri had turned to both the university and to Sick Kids looking for help. The university washed its hands of it by calling it a scientific dispute. Sick Kids chastised her for signing the confidentiality clause. When Apotex threatened to sue her, she says she asked the hospital for legal assistance. The hospital denied that she'd ever made such a request. In any case, it was not provided.

She went on a speaking tour to raise money for her legal defence fund and more than two hundred doctors around the world came together to form Doctors for Research Integrity to help. The next thing that happened is she found herself chastised in the media for becoming a self-promoter.

"I live like a monk. I live in a very ordinary little house in a very ordinary part of Toronto. Basically, I work. I don't have children. I don't have a lot of expenses. All the money I earned on the speaking circuit went to Doctors for Research Integrity to help cover my legal costs."

In the midst of this, she and colleagues began getting hate e-mail. It looked like a concerted campaign had been mounted to discredit her. She asked Sick Kids to investigate, but it found nothing. So she and some colleagues hired a computer forensic expert who quickly discovered the culprit: Gideon Koren.

"He kept denying it," Olivieri says, "but we caught him. Anonymous, harassing hate mail."

When push came to shove, the administrators of Sick Kids fired her. Not once, but twice. Although the hospital denies this version of the events. It says it had originally wanted to move her thalassemia work to another location and that she'd refused to go.

"But the truth is," one senior staff member says, "the bosses here were simply pissed off with a woman being this assertive."

In the meantime, Koren's behaviour was roundly and publicly condemned. Despite the opinion of many people at the hospital that his behaviour was sufficient grounds for dismissal, he was, instead, suspended. That was December 1999. By April 2000, the hospital decided that he should only remain suspended until June 1, albeit the last two months being without pay. He was then invited to return to work.

***

One of the first people with heavyweight credibility to jump to Olivieri's defence was the inimitable Dr. Drummond Rennie of the *Journal of the American Medical Association*. Notorious for refusing even cups of coffee from the industry, Rennie is not one to couch his feelings.

"The good thing about the Nancy Olivieri story is that it brings starkly to the surface what goes on. First of all, the stupid signing of gag orders by researchers. Secondly, the influence of drug companies when they don't like the results. Thirdly, the brutal behaviour of institutions when those institutions believe they're getting a lot of money from a drug company. Fourthly, the power differential in all this. And fifthly, that if you squeeze a young researcher hard enough, she'll turn and she'll bite. We know this goes on, it's great when it comes out because it tells people it mustn't go on."

Rennie says the issue isn't whether Olivieri is right or wrong, it is that the moment she thought she was right, there was a clear-cut course of action she needed to take. "Scientists can often disagree radically and angrily on important points of science. That's just and proper. And though I believe I know that scientists are influenced by money, even scientists influenced by money can legitimately disagree on a scientific question. But as the head of the trial, as a doctor with patients in the trial, if it is her belief that there is a danger, whether she is correct or not, she is morally bound, and actually in the law bound, to tell her patients. The issue is what she thought. Apotex can disagree with her, and they did. But they should have paid attention to her. They should have acknowledged her right and her duty to do what she did."

Rennie is equally outspoken about the hospital's role. "The Hospital for Sick Children is a place with a remarkable reputation. But I think what has gone on there is a cesspit. A lot of people have behaved appallingly. Koren wasn't fired. Why? Because he's distinguished. It angers me a great deal, and I think it's proper to be angered by stuff like this. When you see a volcano erupting, you realize the centre of the earth is boiling magma."

Also rallying to Olivieri's cause were the two greatest experts in the field of thalassemia.

Sir David Weatherall, Regius professor of medicine at Oxford University and director of Oxford's Institute of Molecular Medicine, agrees that her scientific claims are valid. "She has two concerns about this drug from her own work. One was that she found it is not maintaining its effect in a significant proportion of patients, significant being nearly half. And I think that two subsequent studies have proved that to be the case, so there's no question about that. On the second issue of whether it causes liver scarring, she's the only one who's actually ever done a controlled study to look at this. However, the numbers were small. This drug, before it's thrown out to the world, should have a more extensive prospective clinical trial. I think she was absolutely right in her stand against the company. A doctor's first duty is to the patient population. I know this sounds trite, but her responsibility is to her patients and not to the bloody company. If you genuinely believe there's a problem, you have to disclose it. That's what she did."

The second expert is Dr. David Nathan, director of the Dana Farber Cancer Institute at Harvard University.

"There are two separate issues here. The first is how a researcher has been treated by her institutions. The second is Olivieri's science. And, in essence, it is only the first issue that really matters. The science is irrelevant. Whether Nancy is right or wrong, that will come out. But as soon as she concluded that the drug was dangerous and ineffectual, or at least much less effectual than she had originally told her patients, she had to act the way she did, and if she hadn't, her conduct would have been unethical. To her credit, after she got all those kudos from the scientific community for bringing this drug out of the cellar and showing how good it is, once she became suspicious of the drug, once she no longer had confidence in it, she told her patients and told the scientific community. She did exactly what she had to do. Which is when this all hit the fan."

It is the secrecy clause, Nathan believes, that is the nucleus of the problem.

"The gag clause is a no-no. Confidentiality agreements are considered by many institutions, including Harvard, to be absolutely forbidden. In this case, Olivieri was something of an ingenue. She had never dealt with a drug company before. Nor did it help matters that the Hospital for Sick Children had a totally feckless system for monitoring what their researchers signed. Had the proper controls been in place, the incident might have been avoided. Then too, had the hospital not been afraid of Sherman, they might have met their responsibility by correcting Olivieri's mistake in having signed the gag clause. They could have said to the drug company, 'It's too bad that we missed it and too bad if she signed it, but guess what, Mr. Sherman, if you sue her you have to sue us.'"

When Dan Soberman, the former dean of law at Queen's University, looked at the gag clause, he decided "to the extent that such a clause prohibits disclosure of information about a medicine that might reasonably be believed by a researcher to cause harm to the health of a person taking that medicine, the clause is void. Period."

Nathan agrees. "I don't care if she signed the Declaration of Independence. The judgmental mistake was to sign something that was stupid and outside of the policies. It was stupid of the hospital not to immediately say, 'Sign it or not, we're fighting this.' If they'd done that, the whole thing would have been over. Instead, the hospital beat up on her. They wanted the Apotex money and they didn't like Nancy. Then they didn't control Koren's behaviour. He had a lot of open hostility to Nancy. The hospital was lethargic about investigating the hate mail. How embarrassing. How ridiculous. This is the hospital that helped to discover the genetic basis of cystic fibrosis. If they'd wanted to, they could certainly have found Koren."

Nathan and Weatherall had both been called in by the university and Sick Kids to help find a solution. What they found instead was that the two institutions had considered the options – blame Olivieri, which was the easy way out, or blame Apotex, which was the costly way out – and they opted for the easy way.

"You always hope for common sense," Nathan continues, "but what happened in the Nancy Olivieri case was an abandonment of common sense by almost everybody. It became turf protection. Lack of wisdom. Nobody in the structure said, 'Folks, the game is over and you're going to do as I say.'"

As the Olivieri story took on a life of its own, media attention turned to Barry Sherman. When the story reached CBS Television in New York, *60 Minutes* took it up. Leslie Stahl interviewed Nancy Olivieri, who came across as the victim. Then she interviewed Sherman.

For a man who has displayed such remarkable business acumen over the years, he demonstrated a serious lack of media skills. When Stahl suggested that Apotex had launched a smear campaign against Olivieri, Sherman retorted, "That's completely absurd. She is the one who is conducting the smear campaign." Then, as the crew changed tapes, and Sherman wrongly believed that the cameras were not rolling, he blurted out, "She's nuts. Nuts."

Stahl snapped, "What did you just say to me? You just said she was nuts. You just said that to me. You looked at me and you said she was nuts."

Sherman realized he'd been caught out. "I said to you ..."

Stahl reminded him, "You said she's nuts."

"Hold on a sec," Sherman pleaded. "I said I'll say certain things to you off the record ..."

"But that wasn't off the record," Stahl retorted. "We were rolling. The cameras were going. The point is that you are still saying these things and I am a reporter."

Sherman pleaded that he was agitated. "Given that I'm upset I might well say things that in a private conversation, off the record, that I would not say on ..."

"But we're reporters," Stahl reminded him. "We're not your pals."

It was a humiliating lesson in the first commandment of broadcast interviews – there is no such thing as a dead mike or a camera not rolling.

The L1 tests continued in Europe, where the European Union looks set to license the drug. Olivieri had protested but to little avail. If the drug is licensed there, it will quickly gain acceptance around the world. Although she is convinced that the Americans will not license it, because the FDA file on the drug contains all of her objections. Nor will it find much use in Canada, if it ever gets licensed, because she won't prescribe it and she treats most of the nation's thalassemia patients.

The underlying problem with L1, notes Dr. Michele Brill-Edwards, who has seen Olivieri's data and agrees with her contentions, is that the drug itself might be causing more harm than good. Patients taking L1, at least some of them, could be dying faster because they are taking the drug than they would if they were not taking the drug. "It's a very serious situation," says Brill-Edwards, "but it will not be evident. If a drug provokes either the same phenomenon as the disease or something very similar, how are you going to tell? I fear that this drug will keep getting used and people will keep saying it's working."

In February 2000, the university and Sick Kids came to an agreement with Olivieri. While she was reinstated as an active member of Sick Kids staff, she moved her office to Toronto Hospital, reporting to the physician-in-chief there. She retains full access to and responsibility for all of the patients she had been treating and continues to, conduct her research. The terms of the settlement also include Sick Kids' agreement to indemnify her for any uncovered costs of legal actions brought by Apotex and to pay her legal and other costs up to $150,000.

The closest the hospital administrators ever came to any sort of public apology was a concession, in a press release. "The Hospital could have done a better job of providing her with support."

Bizarrely, the release goes on to state, "Over and over again the management of the Hospital backed her right to publish the material. They talked to people at Apotex and told them to back off." The problem with that statement is there's no proof that any such thing ever happened.

When the settlement was announced, everyone at the university and at Sick Kids hoped this would finally go away. That the world might forget how the university had allegedly been looking to the Apotex Foundation – one of the ten largest corporate donors in Canada – to help finance a building project with a $20 million to $30 million gift. And how Sick Kids needed to maintain its relationships with Gideon Koren and Michael Spino.

According to the *Globe and Mail*, "Nancy Olivieri was hung out to dry, and children were put at risk, because the hospital and university were too hungry for Apotex's good will and, more to the point, its cash."

After the scandal broke, Apotex was still willing to go ahead with the donation. But the woman then heading the Sick Kids Foundation refused the overture because she felt it was unseemly at a time when the company was attacking one of their researchers. As it happens, the Apotex gift would have triggered a series of matching grants from the federal and provincial governments worth around $50 million, plus private donations of about $23 million.

Although Sick Kids CEO Michael Strofolino has always denied that Apotex money was at the heart of this, to some of the men running the hospital, Nancy Olivieri and her science had gotten in the way of a lot of money.

Having mishandled the affair from the beginning – not just administratively but also in the media – the Hospital for Sick Children found itself in the midst of a full-blown professional and public relations disaster.

The executive director of the Canadian Association of University Teachers (CAUT), James Turk, labelled it, "The Greatest Academic Scandal of Our Era."

The University of Toronto Faculty Association filed a grievance with the university for violating policies that guaranteed faculty members academic freedom. It also objected to the fact that the university hadn't protected Olivieri and her cohorts from discrimination, harassment, and intimidation.

At one point the hospital tried to slap a gag order on Olivieri, barring her from speaking to the press, which is always a sure sign of having lost control of a situation. Besides being completely stupid – because gag orders never work – in this case it merely signalled to the rest of the world that the administrators didn't want her side of the story to keep making headlines.

Strofolino opted to bring in an outside reviewer to investigate the situation, even though the administrators had already announced they wouldn't go this route. The reason they backed down was, almost certainly, because their public relations was so miserable and without something that looked dramatic, they risked losing those few supporters they'd managed to hold on to.

That man was Dr. Arnold Naimark, professor of medicine and physiology at the University of Manitoba and the university's former president and vice-chancellor.

There can be no doubt about Naimark's credentials as a physician, scientist, and educator. But he brought baggage with him to this assignment that should have been questioned.

At one point during Naimark's term as president and vice-chancellor, Apotex donated C$789,840 to the school. That was the figure used when Naimark's independence was first questioned. But, according to Naimark's own report, from 1986 to 1998, Apotex donations to the University of Manitoba totalled C$6,908,051. That Apotex or its chairman, Barry Sherman, might have donated money to nearly all universities with health sciences faculties – as Naimark would later declare – doesn't erase the fact that Naimark, directly or indirectly, had an admitted relationship with Apotex and/or Sherman.

What's more, Naimark was on the board of directors of the Canadian Imperial Bank of Commerce, whose CEO was on the board of Sick Kids. Having a business association with someone on a board and then agreeing to sit in judgment of that board's conduct doesn't appear autonomous. But then, when a board whose conduct is being questioned gets to set the ground rules and also appoint the person who will ask those questions, well, that doesn't appear independent either.

On top of that, Naimark has, for years, maintained very close ties to the Canadian pharmaceutical industry.

For any independent investigator to be effective, it is not enough to be independent, the investigator must also appear to be independent. So when Olivieri and her closest associates decided that Naimark missed that by a mile, they refused to cooperate with his investigation, relegating him to consider little more than secondhand sources and hearsay evidence.

The criticism of Naimark's independence was intense enough to worry the administrators, who hastily agreed to invite two people to help him. When neither the administrators nor Olivieri could agree who those two people should be, Naimark himself chose law professor Bartha

Knoppers of the University of Montreal and Dr. Frederick Lowy, rector of Concordia University. Both had been previously rejected for whatever reason by Olivieri.

Compounding matters, the two were chosen several months after Naimark began his investigation and only about a week before Naimark actually presented his report, which presupposes that a good portion of the report may have been already written. In any case, as a true recording of the events, it was demonstrably incomplete.

Naimark reviewed 490 letters, including 220 to or from Olivieri, and 30 more written on her behalf. He interviewed 40 people but did not interview Olivieri, Brittenham, or any of their closest associates. He rationalized that away by insisting that Olivieri's lack of cooperation did not invalidate his review. He says he asked himself if her non-participation was so critical that it would render his report useless and the conclusion he came to was no.

So, without having matched independence with the appearance of independence, and being limited to only some of the documents and without having access to the people who really mattered in all of this, he soldiered on. But then, he did have access to one person on whom he based a great deal. Gideon Koren. A man who would later be irreparably compromised.

"The criticism levelled at the review and the report has largely been voiced by Dr. Olivieri and her colleague," Naimark says, seemingly suggesting that because the protagonists protested, their objections must somehow be less valid.

Except that the *Canadian Medical Association Journal* found Naimark's work written unequivocally from the point of view of the hospital administration. The *CMAJ* felt it was based heavily on undocumented evidence obtained during interviews with people on the hospital's side and on Apotex's side but with no one on Olivieri's side. The resulting report, the *CMAJ* stipulated, was, at best, "incomplete."

Dr. Arthur Schafer, author of *Medicine, Morals and Money* and director of the Centre for Professional and Applied Ethics at Naimark's own University of Manitoba, also found the report lacking. "By choosing as the sole reviewer someone with commercial ties to a member of the Board of Trustees and professional ties to Apotex, did the Board show disrespect for the principle of an impartial investigation by a disinterested investigator?" Schafer would eventually conclude, "The danger is either the reality or the perception of a whitewash."

Naimark defends himself by saying, "In the report and in subsequent correspondence I have invited anyone with information that invalidates in any material sense the representations and findings in the review report to provide it to me. No such information has been forthcoming."

This disregards Gideon Koren's subsequent behaviour, which, if the gold standard is the justice system, throws everything Koren told Naimark into disrepute. Because Koren's contribution is vital to the review, being the person closest to the affair to testify, his contribution sullies the end result.

The tone of the report is distinctly pejorative. It is typical, one critic notes, "of the abuse that is visited upon those who publicly disagree with an institution." Naimark appears to regard Koren as a completely independent scientist whose own views were not coloured in any way. The impression one gets from Naimark is that because Koren is an eminent and independent scientist, people should take note when he disagrees with Olivieri. It appears to mirror the attitude of the hospital administrators, suggesting that if Olivieri had been right, Koren would have agreed with her.

Dr. Marcia Angell, then editor-in-chief of the *New England Journal of Medicine*, questioned the attitude of academics and scientists who, like Naimark, don't see their own conflicts of interest as material. "Imagine a judge who has before him a case involving two companies suing each other, and he owns one of the companies. And he says, 'Not to worry. I'm a judge and I learned how to evaluate things in a dispassionate way.' He'd be laughed out of court."

How and why Naimark's various conflicts are different questions logic. What's more, just because the Sick Kids administrators and Naimark himself ruled those conflicts immaterial does not in fact make them immaterial.

The *Canadian Medical Association Journal* certainly didn't think they were immaterial. "Naimark's associations with private industry, while providing a unique perspective on the relation between the commercial and academic sectors, may make it more difficult for his report to be seen as unbiased."

Nor did Naimark's local Alberta Medical Association, which raised the conflict-of-interest question in an editorial in its newsletter.

"In his [Naimark's] professional role as fundraiser for the University of Manitoba Centre for the Advancement of Medicine he had frequent contact with pharmaceutical companies and, furthermore, was a member of the board of directors of the Canadian Imperial Bank of Commerce, whose president also sat on the board of directors for the Toronto Hospital for Sick Children."

In law, a conflict of interest cannot be gotten around by claiming it has no importance. In medicine, all too often, it appears to be part of the wallpaper. When the issue is raised, the reaction is frequently righteous indignation. It's how dare you suggest that a man of my stature would be biased in such a manner? Righteous indignation and a blatant denial of the fact that bias is created.

When asked why he didn't recuse himself, Naimark sang from that hymn sheet. "My only role as Reviewer was to review the facts and circumstances giving rise to the L1 controversy and to report my findings to the Board. It is crucial to understand that I was not a grievance arbitrator nor was I to render a judgment as to any matters in dispute between Apotex and Dr. Olivieri. The Board was concerned with matters related to the Hospital, such as patient safety, conflicts of interest within the Hospital, etc., and not with Apotex per se. The Review was seen by the Hospital as background for a subsequent review and revision of the Hospital's policies and procedures in relation to clinical trials research. Given the foregoing, the fact that I happened to be President during a period when Apotex made occasional donations to the University of Manitoba, as it has done to nearly all universities with health sciences faculties, was regarded by the Board and by me as immaterial."

It might be said that for a person to decide his own conflicts of interest are immaterial is, in and of itself, a conflict of interest. That it entirely compounds the sin. But that's not where these conflicts end.

Naimark's University of Manitoba has five research and service organizations housed on the campus. There is the federal government's Freshwater Institute and the Canada Agriculture Research Station. There is the provincial government's Agricultural Services Complex and the Cadham Provincial Laboratory. But the one that is of most interest in this case is Cangene Corp.

As a good neighbour, the company maintains very close ties with the university, its hospitals, and the various research foundations operating out of the university. So much so that Cangene has been described as a "financial contributor and industrial partner" to the university.

Through Cangene, Naimark – as president and vice-chancellor of the university – had a relationship with Apotex that went beyond the millions of dollars donated over that twelve-year period. And while what Naimark said about Apotex donating money to universities all over Canada might be true, other universities all over Canada do not have the same relationship with Apotex that Manitoba has with Cangene.

That Naimark considers these conflicts immaterial is irrelevant.

The fact is, Cangene is not only involved with the university in a scientific and medical relationship, it leases the land its offices are on from the university.

Cangene is a subsidiary of Apotex.

One of the Cangene directors is Michael Spino.

Cangene's chairman is Barry Sherman.

So the independent reviewer whom the Hospital for Sick Kids chose to judge Nancy Olivieri – the same independent reviewer who regarded challenges to his independence as immaterial – had once been, for all intents and purposes, Barry Sherman's landlord.

CHAPTER 9

THE STREET FIGHTER'S LAMENT

"**W**hen I started in this business," Barry Sherman says with a remorseful tone, "I never would have thought that by the year 2000 the governments would be backing the multinational drug companies who have raped the health-care system."

He stares to make his point. "They take billions a year out of Canada, the prices are twenty times what they should be, and they have this tremendous lobby group that goes around saying, 'Look how wonderful we are, we're investing.'"

Now the passion starts building. "And you've got all the government officials saying, 'Yeah, they're terrific, they're investing.' And, of course, they're not. The number of jobs are very small. Everything's coming into the country at high prices. The trade deficit is in the billions, the health-care system's going broke. And not one word about the largest element of health care: pharmaceuticals. We're not getting value because we're getting raped by having to pay twenty bucks a tablet for something that should be two cents. What the hell is going on here?"

Sherman is a man determined to tell anybody who'll listen the answer to that question.

A generic drug is a copycat version of a branded drug, permitted to come onto the market as soon as the branded drug goes off patent, but only on the condition that the copycat is "bioequivalent" with the original, which means the generic version must be more than just a chemical copy. It has to be as safe and effective as the branded drug and act in exactly the same way. It must contain an identical amount of active ingredient and must be in the same dosage. A generic must also meet standards for "bioavailability," meaning that it must deliver the same exact amount of the active ingredient into the bloodstream and in very nearly the exact same time, within a narrowly defined margin of difference.

However, where branded drugs and generic drugs are allowed to differ is, occasionally, in the inactive ingredients that are of no medicinal value – such as colouring and flavouring – and, always, in price.

Because the generic manufacturers have not had to undergo huge R&D expenses or vastly complicated clinical trials, building a generic costs considerably less than developing a branded drug. Where Merck may spend $300 million on researching and developing a drug, Apotex can get its generic version on the market for around $1 million.

But first the generic company has to get past the branded companies' lawyers.

AstraZeneca owns the patent on one of the world's top-selling drugs, the stomach ulcer treatment, Losec. The generic name is omeprazole. The drug loses partial protection in the United States in 2001, but AstraZeneca claims that patents covering the use and formulation of the drug are protected until 2014. When three generic firms disagreed and announced, in early 2000, that they intended to challenge those patents, AstraZeneca fired back with three lawsuits. Considering that AstraZeneca relies on the drug for around $2 billion a year – almost a third of its worldwide sales – it's understandable that it's not going to give up without a fight.

Included in its tactics is an alternative version of the drug. AstraZeneca claims it's a different drug that does the same thing, but does it better. But it built its original omeprazole market on the claim that the drug is 98 to 99 per cent effective. The question therefore becomes "What's so special about this new version?" The answer has to be "It safeguards the market for another patent life."

At AstraZeneca, management sees this as a logical way for a commercial company to behave. It has a huge market and it's protecting it.

The generic industry takes a different view. It says that what AstraZeneca is doing will not bring benefit to a single patient and therefore this is wasted R&D. Eager to get its hands on the molecule – and perhaps with a twinge of sour grapes – the generic companies see millions being spent developing a molecule that may or may not be as good as omeprazole, and millions more which will have to be spent convincing everybody it's better than omeprazole.

The numbers make an even stronger case. Patients and health-care systems around the world are paying $2.5 billion a year for omeprazole. Once it comes off patent, generic competition will initially reduce that by, say, 50 per cent, and eventually as much as perhaps 80 per cent. That immediately frees up at least $1.25 billion from those same health-care budgets to pay for the next innovative drug. Without the generic, $2.5 billion gets them nothing more than son-of-omeprazole.

But then, AstraZeneca already made one bid to keep the cash flowing by withdrawing the capsule from the market and replacing it with a tablet. The two are interchangeable, otherwise the regulators would have demanded new clinical trials. Suddenly the generic industry can't compare their omeprazole capsule to AstraZeneca's capsule because it doesn't exist on the market any more.

Barry Sherman is an aging street fighter and a mass of contradictions. Portrayed by some as the villain in the Nancy Olivieri affair, he is praised by others as one of the most charitable men in Canada. Said to be worth C$1.8 billion – that's enough to make him Canada's eleventh richest man, behind Terence Matthews of Newbridge Networks and in front of Paul Desmarais of Power Corp. – he shoots from the hip and shows a dogged willingness to scrap with anyone, anywhere, any time. Labelled by business competitors as one of the toughest sons-of-bitches in North America, he can be charming and unnervingly likable. Vilified by many in his own industry, he is courted at arm's length by politicians of all persuasions, at least until he moves in real close and lets them have it with both barrels.

Born in Toronto in 1942, Sherman was ten when his father died, leaving his mother, sister, and him in difficult circumstances. They took in boarders, his mother worked, and they struggled. His father had been running a zipper manufacturing company and when the family share was sold for C$50,000, it helped bring in a couple of thousand dollars a year income. He held down part-time jobs as a student and still managed to graduate from Forest Hill Collegiate High School as the top Ontario scholar that year with fourteen subjects and a first in every one of them.

In Grade 12, Sherman won first prize in a national physics contest and dreamt of studying aeronautical engineering. It was the beginning of the 1960s. President John F. Kennedy would soon announce that the United States intended to put a man on the moon before the decade was over. Six years later, Sherman had a master's degree in aeronautics and a Ph.D. in system's engineering from the Massachusetts Institute of Technology (MIT).

He was still at MIT in 1965 when his uncle died. Lou Winter had a small generic drug business called Empire Laboratories, where Sherman had worked for a few summers. So he got it into his head that he might be able to put together a small syndicate and buy it. The trustees turned him down, explaining that they intended to run it instead.

Following graduation, he returned to Toronto and tried to negotiate with DeHavilland Aircraft to buy its SPAR division, the company that makes the arm for the space shuttle. He'd worked there too one summer. De-Havilland didn't take him seriously and, anyway, he didn't have any money.

In the meantime, Empire Laboratories was in trouble. Sherman called the trustees again, and they sold him the company at net book value, which was a couple of hundred thousand dollars. He didn't have that much either, so a family friend and his mother invested and he wound up buying Empire.

The company was making money within a few months.

In 1973, ICM offered to buy the business, Sherman and his investors agreed to sell it, and he used that money to start Apotex in 1974. Compulsory licensing was in full flow. Sherman brought generic drugs to market, charged 70 to 80 per cent of the brand price, took half the market share, and steered Apotex through sixteen years of strong growth.

"We were doing all the right things," Sherman says, "all the things the government wanted us to do. Then, all of a sudden, everything we were doing was no longer the right thing. According to Mulroney it was the brand-name companies and monopolies that were needed. They took away compulsory licensing, put in draconian regulations, and are on the verge of destroying the generic industry. When we're gone, it will be impossible to replace us. It's not possible to start another industry under these circumstances. We're here because we were able to be here and flourish and make money and build our facilities when the law made sense. Now it's difficult even to keep going because the law doesn't make sense. If we don't invest and do it, nobody will. I'm still here fighting, hoping somebody will wake up and help us. The government together with the brand-name drug companies are intent on putting us out of business and they're succeeding."

Apotex is the largest generic manufacturer in the country and controls about one-third of the market. "The generic industry is vital to Canada. When I say vital I'm talking about high-tech employment, research, and saving money for the health-care system. I've spent thirty years building this fantastic industry in Canada, we employ thousands of people, we save billions of dollars for the health-care system, we've done all the right things, and the minister of industry treats me like an interloper."

Sherman is openly disgusted with Brian Mulroney for taking away compulsory licensing, and just as angry at Jean Chrétien for not putting it back. "The generic industry in this country is in a state of collapse. The government says everything's wonderful. Apotex is now losing money. 2000 is our first year when we're having enormous losses. 1999 was about to break even, but the last six months of 1999 we lost about C$30 million, which takes away our profit from the first six months. The only reason we've kept going, been able to keep going, is that we happen to own a major stake in Barr Laboratories in the United States, which is a successful company. I sold $100 million in stock in the past couple of years, took that money and put it into Apotex to keep going."

The entire generic industry is, Sherman says with obvious frustration, "unsustainable. The combination of the anti-competitive regulations and the pseudogenerics, those two factors make it impossible to continue to invest in the health-care industry in Canada. As a result of which, the monopolies will go on forever. No one will invest in new products because you won't be able to get it onto the market."

Pseudogenerics are the branded companies' own drug, repackaged as a generic, brought to the market a few months before the generic company can launch its own version.

"Or they hang us up in court. When you're in patent litigation, you can't predict the outcome. It's not as if you can look at the thing and say, 'I'm right, the patent's invalid or won't be infringed and therefore I know I will win.' Whether you're right or wrong, when you get to court it's fifty-fifty. You've got a non-infringing process and they'll get a Nobel laureate to swear that the moon is made of cheese. So even if you've got 99 per cent certainty that you're not infringing, you know they're going to sue you anyway and so you're off the market for that period of time with no revenues to pay for the litigation. Under any normal scenario, you just launch the product, then you litigate, and if you lose at the end of the day you give up your profits. In this country it's rigged against us. We have to carry all the expenses, have no sales to deduct that from, and if we're stopped because the court rules against us, then we've lost all of our investment, not just the profit but all of our investment. And that means we can't invest."

Apotex employs some thirty-five hundred people, compared with Big Pharma's total in Canada of around fifteen thousand. But Sherman points out that Apotex produces more than Big Pharma does. "They have all these people in marketing and 30 per cent of their income goes to these glossy ads to doctors. The purpose of the ads, of course, is not to get the best therapy but to get the doctors to prescribe those things on which the drug companies make the most profit. There's never an ad that says, 'Prescribe this because it's cheap and better value for the health-care system.' Then, as soon as there's generic competition, they move on to promoting something that's more expensive, even though it's not necessarily better."

What's more, as soon as anyone in authority tries to challenge Big Pharma, he says the first thing they do is brag about how important they are to the economy, the role they play in Canada, and that if anybody in authority tries to do anything they don't like, they'll pick up and leave.

"Those idle threats," Sherman snaps, "they're absurd. All the more so because the multinational drug companies have nothing of significance in Canada anyway. They're here because our dollar is cheap and we have good scientists in our hospitals. When they suggest they'll only do research in Canada as long as we have strong patent protection in Canada, which is the other thing they keep saying, the more patent protection the more research, I say it's absurd because the research isn't for Canada. You get patents regardless of where the research is done and the research is done for the rest of the world. You don't do it in Canada because there's more patent protection in Canada. It doesn't make any sense. There's just no logical connection. And indeed the Eastman Commission showed that."

The Eastman Commission also showed that after compulsory licensing was introduced, the rate of job creation increased. Sherman says that happened simply because drugs became affordable, the government was able to pay for drugs, which created more consumption, which created more production, which created more investment.

"When you have these monopolies where everything is twenty bucks a tablet, the provincial governments can't pay for them so some things are excluded from the plans. And even if they are paid for, these big drug companies pull C$9 billion out of the budget when the drug bill should be, say, C$2 billion. That's C$7 billion that could create thousands of other jobs."

Since the free trade agreement helped to nourish the globalization of business, the Canadian economy has picked up largely because the American economy has picked up. But, he claims, if you look at the comparative figures, Canada's standard of real income has dropped to about half the American level from what it was.

"I keep saying to the politicians, 'You don't understand,'" Sherman continues. "They say we need a level playing field and we'll attract investors. I say, Canada is a small country, it can never be a level playing field, we're a small country next to a big country and as businesses have globalized, who are the winners? It's the big American or European multinationals. None of them is in Canada. Where do people want to locate their production? Why would anybody want to put production in Canada? You locate it in your home or in your major market. That's where you have your factories, that's where you have your technology, that's where you have your management, that's where you have your planning, that's where you have your research. Canada is simply a market to exploit."

The result, he insists, is that everything comes into the country at high prices and all the money leaves the country tax-free.

"The minister of industry will say that one of the problems is that our taxation is too high. But our taxation has to be high because we have a lower tax base. Our productivity is lower. Why is our productivity lower? Our productivity isn't low, it's an apparent low productivity. Why? Because everything is coming into the country at high transfer pricing and everything's being sold with very little value-added for Canada. And there's an appearance of low productivity caused by transfer pricing. We've lost all of our significant Canadian-owned companies. Apotex is the last significant Canadian-owned company in the pharmaceutical industry. We used to be a branch-plant economy with some Canadian businesses as well. Now we're no longer a branch-plant economy because there aren't any branch plants. We're just a warehouse economy."

The proof of the pudding, according to Sherman, is the job figures. "They take in C$9 billion in Canada. Well, the average industry creates 10,000 jobs for each billion in sales, so there should be 90,000 jobs. But there are only 15,000 jobs. And nobody seems to care. If you look at our figures, Apotex is by far the largest employer in the industry in Canada. We have 3,500 employees, Merck has 900. But Merck takes twice as much money as we do out of the health-care system. Our prices are low and we make everything in Canada. Our jobs per dollar are several times what theirs are and nobody seems to notice or care. I figured I should be a national hero for what I do, but I'm not. If anything, I'm a villain."

There is some basis for his argument, in that multinational industries do tend to put the bulk of their employment – especially their best jobs – in their home country or in their major market. That's especially evident in the pharmaceutical industry, with most of the conglomerates headquartered in the United States. Even those staunchly British-based drug companies, SmithKline Beecham and Glaxo, have been forced to acknowledge the importance of the American market. In all of the public statements about their proposed merger, the boards of those two companies have insisted that the new entity, Glaxo SmithKline, would remain a British company. They even built a new headquarters just outside London on the way to Heathrow Airport. That's where the chairman of the board will be. But the CEO, together with the command and control functions of the new company, will be in Philadelphia.

Much like NATO, foreign drug companies do whatever they have to to appear politically correct at home. But the decisions to pull the trigger come from America. A secondary market such as Canada is of little interest to Big Pharma, other than the minimum amount they have to invest in order do exploit R&D.

"The people most interested in building Canadian industry, one imagines," Sherman goes on, "would be Canadians. But even Canadians will put factories in the United States if that's where the major market is." That's a veiled reference to one of his long-time competitors, Novopharm, who recently built a production plant in North Carolina. "I'm the exception. We built ours in Richmond Hill. Just about everything the brand-name companies sell in Canada is imported. They may make some tablets in Canada, but the value is insignificant."

By comparison, in Winnipeg, Apotex sunk over C$100 million into a company called Apotex Fermentation. The drug he was working on there was a generic version of Merck's Mevacor, an anti-cholesterol drug, which he finally got onto the market using a non-infringing process.

Merck succeeded in delaying them for over two years, which cost Apotex C$100 million worth of lost business.

The next one was a generic version of Bristol-Myers Squibb's Pravachol, which he'd intended to launch when the government changed the regulations, meaning that he couldn't use certain chemical references and had to start all over again. That delayed him another year.

"The point is, we made this C$100 million investment when we still had compulsory licensing and now there's no future in it. We can't invest in factories and can't invest in research, even if we have a non-infringing process or when there's no patent. You can't do it when you know you're going to sit there with an idle factory tied up for years in litigation. The branded companies don't care about doing anything except putting us out of business. So at the end of the day the Canadian generic industry will be a fragment of what it should be. The C$9 billion Health Canada spends on drugs will be C$20 billion."

When Barry Sherman isn't knee-deep in his own battles, he's defending the corner of another fighter who is.

The generic story of the new millennium was the blockbuster drug story of the 1980s: Prozac. And the main event is in the United States. The challenger is Barr Laboratories. Sherman owns 40 per cent.

The development of Prozac began in Britain in 1953, when psycho-pharmacologist John Gaddum suggested that a substance in the brain called serotonin played an essential role in human sanity. Within four years, the National Institutes of Health in Washington were devoting serious research to serotonin. That led drug companies in the 1960s to begin test-ing a new class of treatments, called selective serotonin reuptake inhibitors (SSRI). The Swedish company Astra was first on the market in 1981 with Zelmid, a drug withdrawn two years later for being toxic.

At the same time, scientists at Eli Lilly in Indiana were working on a project called "110140," which was a drug generically known as fluoxe-tine. The FDA approved it in December 1987, and Lilly dubbed it Prozac.

As successful as Prozac was right from the start — its first full year on the market saw Eli Lilly sell 175 million of these green-and-white pills — it was never far from controversy. The FDA was accused of succumbing to pressure applied by Lilly for regulatory approval. Then, despite the agency's approval only for the treatment of chronic depression, it was immediately prescribed for dozens of off-label uses, including PMS, bulimia, and obsessive-compulsive disorders. Next, the price of the drug was ques-tioned. It cost $2 per pill, when the market was filled with antidepressants at 10 cents a pill.

By 1990 it was the most famous prescription drug in the world. Prozac had even made it onto the cover of *Newsweek*. But a Harvard Medical School report in the February 1990 issue of the *American Journal of Psychiatry* reported six cases of what appeared to be Prozac-induced agita-tion leading to violence and suicide. The company denied that there was any link between the drug and suicide. The following year, the FDA agreed that no credible connection existed. Since then, more than 160 cases related to violence and suicide have been filed against Lilly. Most were dismissed. Some have been settled out of court, about which the company will say nothing. The few that went the distance saw Lilly winning them all.

In the meantime, the generic companies had been lining up, waiting for the moment when they could take their chunk of this market.

"Around 1993 or so," says Bruce Downey, Barr's CEO, "it came to my attention that the original molecule patent on fluoxetine was expiring in 1994. The problem was there were two additional patents protect-ing Prozac."

One was a "use" patent, which protected the use of fluoxetine to treat mental illness. That expires in 2001. Then there was an oddball patent, called a "mechanism of action" patent, which describes how the chemical inhibits certain reactions in the brain. That patent expires in 2003.

"To me," Downey continues, "that didn't sound as much like an invention as it did a description, so we had someone look at these two patents and the report came back that they might be vulnerable. We decided to challenge them in December 1995."

The strength of Barr's case rested on that second patent, which Downey and his lawyers believed violated one of the principle rules of patent law, that being, you only get one per idea.

"When you launch a patent challenge, there's a whole ritual you need to go through. You do the R&D for generic approval and file with the FDA. You tell them that you believe the patent on the product is either invalid or unenforceable and that you're going to challenge it. As soon as you make that certification to the FDA, you also send it to the patent holder. They then have forty-five days to sue you, and if they do, they get a thirty-month stay of FDA approval so that the court case can run its course. Regardless of the validity of the patent, they get thirty months."

These challenges, Downey admits, are only worth the effort when the patent is weak and the prize is a blockbuster. "There's no percentage in challenging strong patents. And if it's only a million-dollar product, the challenge wouldn't be economically feasible. But with Prozac, worth a couple of billion, if you can launch your generic even six months early, that can be worth hundreds of millions of dollars to the generic company."

Needless to say, Lilly never intended to let Downey do anything of the kind. It took his challenge to court and also launched a tablet form of Prozac. Because he was only challenging the capsule form, this was a pretty strong defence against the possibility he might win.

"It was a backup plan. If we'd won, they could have switched everyone over to the tablet and there wouldn't have been a market left for our capsule."

Next, they stepped up work on their once-a-week pill. The idea here is to patent the delivery system – the time-release mechanism in the drug – and then shift the market from a daily dose to a weekly dose. That will force Barr back to the drawing board in search of a delivery system that can produce the same effect without violating this new patent.

And even then they were not done.

Fluoxetine is a mixture of two isomers of the compound fluoxetine, one of which is active and the other isn't. The one that isn't active is theoretically the source of some of the drug's side effects. So Lilly came up with a way of isolating the so-called positive isomer from the so-called negative isomer. Its idea was to get that single isomer approved, then switch people onto that compound.

"The key to generic use is substitution," Downey continues. "My Prozac won't be substitutable for the tablet form, the once-a-week form, or the new compound. By the time we get there, that $2 billion might be down to a $200 million market with the $1.8 billion moved to these other forms. Their reps are out there selling them now, convincing everyone that they're better. If they get their timing right, they introduce the new product, move the market, and discontinue the old product so there's no product to substitute."

In January 1999, the Federal District Court in Indianapolis, Indiana, granted summary judgment in favour of Lilly on Barr's claims against the two patents. Eighteen months later, on August 10, 2000, shares in Eli Lilly were halted on the New York Stock Exchange awaiting an announcement. When it came, the shares plunged from $108.55 to $76, a loss of 29 per cent. And Barr's shares surged 68 per cent, from $45.75 to $77.

The U.S. Court of Appeals for the Federal Circuit in Washington had overturned the original decision protecting Lilly's "mechanism of action" patent. Barr would now be permitted to come onto the market with its version in 2001. At $2 billion a year just in the United States, the decision had reasonably cost Lilly some 20 per cent of its global sales over those two years. Whether there is any market left for Barr is another matter.

***

Because drugs are not discretionary purchases, Barry Sherman believes, there must be some mechanism somewhere to prevent patent abuse.

In that regard, he harbours a deep well of anger for John Manley, "who sees his job as helping American industry screw Canadians."

According to Sherman, Manley – as minister of industry from 1993 to 2000 – was supposed to protect Canadian industry and Canadian consumers. "Instead he's a propaganda machine for the American drug companies, giving them whatever they want, pretending that they're investing in Canada when all they're doing is raping Canada, pretending that they're doing good things for Canada, pretending that the generic industry is fine, pretending that prices are fair. None of it is true."

Not that Sherman has, by speaking his mind, particularly endeared himself to Manley.

There was a dinner a few years ago when Queen Elizabeth was in Toronto, and Sherman and his wife were on the guest list. They walked into the Royal York Hotel, and when Sherman spotted Manley, he went over to say hello. He says that Manley refused to shake his hand and snapped, "You son of a bitch, you tried to get me defeated in the last election."

Sherman remains stupefied. "Can you imagine a minister of the Crown saying that to a citizen of this country? 'You son of a bitch you tried to get me defeated at the last election?' But I didn't try to get him defeated. We supported the Liberals."

What had happened was, the Canadian Drug Manufacturers Association, which represents the generic industry, put up posters in Manley's riding because it wanted to show him how upset it was with government regulations.

"We wanted to influence him. But apart from that, even if I had tried to get him defeated, so what? Isn't that my right? What he should be doing is saying to the branded drug companies, 'You bastards are gouging the health-care system. What you're doing is unconscionable. We may have to let you do certain things, but not more than what you're clearly entitled to do, and beyond that we're going to do everything we can to make sure that Canadians get competition at the earliest possible time so that we can build an industry and make health care affordable.' Isn't that what anybody with a brain would be saying?"

Once upon a time, Sherman says, there was a Ministry of Consumer and Corporate Affairs that had been put in place to protect the consumer. But Mulroney did away with it, putting the Competition Bureau inside the Department of Industry. So there is no longer a public watchdog trying to help the consumer.

"When Trudeau was in power, the Ministry of Consumer Affairs fought anti-competitive practices," Sherman continues. "They're the ones who brought in compulsory licensing for pharmaceuticals. Well, that's all merged now into the Department of Industry. They've put the fox in charge of the chickens."

He isn't particularly enthralled with Prime Minister Jean Chrétien either.

During the Liberals' 1993 election campaign, Sherman tried to make compulsory licensing an issue. After all, it had once been Liberal policy. Chrétien agreed to make an appearance at the Apotex headquarters in Weston on the edge of Toronto, where Sherman was helping to raise money for him.

"He gives a speech to our staff in our cafeteria saying how terrible it is what the Tories are doing and it's not fair, the regulations are unfair and says, 'As soon as we're elected it will be our priority to make it right.'"

Sherman spoke to Chrétien about it again, in Ottawa, before the election. He was there with a group of other people and, towards the end of that meeting, he mentioned to Chrétien that he'd appreciate a one-to-one chat. Chrétien said okay, and when everybody else left the room, the two men went into Chrétien's private office.

"I said to him, 'This is very important to us, to Canada, to our sector of the industry. We're prepared to put a lot of money into helping you in your campaign, but I'd really like to know that this is not bullshit and that when you're elected you're going to act on what you say.'"

According to Sherman, Chrétien replied, "I can't give you a specific promise of exactly what I'm going to do, but I'm an honourable person. Taking away a license retroactively is unconscionable. The regulations are unconscionable. I can assure you that as soon as we're elected, it will be our top priority to give you substantial relief in these areas. But I also want to say to you that we're going to do this because it's the right thing to do and what you contribute to the campaign is irrelevant, whether you give us nothing or whether you give us a lot of money, it won't make a bit of difference, we're going to do the right thing."

Sherman told Chrétien, "That's terrific. I'm glad you're principled and we are going to support you heavily in the campaign."

There's no doubt that Sherman made good on his promise because he did raise a substantial sum for the Liberals.

Once they got elected, Sherman points out, "They made it worse."

There was a mandated review of C-91 after four years, and from what Sherman understands, a parliamentary committee was going to recommend that the regulations be set aside. But Manley supposedly strong-armed the Liberal members of the committee into announcing instead that the government should review the regulations. So the committee that reviewed the regulations comes out with a report that says the government should review the regulations without adding its presumed conclusion to get rid of them. When the government followed, it made some major changes.

First, it moved the notification time.

Under the old system, the generic company notified the branded company of its intentions before it submitted a new drug application, and the branded company would then submit a list of patents that, it claimed, would be violated. While lawyers would fight it out in court, the generic company could do as much of its research as it wanted to.

Under the new system, the generic company had to notify the branded company after the new drug application was made. That meant the generic company first had to invest in the product and develop it. They'd have to spend a fortune getting the product ready, at which time everything would stop for years waiting for litigation. It created a cash-flow nightmare for the generic industry.

Second, they moved the goalposts by changing the reference system.

A generic is a bioequivalent of a drug, so there must be another drug to compare it with. In the past, the regulations only restricted generics when the reference was to the patented product. The new regulations restricted generics even if they're not compared to a product with a patent as long as they're comparable and capable of being compared to a product with a patent.

"Unbelievable," Sherman laments, forever convinced that Big Pharma somehow persuaded Chrétien that unless he protected them, or at least protected one of them, it stood to lose C$100 million. The company he suspects at the bottom of this is Merck because the regulations so obviously prevented him from coming out with his version of its Vasotec.

"Nobody says if we do this, it's going to put a generic company out of business and cost the health-care system C$100 million. So where does the C$100 million come from that Merck is going to make? The pockets of the generic industry and the public."

When the government decided to change the regulations, Sherman says, various cabinet ministers from Ontario wrote to the prime minister saying don't do it.

"They were ignored, overruled," says Sherman. He doesn't know whether the Prime Minister's Office ordered Manley to do it or Manley wanted to do it. He does know that the grassroots, the majority of the Liberal party, is on his side. "They know that we're right, they know that it's terrible to keep screwing us at the expense of the health-care system and to the benefit of these foreign-owned companies, but that's what's happening. So the Liberals have become the Tories."

He cites the example of Merck, a company with Canadian headquarters in Montreal. Through the late 1980s and into the 1990s, during the separation discussions, Merck – and the other pharmaceutical companies in Quebec as well – represented multinational interest in the province. By playing their political cards carefully, Big Pharma in general and Merck in particular gained a great deal of influence in Quebec. So even an idle threat of "If something doesn't happen we're going to shut down and disinvest" makes Montreal's politicians very nervous. In turn, those politicians run to Ottawa and say, "If Merck and the rest of Big Pharma leaves Montreal, everyone in Quebec will point their finger at Ottawa and say, 'This is just another example of the federal government not looking after Quebec's interest.'"

It gives Big Pharma their tremendous political clout.

It's hardly a coincidence then that Quebec has what is known as "the fifteen-year rule." The provincial formulary will only list a generic drug, and therefore pay for it, if the branded version has been on the market for fifteen years. This rule applies even if there's no longer a patent on the branded drug. So a generic drug that may be interchangeable in Ontario won't be dispensed in Quebec because the government is willing to pay for the high-priced branded drug for fifteen years. For example, a generic version of Prozac has been on the market in Canada since 1996. Quebec continues to buy the branded, more expensive Prozac and will, until 2004, even though it has the equivalent generic available at 40 per cent less.

Sherman retorts, "And the minister of industry says, 'I don't care if it costs Health Canada more, we have to do this because we're getting all these wonderful jobs from this industry and that protects the jobs.' It's stupid. How do you get more jobs by paying twice the price for the same thing?"

Big Pharma's usual answer to that is "But look at the research we do here. We promised when the government got rid of compulsory licensing that we'd do more research, and that's exactly what we're doing. We spend a billion dollars on research in Canada."

But Sherman contends it's not for the benefit of Canada.

"Merck and others spend money doing research in Canadian hospitals because it's cheap, but it's for the benefit of Merck worldwide. If there's anything discovered, it leaves the country without payment, it's exploited abroad, and then those products come back into the country at very high prices. Meanwhile, they deduct any research money spent in Canada from Canadian income as if it were an expense to earn money in Canada, which it isn't. Anyway, it's subsidized by the taxpayers because the companies get tax benefits for doing research in Canada. If the research is being done in Canada for the benefit of foreign companies, it should not be deductible for Canadian tax purposes. In addition to paying ten times what we should for drugs, we're paying for half the research on them too. Is this good for Canada? It's insane. The industry is right back to where it was pre-1969."

Sherman has seen Jean Chrétien since he's been prime minister. The two men met privately at 24 Sussex Drive. He went there hoping they might have a heart-to-heart and to ask again for Chrétien's help. After the usual pleasantries, Sherman mentioned those regulations and how the generic industry is dying on the vine.

According to Sherman, Chrétien replied, "I don't know anything about these things, I have to leave it up to my ministers."

Sherman now reminded the prime minister that in 1993 when he came to Apotex and spoke to the staff, he'd understood perfectly.

To which, Sherman claims, the prime minister replied, "Oh well, you know, I haven't practised law in thirty years."

According to Sherman, Chrétien blankly refused to discuss it.

These days Sherman just shakes his head wearily. "But in 1993 he understood exactly. He explained it to us and to our staff. When he's saying in 1999 what does he know, he knows it's wrong but will pretend not to know because that makes it easy. He figures, 'I'll pretend there's no problem, or I'll pretend that I don't understand there's a problem, because what else can I say? I can't say, yes, you're right, but I'm not prepared to do the right thing.'"

An attempt to confirm the conversation brought no reply whatsoever from the Prime Minister's Office.

"We're getting gouged by paying enormously high prices for drugs, the money is leaving the country tax-free, and on top of that we're paying for their research fifty cents on the dollar through our tax system. And that leaves the country tax-free too," Sherman summarizes. "I just can't see what's in it for the government. What are we going to do about funding health care? The health-care system is going broke. But not a word about spending C$9 billion on pharmaceuticals when it should be C$1 billion. They're either stupid or they're crooks, I don't see a third possibility."

CHAPTER 10

PLAYING HARDBALL

The first thing was always reconnaissance.

He drove his rental car out to the Spanish factory that afternoon, sur-veyed the main gate, noted that the guard shack was far enough away from the production facilities at the rear of the property, then followed the fence around to the back. He wanted to find a spot where he could safely park later that night and where he could most easily go across the fence.

He assured himself that access would be easy.

That's when he heard dogs barking.

Two German shepherds and a Rhodesian ridgeback raced to the fence.

He waited to see if any others arrived – it was just the three – reassured himself that access would still be easy, and drove back into town to find the nearest butcher.

Much later, in the dead of night, now dressed in black with his face darkened too – the way you always see commandos in the movies – he returned to the factory. Driving slowly and without headlights so as not to attract the guard's attention, he parked, got out of his car, walked along the side of the factory towards the guard shack until he attracted the dogs' attention. Now when they barked and ran towards him, he tossed three steaks over the fence, then retreated back into the night. The dogs ripped the steaks apart and ate them quickly. An hour later, he rattled the fence at the rear of the factory. Nothing happened. There was no barking. The tranquilizers he'd laced into the steaks had done the job. So, now, while the three guard dogs slept, he climbed the fence.

Jimmying a window to get inside the plant was easy. He made his way through the offices and shop floors until he found what he wanted – large chemical drums. He ripped labels off some of them, found paperwork in files that he could take, and photographed the production facilities. On the way out, he stole several bags of office garbage.

Just as he got back to his car, the guard from the front gate started waving a flashlight at the factory. Perhaps he'd heard something. Perhaps he was wondering why the dogs were asleep.

Paul Whybrow couldn't have cared less. It had taken him less than twenty-five minutes to get in and out. And as the guard walked cautiously towards the factory, Whybrow disappeared into the night.

⬤▬

As the market for legitimate prescription drugs has grown to a colossal size, the market for illegal prescription drugs has grown alongside it.

These are illicit generics made by companies in direct violation of patent protection; counterfeit drugs that contain no active ingredients but are packaged and priced like the real thing; and substandard drugs that contain some active ingredients and are sold as the real thing but do not meet pharmacopoeial standards. Because it serves Big Pharma's interests, illegal prescription drugs get grouped together under the heading of counterfeits. When the word "generic" can be tossed into the pot, they deliberately tar legitimate generics with the same brush as counterfeits, trying to confuse the issues of bioequivalence and counterfeit drugs to create the impression that the two words are interchangeable.

Of course they're not. The World Health Organization defines counterfeit drugs as those that are deliberately and fraudulently mislabelled with respect to identity and/or source. The only similarity between legitimate generics and counterfeits is that they both cost Big Pharma billions of dollars a year in lost revenue. Where legitimate generics and counterfeits are decidedly different is that counterfeits present serious health dangers to the public.

When a shipment of diethylene glycol, a chemical found in antifreeze, was deliberately mislabelled as glycerine, it was used to make cough syrup that was shipped to Haiti and killed eighty children. A few years before, the same solution was used to make counterfeit eyedrops that were administered to patients in Bombay. Fourteen people died.

When thousands of doses of a meningitis vaccine showed up in Niger, packaged to look like the genuine SmithKline Beecham product but were nothing more than salt water, people died of meningitis.

When fake Microvlar oral contraceptives flooded the market in Brazil, dozens of women suffered unexpected pregnancies. In this case, the local subsidiary of the German pharmaceutical company Schering AG, which manufactures the pills, had produced a batch of lookalike placebos – 650,000 packages, each containing twenty-one lactose and sugar pills – to test out its new packaging equipment. The placebos were supposed to have been destroyed after the tests, but a criminal gang managed to steal them en route to the incinerator.

Statistics are difficult to compile and therefore not terribly reliable. Many years ago, the WHO reported that 7 per cent of the medicines sold in the world were counterfeit. The International Federation of Pharmaceutical Manufacturers' Associations claims the correct figure could be as high as 10 per cent. A survey conducted by WHO between 1982 and 1997 listed 751 incidents of counterfeit pharmaceuticals appearing on the market in twenty-eight countries. Most of those counterfeits were said to have been manufactured in India, Pakistan, Indonesia, Thailand, and the Middle East, but a source now says that perhaps a quarter of them came from Spain, Italy, and Greece. Another report claims that substandard drugs are pouring into Africa from Vietnam, although it's not clear whether those counterfeits are produced by criminal gangs in Vietnam or somewhere else and merely transshipped through Southeast Asia.

Western health officials currently accuse China of being the largest producer of substandard medicines. While predictable denials come from Beijing, the Chinese continue to flood the Third World with their drugs. India also has plenty to answer for. An estimated twenty-six thousand companies there manufacture pharmaceuticals, a huge percentage of them operating in factories that fail to meet even the most minimal standards of hygiene. Those drugs regularly show up in pharmacies as far away as Mexico, a country said to be drowning in counterfeit medicines. One estimate is that fake drugs, mostly from India and China, make up 10 per cent of the lucrative Tijuana market. That's where Americans stream across the border from California to buy cut-price prescription drugs, medication not authorized for sale in the United States, or drugs for which they don't otherwise have a prescription. One batch of antibiotics, packaged in Mexico, was recently traced from Panama into Venezuela. When the sell-by date expired, the drugs showed up all over Latin America – including Tijuana – now in counterfeit packaging with an extra two years added to the expiration date.

In Indonesia, which has a huge counterfeit drug problem, 60 per cent of the market is supplied from Malaysia and Thailand by organized criminal gangs. In Pakistan, officials publicly admit that 2 per cent of the drug market is counterfeit. Experts privately agree that the truth is closer to 50 per cent. In Bangladesh, $77 million worth of drugs are smuggled into the country every year, most of them outright fakes or substandard. *Time* magazine has suggested that up to half the medicines sold in sub-Saharan Africa could be fake.

More and more counterfeit drugs, especially those ordered over the Internet, are coming into Canada and the United States through the mail. Categorized as one of the top-ten most disturbing forms of high-tech crime, counterfeit drugs have been seized alongside shipments of legitimate imports from several European countries, especially Greece. Glaxo Wellcome became so concerned when manufacturers in India were copying several big-selling drugs, including Zantac, it upped the stakes by designing entirely new, much costlier, more difficult to copy packaging. Adding holograms and security seals has proven to be relatively effective. But it isn't always enough and usually only works when companies also send their reps out into the field to find fakes on pharmacy shelves and then spend money on ads to warn consumers.

As counterfeiters have become more adept at sidestepping those efforts, the multinationals have stepped up the fight. Twenty of the largest drug companies funded the Pharmaceutical Security Institute (PSI). Essentially a civilian police force, its agents are sent into the field to investigate clandestine manufacturers, to identify illegal traders, to gather samples for patent infringement cases, and to liaise with law enforcement.

The PSI are the industry's officially acknowledged spooks.

Paul Whybrow was one of the agents the industry doesn't acknowledge.

Born in 1951 in Kent, England, Whybrow joined the British Merchant Navy right after school, sailed around the world on passenger liners for the next three years, came back to England, and, not having any idea what he wanted to do with his life, got a job selling cars. That lasted nine years, until a strike by British miners, high interest rates, and inflation combined to cripple the economy.

Needing work, he spotted a recruiting ad for the Port of London Authority Police, decided he wanted to be a detective, and at the age of twenty-eight signed on. He completed the standard training courses, but quickly discovered that the port was not for him. He spent ten weeks patrolling the docks along the Thames River at Tilbury, checking seals on the back of lorries and, as they drove out the gate, getting his lungs filled with diesel smoke. As soon as he could manage it, he transferred over to the City of London Police.

After two years of walking a beat, he moved into the criminal investigation division as a detective. In 1984, he was assigned to the fraud squad. In those days, there were no professional undercover cops on the city force. Scotland Yard had a team of undercovers it loaned out to other forces, but these were mostly cops who knew how to buy stolen televisions off the back of a lorry. There wasn't anybody on any force who could play the role of a banker to negotiate a parcel of stolen bonds, or to be a businessman interested in a stock scam.

The medium-height, dark-haired, and fit Whybrow fell into it by accident. When an informant tipped off the fraud squad about a con man looking to unload $2 million worth of Italian bank bonds, somebody decided that Whybrow could look the part. He put his warrant card in his desk drawer, took some petty cash for cab fare, and, without any backup, went to meet a pair of suspects at the Royal Garden Hotel in Kensington. Two weeks later, both suspects were in custody and the stolen bonds were recovered.

Because it worked so well the first time, Whybrow was sent undercover a second time. Within a few months, his superiors realized that he had a real talent for this. So they gave him a new identity, a passport to match, a credit card and a bank account in his new name, and a safe-house address. Just like that, the City of London Police had the first official undercover officer in the entire country specifically to deal with financial fraud.

"The problem was," Whybrow says, "no one at the time fully understood how to run an undercover operative. I'd work three or four weeks under my assumed persona, and when the case came down, they'd put me back on normal police duties. I wasn't taken out of circulation. In an ideal world I should have been. But this isn't an ideal world. It meant I had to learn how to be careful. Not paranoid, but careful. Being paranoid and being careful are two different things."

As far as he knows, he only got burned once. He was doing a job in Gibraltar and part of the script called for him to get arrested with his two targets. They were nabbed picking up £600,000. The idea was that the known fraudsters would lead him from that job to a much bigger one.

"We walked into the bank where we were to get the money and I went up to the manager to ask if the transfer had been made. That was the code. And sure enough, a few seconds later, the cops come through the doors. They cuffed us and hauled us off, including me, and put us in cells cut out of the Rock. The two targets kept telling me that someone stitched us up and I kept agreeing with them. The police interviewed them one by one, with me listening in from another room, then tossed us back in the cells together. Finally they brought us into the superintendent's office. He went through a big theatrical scene where he slammed our passports down on his desk and told us we were three very lucky gentlemen. He said there just wasn't enough evidence to hold us. He said, 'I suggest you walk out of this police station and get off this rock before we find a good excuse to lock you up.' We grabbed our passports, got into my hire car, and drove to Málaga. We were supposed to meet again back in England to plan the bigger job."

But it never happened. The informant who'd originally put Whybrow onto these two suddenly showed up with the news that he was a marked man.

"They'd somehow found out I was a copper. They told the informant they were going to get me. Sure enough, they called me for a meet, but I didn't go. I never saw either of them again."

Over the course of ten plus years, Whybrow was someone else as he chased down stolen American government cheques that were being negotiated by the Camorra Mafia in Italy, as he helped recover huge amounts of counterfeit money, as he rounded up criminals living off the underground economy. There were times when his backups got lost, and times when his targets made sure he couldn't be followed, leaving him alone in situations with heavily armed and very determined criminals. But most of the time he found himself fighting the system. Most of the time he found himself trying to make his handlers understand that being a professional undercover cop wasn't like being a regular cop.

"I wouldn't call it burnout because it wasn't, but I got to a point where I was very frustrated with budgetary constraints and bad management. Senior officers who'd never worked undercover couldn't understand how to manage an undercover. And every undercover police officer you'll ever meet will tell you this. We all think we're a breed apart, but you're bound to feel different and special if you're travelling the world, dealing with top-class international criminals. In the case of some of my handlers, the biggest job they'd ever done was a burglary. They'd taken the exams and been promoted, but they didn't understand someone doing undercover work at my level. They still wanted to talk to me as if I was investigating a petty cash theft."

It came to a head the day Whybrow was paged by a target who wanted to meet him at the London Hilton. Whybrow went to his boss for petty cash. His boss asked why he had to meet the man now and why he needed money.

"I explained that I had to meet him because I was his man in the city and he asked to meet me. The governor wanted to know, 'How long are you going to be?' I said, 'I don't know.' He said, 'We don't have a lot of overtime this week.' I told him it wasn't about that. He wanted to know what I was going to do with the petty cash. I said, 'Because I'll have to buy coffee or something and I need to get a taxi.' He said, 'Why take a cab when the Number 11 bus takes you straight up the Strand and from there you can pop around to the Hilton.' I said, 'The last time this guy saw me I was driving a £62,000 Porsche, and you want me to arrive on a bus?' That's the kind of thing I was up against. It pissed me off. I couldn't understand why I had to argue about cab fare when I was putting my life on the line to catch criminals."

So Whybrow decided to call it a day. "I made a deliberate decision that it was time to go. It was easy because I knew there was a whole corporate world out there looking for people who could do what I did." Within one week, Carratu International, one of Europe's leading private investigation agencies, offered him a job. He was taken to lunch by a man – call him Mr. Jones – who said the firm needed someone to work undercover in its pharmaceutical division to collect evidence of counterfeit drugs and of patent and trademark infringements.

At Carratu, just as they are in so many private detective agencies, pharmaceuticals are a big money ticket.

"I started there on a Monday. By Tuesday I was in Barcelona doing an undercover job. Strictly front-door stuff. We were trying to prove that a company was infringing a drug called captopril. This was for Bristol-Myers Squibb. I went to the plant on the pretext of being a buyer. All I was supposed to do was walk in the front door, give someone a list of my requirements, and arrange to have a sample sent to me in England. Instead, I talked them into giving me a tour of the factory, white coat and safety glasses and all. I saw the captopril being dispatched, obtained a sample the same day, and came back to Jones on the Friday with every-thing he needed."

There were jobs for AstraZeneca, Pfizer, Glaxo Wellcome, Bayer, and Roche. After that, there were also jobs that took him through the back door. While he insists that no one ever asks anyone to do anything illegal, everyone who plays this game knows what evidence is needed. "They always say that they never condone anything illegal. But then, they've got to say that, don't they."

Most jobs were routine and uneventful. During the day he'd go in the front door. At night he'd climb over the wall. He was never armed, except with tranquilizers for the dogs. But the factory guards were armed and, occasionally, shots were fired.

"You know what? The guards doing the shooting were just as scared as I was, except they were frightened that they were going to catch me. The last thing they wanted to do was nab me and have to deal with me. So they didn't shoot at me, they shot over my head to scare me away. They didn't know who they were chasing or how desperate I was or what I was after."

What he was after were those drum labels, which would tell his clients what chemicals were on hand and where they'd come from, who was shipping what to whom, and what the manufacturing process looked like. So he stole labels and rifled desks and took photos and also grabbed as much garbage as he could.

"Garbage was a bit like a lucky dip because you never know what you're going to get. Inevitably, it's in black plastic bags, so you take it away from the scene. I've spent many many hours in hotel rooms with the floor covered in garbage. You rip the bags open, go through them, put the good stuff in a new bag and dispose of the worthless stuff wherever you can. You find invoices, letters, faxes, bank statements, customer lists, minutes of meetings, amazing intelligence. Ten years ago you could get whatever you needed out of someone's garbage. Today people know and they shred. That means you sometimes have to bring the garbage back to London and have the shreddies reconstituted. There are people who do just that, paste all those shreddies back together again. You collect whatever you have to, any way you have to, so that the client can make their case of patent infringement."

For the next nine months, Whybrow's work with Carratu took him all over the world. Those years of police experience had fine-tuned his instincts: never paranoid, always careful. And here, budgets were not a problem. He used different names and had different front companies to back him up. When a client wanted him to check on an infringer in Beirut, he'd fly first to Cyprus, stay there a few days, then book onto a twenty-four-hour guided tour of Beirut. The boat sailed from Cyprus and once in Beirut, passengers simply walked ashore without an Immigration check. The ship's captain held everyone's passport. Because there was never an entry stamp for Lebanon, he could come in and out without anyone suspecting he'd been there before. When the coach pulled up to the ship to take passengers on a tour, he'd slip away from the main party, rent a car and driver, and do his own thing.

One of the front companies he used was registered in Malaysia. When his target, working for an infringing company, announced at a meeting in Switzerland that they were ready to do a deal, Whybrow realized the infringer was nearly trapped. But the target said, as luck would have it, that he was going to be in Malaysia in three days and suggested they meet at Whybrow's offices there to close the deal. Whybrow immediately agreed, even though he didn't actually have an office in Malaysia.

He returned to England that night, spoke to the pharmaceutical company he was acting for, got its okay, and was strapped into a business-class seat on the following morning's flight to Malaysia. As soon as he arrived, he invented an office. Almost as if it was a scene out of *The Sting*, he took over a premises, decorated it with materials supplied by the pharmaceutical company to appear as if it was totally legit, and met with his target.

Once there, the bad guy and his associates saw that Whybrow was who he said he was, and within forty-eight hours of arriving in Malaysia, the office set was struck and Whybrow was on his return business-class flight to London.

As if the world of counterfeit drugs and patent infringement isn't already murky enough, globalization has created an underworld of independent traders who move legal drugs back and forth across borders illegally. Most companies manufacture drugs specifically for export. All over Europe, for example, the multinationals cater to their home markets with one set of prices and then, because Eastern Europe is a huge market in size but a relatively poor one, they export a line of drugs – the same drugs they sell at home – priced lower for the Eastern European market. What those freelance traders try to do is buy drugs destined for Eastern Europe and divert them back into the West at home market prices.

One of Carratu's clients, the German giant Bayer Pharmaceuticals, started finding these so-called grey market drugs in pharmacies only a few blocks from its factory in Leverkusen. So Whybrow was dispatched to Switzerland to gather evidence against the culprit.

Normal surveillance on the target uncovered a way through which Whybrow – using one of his covers – could meet the man. Over the course of several weeks, Whybrow and the target began having lunch together. Whybrow gradually led their conversations around to business and, as trust built up, the target confessed that he'd been playing in this grey market. The way the target's business worked, he'd set up a company to do business in Russia, was buying medicine from Bayer, and supposedly shipping it to Kazakhstan. At least, that's what Bayer had been led to believe. In reality, the products were never leaving Germany. They were being sold there through wholesalers and into the legitimate market.

Whybrow claimed to have a similar scheme set up through his non-existent Malaysian company. The target fell for it and suggested the two do a few joint ventures. To help it along, the target offered Whybrow the use of his offices in Switzerland. Over the next few weeks, Whybrow directed faxes and contracts – all drawn up with Bayer's cooperation – to him in care of the target's office.

Obviously, the target was reading the faxes and, just as obviously, he was believing what he read, that Whybrow was connected well enough to buy shipments from the multinationals that together they could divert.

The target now suggested they form a company together and open a bank account in Switzerland, over which the target himself would have signature authority. Bayer wired $25,000 into a Whybrow account in England, and Whybrow wired it straight out to the new company's account in Switzerland.

Everything was ready to go. Whybrow had even argued with the people at Bayer that, instead of closing down the target right away, they should allow one or two shipments to go through so that they could then track the people doing the target's bidding for him in Germany. But at the very last minute, the whole thing was scrapped.

With hindsight, Whybrow wonders whether it was Bayer that got cold feet, or Jones. He thinks one possibility is that Jones stopped the job because his superiors didn't know what he was doing. "He would have had to explain how we'd compromised the target. That's why I think he pulled the plug. I argued, 'If you genuinely want to catch this man, he's right there to be caught, right now.' But he wouldn't do it. I guess he didn't have a way of explaining to the company exactly what he was doing."

What Whybrow didn't yet know was that Jones had a serious falling out with the management at Carratu. One day, just like that, Jones was gone. Whybrow, together with another ex-cop working at Carratu named Mick Flack, went to see Jones and found him very down in the dumps. They did whatever they could to encourage him, to assure him that he'd find another job somewhere. A few months later, Jones seemed to land on his feet, employed by Carratu's own client, Bayer AG.

Remembering the guys who'd stood by him, Jones offered Whybrow and Flack the opportunity to leave Carratu and form their own agency. He told them he was controlling all of Bayer's investigations, had a budget worth around £1.4 million for patent protection, and that Carratu would never get a penny of it. He told them, "You two start a business and you can have the lot."

They were reluctant at first, but the offer was simply too good to turn down. So Whybrow and Flack set up a company called Temple Associates in Covent Garden, and went back to work for Jones.

One of the first cases he put them on to was Barry Sherman and Apotex.

"As far as Jones was concerned, Barry Sherman was a real thorn in his side. He was obsessed with Sherman, convinced that he was a major infringer, and he wanted him taken down. I'd been out to Canada on behalf of Carratu, gone through the front door of Apotex, and had an interview. Mick and I then went out to Canada together, and sat around watching the trucks going into the loading bays at the rear of the plant. We dressed in overalls and carried clipboards and walked around the loading bays to see what was coming in and going out. Sometimes we even carried a box with some stuff in it, just in case someone asked us what we were doing there. We could tell them we were making a delivery to Mr. Johnson. Make up any name. You'd be amazed at how much you can get away with if you look the part."

Not far from the Apotex loading bay was an area with picnic tables where employees would have lunch. So Whybrow and Flack sat there eating hot dogs for a couple of days, always taking notes.

"Maybe we did a week's surveillance around the back. But the security is pretty tight at Apotex and you can forget about getting in there after hours. In Italy and Spain the places are made out of cardboard and string. But Apotex was good."

They reported back to Jones that they didn't yet have what he wanted. He asked them to try to get a mole inside the company, and they felt they could arrange that. But that wasn't enough for Jones. Now he came to England to meet with Whybrow and Flack.

"We had lunch together at a country pub," Whybrow alleges, "and all the time, Jones is thinking about how he can get Sherman. This is no longer just business, this is personal. He doesn't just want to compromise him in a corporate way. He's talking about playing hardball with Barry Sherman. It was very direct. He said to us, 'We have to get this bastard Sherman.' He said to us, 'What are we going to do about him? Let's take him out of the game. Take him out.' Mick and I both knew enough not to say anything. He could have been wired. We weren't going to commit ourselves to anything. But Jones was suggesting everything."

According to Whybrow and Flack, the conversation then went like this:

Jones: "What can we do?"

Whybrow: "What do you want us to do?"

Jones: "What about your contacts with the police in Canada? Could you get him stopped?'

Whybrow: "Anything's possible."

Jones: "Let's say he had half a kilo in his boot."

Whybrow insists that neither he nor Flack said anything about this.

Jones: "What's his sexual preference? Could we get him hooked up with little girls, or even underaged boys?"

Again, Whybrow says, he and Flack refused to get drawn into this. They knew better. But, Whybrow maintains, Jones was adamant.

Jones: "We've got to take him off the scene. Got to take him out."

On the face of it, Whybrow says, Jones might have thought they'd do it. After all, he was paying them £500 a day, and for that money, they at least looked like they were interested. But, he declares firmly, there was never any question of doing it. "We figured we'd go out there for a few days, then ring him from Canada and say, 'Sorry, it can't be done.' There are, after all, some things we're simply not going to do. You do have to draw the line. But we'd have gone out there and made like we're trying to do it and charge him three grand for it."

In fairness, Whybrow adds, Jones never actually asked them to do anything illegal. All he wanted them to do, they insist, was "whatever it takes." Whybrow thought Jones a bit reckless. But Jones never said to them, do it. Jones never asked them to commit a crime.

Whybrow now thinks Jones was really on some sort of fishing expedition. "He was looking to find out from us what we could do. He wanted Sherman taken out, but I don't know what his solution was. He might not even have had one. Even if he did, it wasn't going to be easy because Sherman is a very sharp operator."

When the conversation was repeated to Sherman, he didn't seem surprised. "The branded drug companies hate us. They have private investigators on us all the time. The thought once came to my mind, why didn't they just hire someone to knock me off? For a thousand bucks paid to the right person you can probably get someone killed. Perhaps I'm surprised that hasn't happened."

⬤

While all this was going on, Flack was working some informants for Jones and Bayer in Cyprus.

The target there was a manufacturer named Pittas, who, Jones believed, was one of Europe's major pharmaceutical infringers. Mick's contacts were a marine surveyor he called Lefty, who had access to the port at Limassol, and Lefty's cousin, who worked at the airport at Larnaka. Between the two of them, they covered just about anything leaving Cyprus, including everything shipped out of Pittas' factory.

Even though it was Flack's dossier, Whybrow had gone out there with him on several occasions. Now, in mid-February 1996, Lefty had contacted Flack to say he had some good documents to show that Pittas was still infringing. Flack got Lefty to send a sample along, it looked promising, and so Flack asked Jones if he wanted anything done about it. Jones told him to go out to Cyprus right away.

Whybrow was working a small deal for an American bank in London, where one of the managers had been compromised by a Russian. Flack told Whybrow he was running over to Cyprus and asked if he wanted to come along. The weather was terrible. A couple of days in the sun appealed to Whybrow, so he said sure.

Flack was already booked on a flight. Whybrow followed the next day. The two had rooms at the Four Seasons in Limassol, but there was a lot of construction going on across the street and it was noisy. They moved to a hotel next door. But there, they encountered insurmountable troubles with the plumbing – the toilets wouldn't flush – and for the third time in three days, they changed hotels again.

Lefty's documents weren't as good as Flack had hoped, so he pressed him for more. Lefty's response was to set up a meeting with a chain-smoking, gold-bracelet-bedecked character called Georgio.

Now Whybrow started to smell a rat. "He gave us the documents and left. But they were pretty useless. Lefty then told us that he had to pick up more documents from somebody's office the next day. We kept asking, 'Are they going to be better?' and he kept assuring us they were. He said the guy who had the documents couldn't get them to us, that we had to go to him. So we hired a car, drove up to the offices, went in, some guy gave us more documents, and we left. On the way out, I noticed there was some broken glass on the floor. But I didn't think anything of it. We just went back to the hotel, looked through these documents, there were some that were okay, packed them in my suitcase, checked out, and drove to the airport. As far as we were concerned, that was the end of it."

It was now late on Wednesday night, February 14, 1996. The airport was pretty much deserted. They parked the rental car, checked in, and headed for the gate. That's when Flack remembered he still had the car keys. What they normally would have done is what they'd done hundreds of times before: wait until they got home to shove the keys into an envelope, address it to Avis, and post them back. But because they had half an hour before the plane left, Flack looked around, spotted the Avis desk about a hundred yards away, told Whybrow to go through, and took the keys back.

When he didn't find anybody at the Avis desk, Flack banged on the counter. The clerk, sleeping in the back room, woke up and took the keys. But just as Flack turned around to leave, the fellow called him back. He told Flack he had to wait a minute because there was a problem with the car. Flack stood there while the fellow made a phone call.

Whybrow was waiting for him at the gate. When the flight was called, he got onto the plane. He told himself that Flack would be there any minute.

The flight attendant came through the cabin with orange juice. Whybrow took one and settled down to read his newspaper. Then she returned to do a head count.

Whybrow realized something was wrong. "Once that happens, your instincts tell you not to get off the plane. I wasn't going to look for him because so much can happen on that island. I knew to stay put."

The cabin crew started to shut the door. Just before they got it closed, someone knocked on it. They opened it and a man came into the plane. He looked around, then went straight to Whybrow and asked to see his passport. He looked at it, gave it back to Whybrow, got off the plane, and, again, the flight attendant counted heads.

All this time the engines were running.

The crew went to shut the door again and, just like the first time, before they could get it closed, someone banged on it.

Now several men came onto the plane, went straight for Whybrow, and dragged him away.

A police car was parked at the bottom of the steps, with its headlights shining on the underbelly of the plane. Flack was standing there, guarded by two men. The police had the cargo bay opened, and Whybrow's bag was pulled off. They put it in the car's headlights, opened it, and yanked out the papers Lefty's contact had given them.

One of the cops asked Whybrow, "What are these papers?"

He answered, "Business documents."

The cop said, "These are stolen and you are both under arrest."

Whybrow and Flack were handcuffed behind their backs and taken to the police station at the airport. They were left sitting in the CID office under police guard, without water or food, all night. Late the next morning, an officer arrived from Limassol, bundled them into a car, and drove around the countryside for what seemed to be several hours, until he found a woman hoeing her garden. She turned out to be a magistrate and was the one to sign the papers that kept them in custody. Whybrow was then taken to Limassol Central Police Station. Flack was driven somewhere else. And for the next twenty-three days, without ever being charged, they were held in solitary confinement.

The cell was very small and had no light. They were not allowed to wash or to shave. The bed was one plank of wood, the blanket was filthy and moth-eaten. There was a Coke bottle in the corner that served as a urinal. If they needed a toilet, they had to wait until one of the guards took them to it. The food was mainly stale bread.

Sometime around the seventh day, a lawyer showed up. He was British, from London, and the first thing he told Whybrow was, "I'm from the B people. I've been sent to help you. Is there anything you need?"

Whybrow took that to mean Bayer.

This lawyer arranged for a local attorney to take the case. Whybrow says he later learned that Bayer paid the local attorney £12,000 for each of them, and was never seen by either of them again. It was only later that he also learned how Lefty had been compromised by someone close to Pittas and, to save his own butt, had handed Pittas the two operatives from Bayer.

It was another week before Whybrow was able to get word out of the jail that they needed another lawyer. This time a young Cypriot attorney named Nicos Clarrides showed up and took over their case. But justice moves slowly in Cyprus and the two stayed on remand, waiting for a hearing from the night they were arrested until June 20.

Because there was no statute for industrial espionage in Cyprus, they were then charged with burglary and conspiracy to undermine the economy of the island to the tune of $70 million.

Both Whybrow and Flack went into shock. "Our lawyer came to us and warned, 'You'll get seven years if you try to contest this and it doesn't matter what you say because this is now political.' He told us that Pittas had paid for the attorney general's political campaign and spent weekends with the president. Our lawyer said there really wasn't much he could do because they were putting such pressure on this. He said the only way he could help you was if we pled guilty to the burglary. He said, 'They want to have you labelled as criminals who have come to Cyprus to undermine the economy.' But if we plead guilty to the burglary, which is set at only £44, he said he'd do his utmost best to get the conspiracy charge dropped."

The £44 was for the broken glass, which was supposed to prove forced entry, that Whybrow had seen on the way out of the office the night they got the papers.

"Mick and I felt that as much as it goes against the grain, we'd take the burglary charge. By this time, we're in prison together. I figured we'd already done four months and that if we pleaded to the burglary we'd be going home. So that's what we did. Then there was that terrible period of waiting for them to drop the conspiracy charge. That must have been three weeks."

When they finally had their hearing, they walked into court thinking they'd be going home that day. Even their attorney said that for a £44 burglary they probably only should have done three weeks. So Whybrow and Flack sat in the courtroom thinking it was all over, at least until they heard the prosecutor outline their crime. He told the judge how the two men had flown in separately and changed hotels three times. He never said the hotels were twenty yards apart and they had a good excuse each time. He made it sound as if they were trying to stay one step ahead of the police.

The judge sentenced them to eighteen months.

They were thrown back into their cells, totally gutted.

Clarrides reassured them they would win on appeal. But until the case came up again, they were stuck in their cells. No toilet paper. No doors on toilets. No glass in any of the cells. Bare bars. Temperatures up to 32°C during the day and not much cooler at night. Boiled courgettes and fatty old meat for food. Nothing to do all day.

The prisoner in the cell next to Whybrow ate the light bulb. There was nothing left in his cell that he could use to do harm to himself, so he unscrewed the light bulb and ate it to kill himself. When that didn't work, he somehow got hold of battery fluid and drank that.

At night, the Iranian drug traffickers who were there would start chanting, then slashing themselves with little pieces of flint they sharpened on the floor. Down the cellblock were Russian hitmen, who walked around scowling at everybody. They were all ex-special forces soldiers – Cyprus is infested with Russians – who were serving life terms for shooting people in the back of the head.

The only other Brits were three soldiers who'd raped and then murdered a Scandinavian tour guide. They chopped her up and buried her in the sand.

Whybrow shakes his head. "Those are the guys you had to sit and laugh and joke with. The guys you played Monopoly with. They expect you to be their friends. They spoke English and they were reasonably clean. It was them or the Iranian drug dealers or the Russian hitmen. At least with the Brits you could talk about cricket."

Their appeal was heard on September 23, and the three-judge panel reduced their sentence to nine months. With a little bit of remission time, they were out three days later.

Handcuffed again, Whybrow and Flack were put on a plane to Zurich. Whybrow had lost more than forty pounds. Flack had lost more than fifty. Both were also totally hooked on Mogadon, sleeping pills that the guards handed out every night like candy. It was the only way they could cut out the noise. The British soldiers put the sleeping pills under their tongues and pretended to swallow them – because the guards had to see you take them – and then went back to their cells, spit them out and saved them up so they could bomb out on weekends.

From Zurich, Whybrow and Flack were flown to London. Flack went into a deep depression. Whybrow heard his wife of twenty-eight years say she was leaving him.

A few weeks later, Jones made contact.

He begged Whybrow not to throw this stuff back at him. He said that there was a willingness to help, but warned that it had to be managed in a professional way. He said there might even be a job at the end of it for the two of them. "All I ask," he said, "is that you don't throw stuff back at me."

Whybrow agreed to a face-to-face meeting.

It never happened and he's never seen Jones again.

He was, however, contacted by a lawyer who said he was representing Bayer, hinting that the company wanted to settle with him, somehow to make it all right. That lawyer arranged a meeting with people who were apparently Bayer's corporate lawyers in London.

Whybrow then discovered that as soon as the arrest hit the papers, someone claiming to be from Bayer had contacted his wife and Flack's wife and told them that if they kept their mouths shut, they'd be taken care of. The media cottoned on to the wives immediately, but they refused to talk.

"We were all told," Whybrow insists, "that we would be looked after. That's why we felt they owed us. Not because we got nicked working for them. Those are professional risks. They could have compensated us for going to prison. But our wives had been warned not to mention the word Bayer to anybody and they didn't. They kept their part of the bargain and so did we. We could have said that in court in Cyprus. That's all Pittas wanted to hear. He wanted us to say we were working for Bayer. He wanted to hear someone say that Bayer had instructed us to take covert actions against him. But we didn't. All we wanted to be recompensed for was keeping our mouths shut. We were asked a million times who we were working for and we kept our mouths shut. That's why Bayer owed us."

In Whybrow's mind, there's no doubt that Bayer, or at least someone acting for Bayer, paid all their legal bills. But he says that when he met with the lawyers and told them the story, they seemed shocked. He says he told them about the way they operated, about how they'd set up a company in Switzerland with a $25,000 bank account, and about the jobs he'd done for Jones. He even showed them his Bayer ID card.

Now, he says, the lawyers got really nervous.

He claims they told him that, as a sign of good faith, if he returned that ID card to them, they would see that he was taken care of. So, in front of a witness, he handed them the card.

"That's right, because I had a witness, I handed it back to them. It never even touched the table. They scooped it up, and you could see the look of relief on their faces. That's when they got aggressive. How do we know about this and about that? I showed them all the papers. They wanted

copies of the papers, but I wouldn't give t[...]
them. In return for all papers and a total gag [...]
they offered us about £12,500. Mick and I both sa[...]
an insult. And guess what? They decided they didn't k[...]
that they'd never heard of us, and we've never heard from[...]

Whybrow is married again and runs his own agency bu[...]
any pharmaceutical work. Flack is out of the business entire[...]
left Bayer, ran a pub for a while – Whybrow believes Bayer might[...]
bought it for him – but got out of that and moved back to German[...]
where he now lives within walking distance of Bayer's main office.

The infringers are still infringing.

And, one presumes, Bayer is still doing whatever it takes to fight back.

hem any. They offered to buy
on what we did for Bayer,
id no. We said that was
now who we were,
them since."
t doesn't do
y. Jones
have

TAKES

"The U.S. market is the critical market for the pharmaceutical industry," says Morgan Stanley Dean Witter's star analyst Duncan Moore. "That's where you've got the highest rate of receptivity to new products, and also the highest prices. What's more, it's a market that has demonstrably shifted away from being entirely professional to becoming consumer-driven. The physicians' role as God is diminishing all the time."

Because drug companies in the United States can directly target consumers through advertising, patient input into treatment is playing an increasingly important role in drug company marketing. The result is an expanded market.

"Much of the value created by new pharmaceutical products is value recognized by the consumer and not so readily by the payer-provider industry."

Moore says that if you had a stomach ulcer in the 1960s, it was usually removed by surgery and that was very expensive. When Tagamet came along, you could get treatment for your ulcer for a relatively modest cost and avoid surgery.

"Clearly, the insurance industry in the United States and the government-sponsored health systems in Europe benefited enormously from that. Tagamet and Zantac between them got the incidence of stomach ulcer surgery down to virtually nothing."

Now, with the advent of proton-pump inhibitors, the cost of treating acid disease has gone up dramatically.

"But you and I, instead of having to spend four weeks in pain waiting for the ulcer to be cured by Zantac or Tagamet, now only have to endure two weeks of pain if we take a proton-pump inhibitor. It's more effective but more costly. There is a benefit to the consumer but none to whoever pays the health-care bills. The drug companies recognize this consumer angle to prescription pharmaceuticals and have targeted their marketing to the consumer rather than just to the health-care professional."

He suggests that government resistance to direct-to-consumer advertising becomes irrelevant as we become increasingly tech literate.

"Educated people are already finding out about diseases and treatments on the Internet. They're already no longer entirely dependent on the physician."

"If you're a Glaxo and you're the only company promoting a migraine drug, then obviously it doesn't cost you a huge amount of money to have quite a high awareness of your product. When there are four companies doing exactly the same with direct-to-consumer marketing, then the cost of making the same relative noise goes up. That's happening in most categories. Costs are going up as health care becomes more and more a consumer product."

Big Pharma knew it was coming, because it had been lobbying for it for years. But when it happened, when the FDA finally lifted the ban on direct-to-consumer advertising (DTCA) on television in August 1997, the drug companies still weren't sure how the public would react.

DTCA had been around for years. The first prescription drug ad directly aimed at the public was to sell Eli Lilly's new anti-arthritic drug Oraflex in 1982. The company's claim that Oraflex prevented arthritic progression turned it into a $1-million-a-week drug. But five months after it hit the market, the drug was pulled because of renal failures and deaths. It turned out that there had been such a serious failure to report problems before FDA approval, prosecutions followed, including that of a British medical director working in the United States. There was also litigation in the U.K. The FDA put a halt to DTCA for two and a half years to revise its guidelines and tighten controls. It set all sorts of limitations on what could and could not be said, straitjacketing advertisers with rules, regulations, and FDA scrutiny.

But now, in August 1997, Big Pharma could advertise products by name, make claims about a drug's efficacy, and didn't have to fully list side effects. The main precautionary notes that once had to be included were reduced to a mention somewhere that only doctors could prescribe the drug and a Web site address or free phone number where the public could get more information.

The companies had been advertising to doctors forever and knew how to market cholesterol-lowering drugs and antidepressants to physicians. Selling to the public in what would soon become a marketing free-for-all was a very different game. To begin with, the public had no understanding of the science. Pharmaceuticals would have to be sold like breakfast cereals. But unlike breakfast cereals, the public couldn't just go out and buy the stuff. All ad campaigns are crafted to create or reinforce a need for a product and then create a response. In this case, the need would have to be explained in a language that the average guy could understand and the response would have to be, "Go see your doctor about this." So Big Pharma, not having any idea how this would work, stuck its toes into the water with a series of ads for a small number of relatively benign drugs.

And the response was far beyond anything the drug companies could ever have hoped for.

The floodgates were open. And the ads poured across the border into Canada. Patients already taking drugs asked their doctors for a change in prescriptions to the advertised drugs. Patients not taking drugs decided they needed drugs and went to their doctors to get them. Doctors, being in business and needing to keep their clients happy, began prescribing more drugs.

Ad spending soared to more than $100 million a month, an increase of 500 per cent in just three years.

Schering-Plough hired Joan Lunden, formerly of *Good Morning America*, to help sell Claritin, making her the first TV celebrity to endorse a prescription drug. They added the chance to win a vacation in Hawaii contest to the campaign. Within six months of the FDA ruling, Claritin was the number-one prescription drug being advertised, its sales having risen by almost a third. Other allergy drugs fought back with ad campaigns and showed huge increases in sales – sales of Allegra doubled, sales of Zyrtec rose 56 per cent.

The industry quickly realized that certain categories of drugs lend themselves more easily to ads, at least they sell better when advertised. Lifestyle drugs – such as Viagra, for sexual dysfunction, and Rogaine, which promises to grow hair – were among the first. Non-smoking aids were also heavily advertised. Then came instant gratification drugs, especially allergy treatments, analgesics for pain, and cures for stomach problems. So too "fear of the future" antidotes, medications that reduce high blood pressure or high cholesterol and therefore comfort consumers into thinking they are reducing the risk of heart attacks. Some full-page newspaper promotions even offered money-back guarantees for cholesterol-lowering drugs.

Within just six months of the FDA ruling, and counting only the seven most heavily advertised health problems – cholesterol, smoking, osteoporosis, hair loss, ulcers, menopause, and depression – 3.2 million more Americans had gone to see their doctor than in the six months prior to the FDA ruling, which was an increase of 22 per cent.

Within a year, a Harris Poll survey for Harvard University's School of Public Health reported that almost 30 per cent of the patients taking a prescription drug had spoken to their doctors about a drug they'd seen advertised. Although, of the same people surveyed, only around 12 per cent actually received a prescription for the advertised drug. That led critics of DTCA to conclude that one very real effect of the FDA ruling was to increase visits to doctors by people asking for drugs that their doctors didn't feel they needed.

"Direct-to-consumer advertising for certain drugs has had a dramatic impact in volumes of prescriptions and expenditures," observes Dr. Steve Schondelmeyer at the University of Minnesota's Prime Institute. "But even more than the impact on drug expenditures, it creates added costs in the health-care system. I've talked to many physicians who tell me that the number of visits by patients just inquiring about a drug that they've seen advertised has gone up dramatically. Now, some of those patients might have needed treatment and they weren't getting it, so that's fine. But a number of those patients didn't need treatment. They're the 'worried well.' The ad induced a visit that wasn't necessary. So the drug companies, advertising for their benefit, are creating additional costs in the health-care system. Then, with some of those are people who don't need any treatment, the doc figures, 'Oh well, maybe a little something isn't going to hurt them so I'll give them a prescription anyway.' It's difficult to argue that this is acceptable."

It is precisely that – prescribing to the worried well – which has made DTCA the overwhelming success it has been.

"The drug companies are banking on a synergy between the direct-to-consumer and the direct-to-provider advertising," notes Dr. Eric Rose, a member of the University of Washington School of Medicine faculty who has extensively researched pharmaceutical marketing and the drug company–physician relationship. "The patient sees ads with the name Lipitor and a picture of someone running happily in the grass. The doc sees ads for Lipitor proclaiming, 'Better than Mevacore – 20 milligrams a day' and some simple little graphs. What the drug company is hoping is that when the patient mentions Lipitor, that triggers the doctor's decision."

There is also, Rose says, the any-banana-in-the-bunch syndrome.

"If the patient mentions a specific drug and there really is no significant difference among different drugs in a given category, then the doctor is more likely to choose the one that the patient has mentioned just because he's more likely to want to satisfy the patient."

Drug company market research shows that when people go to their doctor and ask for a specific prescription, as long as the patient's analysis is correct and the medication is needed, the doctor tends to prescribe it. But there are times, when an indication is moderate for a medication, that doctors are still willing to meet patient expectations.

"Especially," Rose says, "where that will foster compliance with other aspects of treatment that the physician feels are also important. The practice of medicine is, after all, salesmanship and negotiation. It is trying to get someone to agree to do something that's going to keep that person healthy."

A patient paying a doctor for a visit creates a business–client relationship and, as such, it is understandable that the client would want to have some say in the results of that visit. Asking for a particular drug or treatment might well be part of the process. And the doctor involved might well feel that he needs to satisfy his client. In a government-run health-care program, where the patient doesn't pay for the visit or, perhaps, not for the prescribed drugs either, the relationship is different. It probably doesn't affect the medicine, but it certainly can affect other aspects of the doctor-patient relationship, such as trust.

Many doctors report that much of what gets fed back to them by patients who learn about drugs through DTCA rarely applies to their specific case. They say that DTCA can lead to unnecessary patient concerns about some drugs and misguided notions about others. Additionally, it can create a sense that only the more expensive drugs – i.e., those advertised – will work. In turn, that can lead some patients to seriously doubt the efficacy of less expensive, older drugs, especially generics.

A spokesperson for PhRMA, the industry's Washington lobby, insists that advertising just gets patients to consult their physician, that it doesn't dictate the result of that consultation, and that it doesn't necessarily mean patients are going to wind up taking the advertised drugs. Yet, while the industry measures the success of DTCA by claiming that people are going to see their doctors in record numbers to talk about their health because ads have made them aware of problems they need to deal with – and see that as a good thing – there is yet another side to this that some physicians feel is not such a good thing. It is that the criteria necessary to make an informed choice do not appear in the ad. If such information were included, they insist, it would be far beyond the understanding of the average person.

Responding to PhRMA, Public Citizen's Health Research Group has stated categorically, "We are aware of no valid scientific evidence that suggests DTC prescription drug advertising leads to better health outcomes for the public." On the contrary, the group believes that the prevailing evidence shows clearly that DTCA may induce needless economic hardship and perhaps physical harm to consumers.

Now that the genie is out of the bottle, it is near-impossible for anyone to control the genie's behaviour.

"You can either try to regulate the drug companies' marketing efforts and encounter a tidal wave of resistance," Eric Rose believes, "or the profession can prevail upon itself to behave in a professional manner. The responsibility is 100 per cent with docs to educate themselves about the promotional techniques of these companies and to insulate themselves at least from the effects of them. I wouldn't go so far as to say that it's unacceptable for docs to expose themselves knowingly to any type of promotional presentation, but I think it's unconscionable not to check how that content jibes with the peer-reviewed medical literature."

Drug companies argue that advertising isn't really advertising, it's education. That by making the public more aware of illnesses and treatments, they're also making people more conscious of their own health and, hopefully, getting them to discuss it with their physicians. They argue that when patients are educated about health, they are healthier consumers.

To suggest that direct-to-consumer advertising is educational is, according to Dr. Christophe Kopp, a GP and editor at the independent French drug bulletin *La Revue Prescrire*, "Like counting how many angels can dance on the head of a pin." He says he spends a lot of his time deconstructing misinformation from ads and resisting patient requests for hyped-up and costly drugs. As for the argument that DTCA of prescription drugs "empowers people" and that "reluctant doctors are just paternalistic," he insists, "that's simple demagoguery."

Merck had turned its promotional guns away from Mevacor in favour of Zocor, its new anti-cholesterol drug, to do battle with Warner-Lambert's Lipitor. When Bristol-Myers Squibb came in with Pravachol, $126 million worth of ads over two years earned it only the third-place position. It abandoned the campaign, raising the question, "If those ads were merely about providing information to the public, why were they stopped?" But no one at BMS cared to answer the question. Two phone calls to the company, one in the United States, one in the United Kingdom, elicited the response "We'll have to get back to you on that one," but nothing more.

It seems apparent that drug companies only spend the vast sums of money they do on advertising when ads result in more prescriptions being written. That the patient is not being turned into an educated consumer but rather a foot soldier in Big Pharma's battle to get doctors to prescribe.

Why else would the companies spend money trashing competitors who have already been ruled dangerous?

When the FDA announced in 1997 that studies were showing how phenolphthalein, the active ingredient in many over-the-counter laxatives, presented a cancer risk for humans, Bayer recalled stocks of its phenolphthalein laxative, Phillips' Gelcaps. Within a day or so, Schering-Plough was running full-page ads in *USA Today* and the *New York Times* reiterating the FDA's findings, noting that a Novartis laxative contained phenolphthalein and that Schering's laxative did not. Its product contained bisacodyl, which was also being looked at by the FDA, but the ads didn't mention that.

Also not publicized by the drug companies are the side effects of DTCA, like wasting doctors' time with unnecessary visits. One drug marketing research firm found that while patient visits increased overall 2 per cent in the ten months following the FDA ruling, patient visits just for allergies – in the wake of the Claritin, Allegra, and Zyrtec campaigns – increased by 10 per cent. A survey of one thousand adults, commissioned by *Time* magazine in association with *Health Magazine*, found that one-third of the consumers who saw a drug company ad mentioned the drug to their doctors.

Now factor in increased prescribing, a certain percentage of which is obviously not warranted. In 1998, Claritin's American sales climbed to $1.9 billion after Schering-Plough spent $136 million advertising the drug. And, because the advertised drugs are almost always the most expensive ones, drug costs rose an estimated 12 to 15 per cent during the first year of DTCA alone.

Time magazine demonstrated this by showing that nearly 30 per cent of the people it surveyed said that if a doctor did not give them the drug they wanted – as opposed to no prescription or a prescription for another drug – they would consider switching doctors. Research has also shown that scientifically unsupported information that appears in drug advertising has greater influence on prescribing decisions than the scientific literature.

The watershed study was done in 1982 by Dr. Jerry Avorn at Harvard University. Some eighty-five doctors in the Boston area were presented with drug company ads and scientifically peer-reviewed literature on two classes of drugs: propoxyphene-based analgesics, which were supposed to be the most advanced on the market for reducing pain; and cerebral vasodilators, which supposedly brought more oxygen to the brain and were therefore said to be a practical way of treating senile dementia. Both classes of drugs were heavily touted by their respective companies and made to look effective. The scientific literature, however, showed propoxyphene-based analgesics to be no more effective than Aspirin and cerebral vasodilators not at all effective in treating dementia. When first approached, 68 per cent of the doctors in the test sample rated drug company marketing as only minimally important in influencing their prescribing, while 62 per cent said scientific papers were very important.

But when Avorn and his team questioned them about the two classes of drugs, 50 to 70 per cent of the time the doctors repeated information that only came from drug company promotional materials. Avorn's conclusion was simple: clever promotion, even when it contradicts the medical literature, can fool a majority of doctors.

With the exception of the United States and New Zealand, most western countries limit prescription drug advertising to professional medical and pharmaceutical journals. Direct-to-consumer advertising is not permitted in Canada. Drug companies get around the embargo by designing DTCA to appear as anything but an ad for a drug. Instead, they advertise diseases – the pharmaceutical version of an infomercial – and hint that the cure is the company's unnamed drug.

In September 1998, Novartis launched a campaign called Living with Heart Disease. The copy reminded the public that Novartis was a world-leading life sciences company and, as such, was developing treatments to help people suffering from hypertension and to reduce the risk of heart attack. The ad didn't name a product – that would have been illegal – but the very obvious implication was that anyone interested in knowing the name of the drug and, consequently, getting a prescription for it, needed only apply to their own family doctor.

Comments Dr. Joel Lexchin, a Canadian physician who has been highly critical of DTCA, "This is a very common tactic that companies use even in advertising to physicians. They either make vague general statements like the one in this ad and let people draw their own, usually erroneous, conclusions or they cite relative risk reductions rather than absolute risk reductions in order to make the product look much more impressive."

Because Canadians are bombarded with media from the United States – and are perfectly free to ask their doctor for a prescription that they've seen advertised illegally but unstoppably in Canada – they represent a significant bonus to the American catchment area for advertising. If nothing else, Canadians can take some solace in the fact that the ads they see must be cleared by U.S. regulatory officials. In the Third World, however, where regulatory agencies are inefficient and have little power, European and North American headquartered companies get away with things that are much too dubious to try at home.

For instance, to sell antidepressants in Pakistan, doctors were provided with a brochure to hand out to patients. Inside was a questionnaire – containing vagaries such as sleeping too little or too much – so that consumers literally could diagnose themselves with depression. Anyone passing the test was encouraged to take a certain antidepressant every day. Because Pakistan, like many developing countries, doesn't enforce prescription-only regulations, it's very easy to buy Prozac or, for that matter, any other prescription medicine. Professional medical associations in Pakistan labelled the promotion deplorable and it was eventually stopped.

Another drug company looking to sell into the Pakistan market – where more than two hundred thousand children die from diarrhea every year – heavily advertised its anti-diarrhea drug as suitable for all cases. When the government realized that the advertised use of the drug might be harmful to patients and, in any case, manifestly contravened World Health Organization advice on treatment of the illness, the company withdrew the ad.

One wonders if they would have had they not been forced to.

The trade magazine *Medical Marketing & Media* gave the game away in the November 1995 issue when it confessed, "In the old marketing model, pharmaceutical companies created patient demand by influencing doctors to write prescriptions. In DTC promotion, companies listen to the patient, respond to their needs, and hope to increase sales by driving consumers to a doctor's office and requesting their product."

Public Citizen points out that if the purpose of DTCA is to educate and inform the public about drugs, why isn't the information complete and accurate? In fact, the industry has a pretty miserable record with respect to the accuracy of its advertising.

The University of California at Los Angeles conducted a study in 1992 of 109 ads, randomly selected from major medical journals. It asked doctors on a panel of recognized specialists to evaluate which ads related to their particular field of medicine. A majority of the doctors decided that thirty of the ads should not have been published because of serious medical inaccuracies and thirty-seven of the ads required major revisions. Only nine of the ads were considered to be in compliance with regulations on medical advertising. In the end, 100 of the 109 were in some way in violation of FDA statutes.

If they advertise that way to doctors, who presumably have the knowledge to decipher the claims, what then of the unsuspecting public?

Adbusters, a magazine based in Vancouver, has an international reputation for debunking advertising. It dissected a Bristol-Myers Squibb ad for Pravachol.

It featured a picture of hockey star Darryl Sittler and his family, with the headline, "DARRYL SITTLER KNOWS ABOUT THE RISKS OF HEART ATTACKS — SO SHOULD YOU."

The copy read, "Darryl lost his father to a heart attack. He believes in knowing your cholesterol risk. One out of three first heart attack victims die not knowing their risk. One particular medication, with a good diet and lifestyle, can reduce the risk of first heart attacks by 31% and second heart attacks by 62%. Call now if not for you but your family."

No product is named, giving the ad the look of a public service announcement. There is also free a phone number for the "Heart Attack Prevention Line." Bristol-Myers Squibb's name only appears in small print at the bottom.

Adbusters attacks the ad on three grounds.

First, in technique. Here's a sports star who seems to be in great shape and the inference is, if he's worried about having a heart attack, the rest of us who aren't in such great shape should be terrified. Making that sort of association is a common ploy.

Second, by inferring there's an easy way to become less susceptible to a heart attack. In order to become 31 per cent less likely to have a first heart attack, we need only take this medication, eat plenty of vegetables, and jog. To say the least, this oversimplifies a problem that is both complex and important.

Third, the use of the figure 31 per cent is suspect. It comes from a study published in the *New England Journal of Medicine* in 1995 that looked at sixty-six hundred men from western Scotland. The average age was fifty-five. All had high cholesterol. Some 45 per cent smoked. Half the group took Pravachol. The other half took the placebo. The *NEJM* results noted that those taking the placebo had a 7.9 per cent chance of a first heart attack. Those taking Pravachol every day for five years had a 5.5 per cent chance of a first heart attack.

The difference therefore is 2.4 per cent. The way Bristol-Myers came up with 31 per cent was by dividing the 2.4 per cent difference in risk by the placebo group's 7.9 per cent.

Adbusters calculated that a fifty-five-year-old woman with high cholesterol but no other risk factors has a 3 per cent chance of a heart attack in the next five years. By taking Pravachol every day for five years, she may reduce her risk by 31 per cent – although you can't tell that from the survey because it didn't look at a fifty-five-year-old woman with high cholesterol – which brings the 3 per cent figure down to 2 per cent, or a benefit to only one in one hundred fifty-five-year-old women.

But that's not what the ad suggests.

It implies that Pravachol increases everyone's chances of avoiding a first heart attack by one-third. How many Pravachol prescriptions would have been sold to North Americans if the ad had read, "For Scottish males with high cholesterol, half of whom smoke, a medication which costs approximately $4,000 for five years of therapy, with a good diet and lifestyle, can reduce the risk of a first heart attack by just over 2 per cent."

Wyeth-Ayerst promoted its antidepressant Effexor in a newspaper campaign with headlines such as "I GOT MY MOMMY BACK" and "I GOT MY MARRIAGE BACK," hinting that life would get better for children and other family members as soon as a depressed adult seeks treatment. Reinforcing the notion that there is a pill for every ill, the ad did not say that there might be equally effective, less expensive alternatives.

"People who may or may not be healthy but don't believe that they're healthy are being encouraged to see their doctor because they've been encouraged to think they might have a problem," says Dr. Peter Mansfield, the Australian physician who founded the Medical Lobby for Appropriate Marketing (MaLAM). "They've made up their mind on the basis of the advertising, which of course has been designed to persuade them that something might be wrong. The doctors are then under a lot of pressure to do what their patients want. Drug companies know that doctors are always looking for simple solutions, that we're under pressure to see a lot of people in a short period of time, that we're looking for something we can do for people and do quickly."

When Eli Lilly started promoting its cancer drug Evista in the United States as a way of reducing the risk of breast cancer, AstraZeneca, maker of Nolvadex – the only drug approved at the time by the FDA to promote itself as proven to reduce risk of breast cancer – filed an injunction under the Lanham Act that prohibits false advertising. The court agreed with

AstraZeneca's claim that the dissemination of false information creates a "grave public health risk."

In a press release acknowledging the court's decision, AstraZeneca noted, "It is imperative that the public and physicians be able to trust the information presented to them by pharmaceutical companies."

To sell Prilosec, an Astra-Merck joint venture, ads were used to strike fear in anyone with a stomach ailment. "People who have heartburn two or more times a week probably do not have ordinary heartburn, but the potentially serious condition of gastro-oesophageal reflux disease." Then, too, they may also just be eating too much.

Similarly, Merck opted for the fear factor to sell Fosamax, a drug aimed at the postmenopausal market. "Thanks to Fosamax and its power to rebuild bone," the ad read, "Susan Brenner is still paddling her own canoe after fifty." The ad featured a picture of a nice-looking, presumably healthy fifty-ish woman next to a lake at sunset.

The text explained that menopausal women may have osteoporosis and because of that are susceptible to breaking bones. What the ad didn't say was that statistics show most osteoporotic fractures not at fifty, but after the age of seventy-five. Nor did the ad provide any hint of what happens when a woman at fifty takes Fosamax for the next twenty-five years. There may not be a long-term study available to show what happens, or if there is and the results are negative, they may have a reason for not saying. From the ad it would be fair to conclude that women will be better off for taking the drug. In fact, there are long-term studies of estrogen, which is also prescribed to prevent fractures by increasing postmenopausal bone mass, indicating that the effect of the drug is reversed after discontinuing use, and showing no long-term gain if used for less than ten to fifteen years.

When Eli Lilly started advertising the antidepressant Prozac, it already had a huge share of the market. The ads were designed to expand that market. Its Welcome Back campaign was aimed at people not being helped for depression who would, through Prozac, be welcomed back to a normal state of mind. The text tried to demystify public perceptions of tranquilizers while all the time reassuring potential customers that Prozac was not a tranquilizer. "It won't take away your personality. Depression can do that, but Prozac can't."

When Pharmacia & Upjohn's Rogaine went from prescription only to over-the-counter status, meaning that anyone in the United States who wanted to stimulate hair growth could simply walk into a store and buy it, ads for the product took on the look of a shampoo ad. "Hair care you need . . . right now." Obviously, from a marketing standpoint, it's easier to sell a general beauty care product than a medicine.

In 1995, the magazine *Consumer Reports* sent twenty-eight ads for prescription drugs for evaluation by thirty-two medical specialists. The experts judged that only about half the ads presented a balanced view of effectiveness, potential benefits, and risks. Only about half the ads spelled out side effects in the body of the ad, as opposed to putting it at the bottom in minuscule, nearly unreadable print. Eleven of the ads were judged by at least one member of the panel to be more harmful than helpful. And one-third of the ads contained errors of fact or made claims that could not be scientifically defended.

After an ad for Cortaid ran in *Parade Magazine* containing this claim – "Only Cortaid is recommended most by doctors. That's because Cortaid stops the persistent itching, then goes beyond to help heal the blotchy, allergic skin rash. Trust the brand doctors prefer over all other brands" – a man in Washington, D.C., wrote to the CEO of Pharmacia & Upjohn, makers of Cortaid.

His letter read, "I assume the statements about doctors' preferences and recommendations were based on one or more surveys of doctors. I would be obliged if you could send me information about the survey(s) on which these statements were based, including the specific questions that were asked about preferences and recommendations for Cortaid, the statistical results for those questions, and details of the survey design(s), including sample sizes, method of data collection, and survey response rates."

The reply, from a brand group director, was right to the point. "While the statement you cited from the advertisement is correct and we have substantiation for the claims made in the statement, it is not our practice to publicly disclose the information you have requested, absent a compelling business need to do so."

The question is not what will happen *if* DTCA ever comes to Canada. It is, instead, what will happen *when* it comes to Canada because it surely will.

In the meantime, stories placed in newspapers are often little more than in-house press releases. Drug companies look for publicity from patient groups they themselves have formed for every disease in which they sell drugs. For example, the Viral Hepatitis Prevention Board helps promote awareness of the need for vaccinations against hepatitis B and is largely backed by SmithKline, which happens to make a hepatitis B vaccine. Drug companies also sponsor "awareness weeks": Influenza Awareness Week, Meningitis Awareness Week, Cholesterol Awareness Week. They pick a health problem and flood the papers with news stories about it, knowing that some awareness of the company product will rub off. The more sponsors there are, the greater the credibility, so it's understandable that a company such as Glaxo would gladly team up with the Migraine Foundation to fund Migraine Awareness Week just when Glaxo was promoting a migraine drug.

This is not to suggest that there is anything dishonest in promotion stunts such as "awareness weeks," but it is difficult to take the corporate view that they are only about education.

Then there's Big Pharma's back-door approach.

After the minister of health for British Columbia discovered that three hundred pharmacies were selling prescription information, including doctors' names and their prescribing habits, to an international drug marketing company – who in turn sold the information to Big Pharma – he actually ordered a rewrite of the bylaws of the College of Pharmacists making the practice unacceptable.

A similar ban has also been extended to Quebec. But the marketing firm in question, IMS Canada Ltd., says it continues to collect such information from three thousand pharmacies spread out across the other provinces.

If someone walked in off the street and requested the same information that the pharmacies and drugstore chains are giving to IMS, one assumes that he wouldn't get it. It seems outrageous that this kind of cooperation is extended by retailers. Presumably, there is an element of self-interest at work.

A large chain running supermarket drugstores in the United States employs a company to manage its prescription database. That company then acts as a marketing middleman, selling information from the pharmacy database – with the pharmacy's permission – to drug companies that then target customers with direct mail. The letters are personalized and made to appear as if they came from the pharmacist.

The most spectacular effect of globalization in the Internet era is the evaporation of geographical boundaries. In some areas they are merely fading fast, in other areas they are already gone. DTCA of pharmaceuticals is one of those areas where they have totally disappeared.

After sexually related material, health sites are said to be among the top-three most popular Internet destinations. What you find when you get there is anything and everything. In 1995, hardly any pharmaceutical company had its own Web site. Now they all do. There are also online pharmacies that respond to the increased demand for "lifestyle" products. There is information on every disease imaginable, on every treatment imaginable, on every drug imaginable. There is advice and there is chicanery.

The *British Medical Journal* Web site is a good example of how the Web creates an arena for opposing agendas. Although the journal has condemned drug company marketing on its editorial pages, it has recently begun to accept drug company ads on its Web site. The U.K. Medicines Control Agency has ruled the use of the Web site for drug company marketing is acceptable because the intended audience is doctors. However, access to the Web site is free and open to anyone, and the *BMJ* reports that around 5 per cent of the hits are from members of the public. The journal's rationale is that advertising allows them to provide a huge, searchable database of high-quality information on all aspects of medicine free to everyone. But if consumers can see the ads on the Web site, some might draw the conclusion that the advertised drugs must be good, otherwise the *BMJ* wouldn't have a commercial relationship with them.

A study in *Scrip* magazine found that the Internet is not yet a major force driving drug sales, which might be why governments have so far left DTCA alone on the Internet. People have to go looking for a site. It's not like television, which comes right into someone's home and gets to people who are not actively seeking information. Also, television by its nature more easily creates emotional images that have been shown to create behaviour change. That's why it is the most powerful – and economically viable – advertising medium in the world. But by 2010 or so, television and the Internet will have digitally fused into one, and at that point, effective and influential DTCA by the drug companies on the Internet will be an uncontrollable reality.

There has always been a market for pharmaceuticals purchased without a prescription and drugs not approved by a regulatory agency. But in the past, obtaining them has meant buying from a local smuggler or going offshore. Now, the Internet brings you right to the source. Suddenly, borders don't exist. Anything you want can be found with the click of a mouse. Americans looking for cheaper prescription drugs no longer have to come to Canada or go to Mexico. Cheaper drugs are right there on the Web. For a Canadian who wants drugs the family doctor won't prescribe – Viagra, Prozac, Valium, and diet pills are the most prevalently sought after – the Web is the obvious source of supply. Because the drug itself can't be transmitted, once it's ordered and paid for – which brings up the real risk of credit card fraud – the pills have to come into the country in a traditional manner.

A package addressed from somewhere in western Europe is rarely looked at by Canada Customs. A package from New Zealand labelled "gift – no commercial value" probably won't get looked at either. But even if someone does inspect it, the recipient can always say he has no idea who sent it or why, reorder, and play the percentage game that the next package will get through.

"One of the things we discovered," says Kevin Della-Colli, who runs the U.S. Customs Cyber-Smuggling Center in Washington, D.C., "is that when you order one thousand units, the company may ship it in one hundred unit batches, thinking two may get seized and eight hundred pills will get through."

Part of the problem is that the Internet has eliminated the middleman. "In the past, we'd always go after the person who filled up the trunk of his car with a thousand Valium tablets and we'd prosecute that person as a smuggler. But the smuggler has disappeared from the picture."

Della-Colli concedes that a lot of pharmaceuticals sold on the Internet might be legitimate. "Countries have different ways of dispensing prescription medication and different laws in respect to how it can be transported or sold. They might not be doing anything illegal in, say, Thailand by offering these drugs for sale. And we have no way of preventing anyone from going to a Web site and ordering prescription medicine."

Some of the sites offering pharmaceuticals for sale are perfectly legitimate. Others openly indicate they will deliberately misdescribe the contents of a package to make it difficult for Customs to find it. "When you buy off the Internet," Della-Colli continues, "how do you know what you're getting? You may be dealing with a company two blocks away, or in Thailand, in Amsterdam especially for steroids, in Mexico, in New Zealand, or in Indonesia. You have no way of knowing. And these companies aren't necessarily selling pre-wrapped blister pack boxes. Some of them are sending you a zip-lock bag filled with little blue pills or little green pills. The pills may be real. They may be counterfeit. They may be product that has passed its sell-by date. Or they may be shipments stolen overseas that are being offloaded on the Internet. There's no way of telling, and there is a real public health risk."

The packaging of Internet drugs raises an interesting point. In some cases, they are, or at least appear to be, properly packaged. Counterfeit drugs sometimes come in counterfeit packaging too.

There is also a market for legally manufactured drugs that are exported to a foreign country only to be imported back. While this is not to say that the drug companies themselves are actually engaged in this practice, they do keep track of sales around the world and you need look no further than Tijuana to start asking questions.

In the Mexican border town just south of San Diego, pharmacies will sell you anything, in any quantity, and without any paperwork. It is, of course, illegal to bring undeclared drugs into the United States and Canada. But anyone who's ever tried to drive into the United States through the Tijuana–San Diego Customs checkpoint on a late Sunday afternoon knows what a real traffic jam can look like.

Every car is stopped. Very few are ever searched. Customs simply doesn't have the manpower to look closely at more than a very tiny percentage of the people coming through. The amount of prescription drugs purchased in Tijuana and brought north across the border is huge. It's because drugs are cheaper there and because some people want drugs their doctor won't prescribe and because there are drugs available in Mexico, especially AIDS drugs, that are not necessarily licensed in Canada or the States.

The question has to be "Doesn't Big Pharma know where these drugs are going?" If they were counterfeit, the drug companies would go after them. One therefore can assume that the same Big Pharma companies that have desperately fought parallel-import legislation wherever it's come up are actually playing the game themselves. A logical conclusion is that if it's not the drug companies selling direct to wholesalers in Tijuana and in cyberspace, it's the drug companies selling to wholesalers, who are then reselling the drugs.

Either Big Pharma does know what's happening or it should know because it has every reason to know. Prescription drugs are not like other products. If you ship a load of blue jeans somewhere, there is no requirement to track them around the world until they're sold. But if you ship out a load of prescription drug products, there has to be a paper trail until it reaches the consumer. The drug companies know the procedures and their obligations. They're also pretty good at finding new ways to sell more product.

CHAPTER 12

TAKING AIM AT THE DOCTORS

Drug companies and doctors are joined at the hip by their closely related interests, but closely related doesn't mean identical, and the two often find themselves, decidedly and deliberately, pulling in different directions.

Where agendas meet, science is served. Yet good science is not necessarily good business, any more than the best business will automatically produce the best science. In a perfect world, doctors and drug companies would have only one agenda: the advancement of their patients' health. But this is far from a perfect world. While every doctor's first and foremost responsibility is – by oath and by law – to his or her patients, by design, every drug company's primary obligation is to its shareholders and employees.

Their ultimate objectives are fundamentally different. And that difference manifests itself every time a doctor writes a prescription.

If diagnosis is the art of medicine, then the selection of treatment is the application of that art. But for doctors who have been practising for, say, fifteen years, an estimated 75 to 90 per cent of the drugs available have come onto the market since they attended medical school. Consequently, they have had no formal training in the function and utilization of those drugs. Whatever those doctors know about these drugs is down to whatever those doctors have taken upon themselves to learn. Homework, which is absolutely essential in order to stay current with the accelerated pace of modern medicine, is an important part of the profession that the patient never sees.

To keep up-to-date, doctors today are spoiled for choice. There are, literally, thousands of journals, magazines, newspapers, research papers, and reviews covering every conceivable aspect of medicine down to the most minuscule specialization. Every day of the week, there are hundreds of lectures, continuing medical education (CME) seminars, and professional association congresses that doctors can attend. Add to that several thousand medical sites easily available on the Internet. Stanford University's High Wire Press, for example, has an online archive of nearly one hundred and fifty thousand free full-text articles and half a million pay-per-view articles.

But not all information is created equal. In this case it runs the gamut from good to bad, from evidence-based truth to honest errors of fact, to deliberate manipulation of facts, to statistical mumbo-jumbo, to half-truths, and to outright lies. Doctors must sort through this minefield and somehow make sense of it. After all, lives are at stake. At the same time, a drug company's ability to control the information that a doctor receives can affect its bottom line. After all, profits are at stake.

"At the heart of the relationship between drug companies and doctors," says Dr. Peter Mansfield of MaLAM, "lies a critical contradiction. Drug companies know very well that their marketing is influential, but they won't admit that it's harmful. Doctors know very well that it's harmful, but they won't admit that it's influential."

Enter here the drug company representative.

The top-forty pharmaceutical companies globally employ approximately 100,000 full-time sales reps and are the bread and butter for another 10,000 to 15,000 people employed independently as direct-to-physician marketing specialists. Although personal selling is the most expensive way of promoting prescription medicines, it remains the industry's choice because it is the most effective. As 80 per cent of a drug's market is said to come from 20 per cent of the prescribers, a small increase in prescribers translates into a much larger increase in market share. That's why the drug companies commit $15 billion to $20 billion a year to the effort, a figure that roughly translates into one drug company rep for every nine to eleven practising physicians in the industrialized West.

Put another way, Big Pharma budgets its direct-selling marketing efforts at between $8,000 to $13,000 per physician.

Company reps – officially known in the trade as "detailers" – are the modern-day descendants of the snake oil salesmen of the 1850s. But unlike their predecessors, many of them come to the job with college-level science degrees, which makes sense, because the rep has to be able to understand how drugs perform. They are further trained – with constant refresher courses – in the company's drugs. But the business of detailing is not about science, it is about peddling drugs to doctors.

At Merck, the career brochure explains that a sales rep's role is "to effectively promote Merck products through a needs-based selling approach. Representatives provide accurate information to physicians and other health-care personnel so that Merck products will be prescribed when indicated." Among the skills the company looks for are "sales and persuasion skills, communication, leadership, planning and organization, self-motivation and initiative."

At Eli Lilly, reps are given the goal of "achieving sales growth in their respective territories." They may also be called on to conduct market analysis, "with a focus on key growth areas, product/market trends, and key influencers." Included in the list of Lilly's requisite skills are communication and interpersonal skills, negotiation skills, project selling, and a "return on investment mentality."

At Bayer, "the Sales Representative will be responsible for supporting and achieving the sales target objectives within the assigned territory . . . will also assess prospective and existing customers/business opportunities to ensure optimal utilization of resources . . . [and] will collaborate with other Sales Representatives on an ongoing basis to assess business opportunities for the development and presentation of the annual territory business plan, actively pursue new business opportunities, as well as record and maintain an accurate customer list for the assigned territory."

They go through courses at the company to learn sophisticated selling techniques through videotaped roleplaying. Once out in the field, they may be assigned to look after a list of physicians, or to work a list of hospital residents and pharmacists. The more experienced they get, the more likely they are to be further trained to work in a specific therapeutic area – say, coronary care, or oncology, or arthritis and anti-inflammatory disease management – to match the specialized interests of more senior physicians. Reps are also matched with their clients, where possible, by personality type. A low-key conservative doctor is less likely to get along with a hard-driving flamboyant rep, so that doctor is placed on the list of a more suitable rep.

Much to the ire of the industry, a former Abbott Laboratories representative has recently been widely quoted as saying, "Prescription drugs are marketed now as if they are cosmetics or candy."

"It simply isn't true," snaps a Wyeth executive. "If we violate accepted practices, a lot of people will have a lot to say about it. But the last word really belongs to the doctors. If they don't trust us, we won't get back in to see them and they won't prescribe our drugs. They are the ultimate gatekeeper."

Dr. Alastair Benbow, a vice-president and medical director at Smith-Kline Beecham, agrees: "We have to be pragmatic because the time doctors have for all the information they need is limited. If they have a drug company representative in front of them with whom they have built up a relationship over a period of time, and they trust that person's judgment because they have found that the information is balanced and useful, then getting information from a drug company representative is perfectly acceptable. After all, you only need to make one mistake as a representative. If you lie or mislead a doctor, you're not going to be invited back, nor should you be."

The number of visits each rep must make varies, but generally they call on four to eight doctors a day. The average visit lasts about eleven minutes.

"Doctors need to be up to speed with all the rights and wrongs of prescribing a particular therapy," Benbow continues. "We think we know our drugs best. We think we can best educate and inform doctors about new medicines. We also want to ensure that our medicines are used correctly. It's in nobody's interest to have somebody using the wrong dose, or prescribing a drug inappropriately."

To back up their reps, all of the major drug companies operate some sort of Medical Information Department (MID), a service-after-sale helpline that a doctor can phone to ask questions about a specific drug or treatment. Additional backup is also provided by a team of staff physicians to handle clinically orientated questions. Still, all of the major drug companies rely first and foremost on their reps to be their conduit between the doctor and the company, creating an enlightened relationship in which the company is perceived to be a full partner in health-care solutions.

The problem with this model lies at the very root of it, the reason Big Pharma spends an estimated one-third of its marketing budget on reps. The expenditure reflects an unmistakable reality – that the main task of the drug company detailer is, simply, to sell more drugs.

"Physicians are human, they can be influenced," notes Dr. Ashley Wazana, a researcher at Montreal's McGill University and author of the study *Physicians and the Pharmaceutical Industry*. The paper insists that drug companies know what they're doing and do it because their investment reaps returns.

Especially worrying is the revelation that while doctors recognize drug companies are trying to influence their prescribing practices, many of those same doctors continue to believe they are immune to influence.

"People are often so busy that they're willing to get their information from the most convenient source regardless of considerations of who prepared what," explains Eric Rose, the University of Washington School of Medicine faculty member who has extensively researched pharmaceutical marketing and the drug company–physician relationship. "The drug companies know that it won't take much to make a doc favour one drug over another. If you've blasted a doc with advertising that includes the starting dose, and the doc sees that everywhere he looks, in every piece of mail he gets, in every magazine he reads, then when he's in the middle of a busy clinic day and he knows that there are three different similar medications he can prescribe and he remembers the starting dose of one right off the top of his head, maybe that's the one he's going to prescribe. It's subtle and the effects are not necessarily pernicious, not necessarily harmful to the patient, but doctors are supposed to make their decisions based purely upon the best scientific data. Not what's easiest to remember, but what's best for the patient."

The industry responds that its critics are confusing the issue by suggesting that just because some information is easy to obtain, the quality of it – in other words, its accuracy – must be questionable.

"Not true," says that executive from Wyeth. "We make it easy because it's in our commercial interests to do that. At the same time, it's totally obvious that supplying anything but high-quality information would be stupid because it's incompatible with our commercial interests. There is so much scientific literature readily available, if we told anything but the truth, we'd be exposed immediately. On top of that, the legal ramifications of unethical sales promotion could be catastrophic. Believe me, any detailer who lies to a doctor-client in the morning is not going to have any doctor-clients by lunchtime. These are intelligent people we're dealing with and if the element of trust is breached, if they don't believe what the detailer is saying about a drug, if they think we're trying to pull the wool over their eyes, they're not going to prescribe the drug or ever let that detailer come back. Who loses if we don't supply the highest quality, most accurate information? We do."

It's an articulate defence but belies the fact that salespeople don't need to resort to untruths when partial truths will do. It's like the tale of the used car salesman whose jalopy has no reverse, so he stresses the advantages of the forward gears.

This defence also ignores the industry's reliance on "the myth of progress." Reps are coached to play up the newness of their products and how advances in medicine are making lives better. And while it is absolutely true that advances in medicine are making lives better, the newest drug isn't necessarily the best drug, any more than newest means most effective or cheapest.

Warner-Lambert launched Lipitor, their me-too cholesterol-lowering drug, in 1997 to go head-to-head with Merck's market leader, Zocor. Lipitor's unique selling points were that it was more potent than Zocor and that it was newer. A beefed-up rep force hit eighty-one thousand doctors' offices every month for several months. Newer won, and Lipitor aptly toppled Zocor from the top of the cholesterol-lowering best-seller list.

Finally, the defence flies in the face of the scientific evidence. Studies conducted over a thirty-year span that have looked at drug company reps and their sales pitches all seem to draw the same conclusion: there is a deliberate lack of balance in the information companies supply to doctors, and, because of that, doctors who rely on drug companies for their information are more prone to inappropriate prescribing.

A survey of faculty and house staff at hospitals in Minnesota and Wisconsin revealed that more than a quarter of the doctors had changed prescriptions at least once in the preceding twelve months after a conversation with a drug rep.

A survey at the University Hospitals of Cleveland found that doctors who attended drug-company-sponsored meetings, or had meals with drug reps, or had received research funds from drug companies, or had been paid by drug companies for a speaking engagement were more likely to ask a hospital to add drugs to the formulary. In most cases, those drugs had little or no advantage over drugs already on the formulary.

A survey of ninety-six British GPs revealed that 90 per cent of them had attended a pharmaceutical-company-sponsored meeting, even though only 17 per cent of those who attended felt the event was valuable.

A survey of 106 statements recorded during thirteen drug company presentations revealed that 11 per cent of the statements were inaccurate in favour of the promoted drug.

A survey at the University of South Australia's School of Pharmacy recorded sixteen pitches made by drug reps to doctors and compared their claims with the data in the Australian Approved Product Information Guide. Contraindications were not mentioned in any of the presentations. Some thirteen of the sixteen pitches contained inaccuracies, which included the promotion of unauthorized applications of the drug. And where supplementary literature, such as comparative product information and scientific data, was given to doctors along with the company's promotional literature, those materials were usually incomplete and sometimes inaccurate.

A survey of primary care physicians revealed that 34 per cent doubted drug company representatives had sufficient knowledge of the products on offer; 65 per cent believed reps did not sufficiently explain side effects; and 57 per cent believed reps often "extended the indications" of drugs, meaning that the rep either promised more than the drug might reasonably be expected to deliver or tried to promote off-label benefits.

A similar survey found that physicians who saw drug company reps more than once a week were statistically more likely to prescribe higher-priced drugs.

Yet another survey, this one published in the *Journal of the American Medical Association*, looked at sixteen previous surveys and reiterated that doctors who regularly saw drug company reps were more likely to engage in "non-rational" prescribing than doctors who did not see reps.

The French medical journal *La Revue Prescrire* established an anonymous network of GPs and hospital pharmacists to monitor the information drug company reps were providing. After each detailer's visit, the doctors and pharmacists were asked to fill in a form, noting: whether the information given on drug indications and doses differed from the official data sheet; whether side effects, contraindications, and interactions were mentioned; what evidence the rep used on which to base his claims; and whether any incentives were offered, such as gifts or payment for participation in a clinical trial.

Eight years' worth of data led *La Revue Prescrire* to conclude in 1999 that in 27 per cent of drug rep visits, indications did not correspond with the scientific literature; that 15 per cent of the time stated dosage was not correct; and that 76 per cent of the time side effects were not mentioned.

What's more, off-label use was a common selling technique, meaning that reps made claims that were either not supported by clinical research or were simply invented to suit their own purpose.

For example, a contraceptive pill was lauded for its off-label benefit of curing acne; a drug used to treat attention failure in the elderly was described as a suitable stimulant for anyone; and a medication prescribed for benign liver symptoms was touted as a cure for bad breath.

"From medical school on," observed *Consumer Reports* in 1992, "physicians are taught to regard medical school faculty, medical journals and professional meetings as sources of unbiased information. Pharmaceutical companies have found ingenious ways to influence all three. In the process, the distinction between promotion and true scientific exchange has been blurred and, in some cases, totally erased."

There's no doubt that when it comes to toothpaste, dishwasher powder, and running shoes, marketing influences consumer decisions. And yet surveys show that doctors almost overwhelmingly insist that when it comes to their prescribing habits, they rely more heavily on scientific training and objective literature than on marketing. Surveys also show that most doctors feel they are invulnerable to commercial manipulation.

At least to some extent, that sense of immunity is a direct result of drug company spin. The best marketing always reinforces empowerment. Just as a magician forces a playing card on an unsuspecting member of the audience, it's up to the rep to make the doctor feel that the choice of a particular drug is his own idea. If the rep can manage that, the doctor is more likely to prescribe it more often.

As every magician knows, the less the audience realizes they're being manipulated, the greater the trick.

It is estimated that as many as 85 per cent of general practitioners see drug company reps three to six times per week. Concerned that so many doctors were devoting so much time to drug company promotion, in July 1999, the *British Medical Journal* took a firm stance against detailers.

In "Reasons For Not Seeing Drug Representatives," a *BMJ* editorial reminded physicians, "Their job is primarily to sell their company's product. They are an important part of the pharmaceutical industry's promotion methods, and they are highly successful in altering doctors' prescribing habits."

Cited was a Northern Ireland survey that demonstrated that prescriptions of various drugs increased in the wake of drug reps visits.

"At the time that new drugs are licensed," the *BMJ* continued, "there are often no published comparisons with existing standard treatments and rarely any economic evaluations. Thus the really useful information is often unavailable at this stage, and by the time it is, the sales force has moved on to talk about other, newer products."

The author of the *BMJ* editorial was Dr. David Griffith, a consultant geriatrician.

"There is a plethora of very good information available to doctors today," he said in an interview for this book. "It's just a question of taking the time to access it. Yes, getting information from a drug company representatives may be the easiest way of all, but easiest is not necessarily best, the quality of the information is questionable and seeing drug reps in order to save time is a cop-out. I'd be very surprised if they actually lied about a product. But I know they are selective with their facts and economical with information. I believe drug company representatives and the bias that they bring to health care is disadvantageous to health care."

Letters poured in to the editor of the *BMJ* in response to Griffith's editorial.

Dr. Harvey Rees, a senior registrar in psychiatry in Bristol, England, warned, "It is naive to suggest doctors underestimate the goals of drug companies in promoting their products within a highly competitive market."

Dr. Chris Sedergreen, a family physician from British Columbia, reported on a conversation with a drug rep twenty-five years ago. "During a particularly sumptuous dinner and no doubt emboldened by generous helpings of Beaujolais, I told him, 'You know, Allan, your product really isn't any better than anyone else's.' To which he replied, 'I know, but as long as you go on prescribing it I can go on taking you out for dinners like this.'"

Dr. Steven Reidbord, the medical director of an outpatient psychiatry clinic in San Francisco, wondered, "Would companies spend so much if these efforts didn't work?"

Dr. David Evan Morris, a GP from Wales, reported on a conversation in which a detailer added to a particular drug's benefits its nutritional value. Morris immediately questioned the claim. The drug rep replied, "If you prescribe enough of it, my family gets to eat better!"

Gert Hubertus, a drug company rep, was fast to point out, "I like to think that the service I give to doctors is valuable. I meet whatever educational needs I can, and I make sure I know all about my product and competitors. In return the doctors [my customers], time permitting, listen to my argument." He continued, "It is not rocket science, there is no need to do gigantic multicentre analyses of prescribing data, and nor is it an industry secret. Reps influence doctors. I, however, do not believe for one moment that doctors are so unprofessional as to allow their habits to be influenced in a way that is detrimental to the health of their patients."

Another drug rep, Melissa Gorgei, also joined the debate. "I have never misrepresented a feature of my drug, nor have I ever knocked another product. I can assure you, however, that there are those reps who do engage in these types of practices. Just like any other field, though, the pharmaceutical industry has both good and bad seeds."

SmithKline's Alastair Benbow takes a different tack. "Should the representative be a doctor's only source of information? Absolutely not. If a doctor chooses not to see company reps, and gets the relevant information he needs from other sources, great. But the reality is that many doctors don't take the time, or don't have the time, to get their information from other sources. Therefore we provide a very valuable service."

When pressed about the collision of interests between the medical side of Big Pharma and the commercial side, Benbow admits, "There's no doubt that commercial people are more interested in the short-term view. And the scientific side of the business, I think, always needs to take the longer term, broader view. As a guardian of the research and medical side of the business, it's my responsibility to say to the commercial people, this is in the broader interest and we need to get that information out there. We have a duty as scientists to inform and educate the commercial parts of the organization, to say forget the here and now and the fast buck you want to make. What we want to do is good science, and good research done in an appropriate way will sell. Sure, there is a constant pulling and pushing in certain directions. There are commercial tensions within the business, and you cannot just flick a switch to change them. I think it is quite possible for the two sides to be married up, but you have to keep working at informing and educating them."

There was a time when drug companies offered incentives to their reps based on sales volume. Contrary to what many industry critics believe, the practice appears to be in decline. Reps have a base salary that can be topped up with performance-related incentives, but in most cases the additional income tends to be relatively small in proportion to the base.

That might be because the companies see a major difference between drug reps and salespeople. According to them, if you're a used car salesman, you know whether you've sold somebody a car. If you're a rep who visits a doctor to detail your product, the doctor may or may not prescribe the drug. You have no way of knowing. So the companies train their salespeople – and pay them accordingly – to approach the job as one that wields influence rather than clinches a sale.

What it all boils down to, Benbow insists, is that a rep is only as good as the product. "If the product is not particularly effective or has a poor safety profile, then no amount of detailing will influence that. As a profession, we are science-data-driven. Unless the science and data are good, you haven't got a chance."

Most drug reps freely admit they keep a diary or profile dossier on their doctors, recording various degrees of intelligence, from the names and birth dates of a doctor's children, to golf handicaps, favourite movies, favourite music, foods the doctor doesn't like, and restaurants the doctor's spouse does. These diaries also give space to the people working in the doctor's office – with the names and birth dates of their children as well – because so much can depend on the staff, such as whether the rep can actually get in to see the doctor.

Although many drug companies themselves deny that they keep data on doctors' personal lives, there is sufficient reason to believe that such dossiers exist, and in a few cases they are worthy of the CIA.

One doctor, using an online Internet forum, warned his colleagues that he'd personally seen a drug rep's database and that it contained detailed listings for nine hundred doctors. Among the fields were age, medications prescribed – broken down by week, month, and year – general prescribing habits plus undergrad and medical school records, in addition to the predictable information about family, friends, and even pets.

The rep explained to this doctor how she once did a search by birthdays in April, limited it to physicians thirty-five to sixty-five years old, then further limited it to the number of prescriptions written for one of her company's drugs. When she'd whittled it all down to a single name, she threw a surprise office lunch party for the doctor. When asked how she'd managed to get her information on doctors' prescribing habits, she confessed that her company bought it from certain pharmacies.

Obviously, it makes sense that drug reps who have worked a territory for a long time get to know their doctors well. And the better the database, the better the company can target those doctors for promotional reasons. Those who see drug reps are reminded through mailings that the company appreciates their time. Those who don't see drug reps are encouraged through mailings to rethink their stance. Company literature of all sorts – including personalized "Dear Doctor" letters – shows up in just about every doctor's mailbox just about every day. More and more, snail-mailings are supplemented by regular e-mailings.

Databases decide who gets what unsolicited non-peer-reviewed journals. And who gets what Christmas greeting. Sometimes that's just a card. Sometimes it's more. One company, with a new osteoporosis drug, sent candy to high-prescribing doctors on their database, whether they saw company reps or not. So those physicians got the point, it was white chocolate in the shape of the top end of a hip bone.

Sweets notwithstanding, feeding doctors is a true and tried drug company method for starting and maintaining relationships. It begins, usually, when doctors are in their first year of hospital residency. Reps juggling briefcases, pizzas, and quart bottles of Coke are one of the most common images in the medical profession. Reps target residents because young doctors haven't yet established prescribing habits, and the drug companies know that once prescribing habits have been formed, they're very hard to break.

Disturbingly, there is anecdotal evidence to suggest that these casual lunches have become such a powerful weapon that some young doctors have actually turned to drug reps for treatment advice, finding "the pizza-man" more easily accessible than the physician in charge.

One doctor in Atlanta, Georgia, became so incensed at how demonically effective these reps were at beguiling residents, he described pizza as "the most efficacious marketing tool ever devised."

Various hospitals have reacted in different ways. Some allow the reps free reign. Some allow limited access to residents, confining them to certain hours or designating a table somewhere for their brochures. Some have banned drug reps outright, albeit not without consequences.

When the director of the student residency program for internal medicine at McMaster University in Hamilton, Ontario, announced that the pizza parties were finished and that his residents were off limits to reps, two companies demonstrated their displeasure. One company threatened to withdraw industry funding of certain projects, while the other denied a request to support a residency research project.

Replacing pizza is a trend towards "information management," in which hospitals allow drug reps to make presentations on a regular basis – but without anything free on offer – and then follow those presentations with a briefing by an unbiased pharmacologist who compares what the drug rep said with the peer-reviewed literature, discusses what issues the rep has significantly ignored and what other medications are available that may work better and also be cheaper.

Perhaps not surprisingly, the more senior the physician, the better the food. Instead of pizzas, bottles of wine and champagne may be offered. Flowers and cakes have been known to show up for birthdays, and more than one physician's nurse has found a drug rep waiting for the office to open with a bagel breakfast.

Reps also show up lugging cartons of product samples.

Some doctors say they see drug reps only for the samples, so that they can administer expensive drugs to patients who can't otherwise afford to pay for them. Others take samples to put patients on a trial so that they can see first-hand how the drug works. That's fine. But often what happens is that a doctor decides to administer the sample because it's readily available, instead of administering an equally effective, less expensive drug.

Once a patient is started on a treatment, both doctor and patient are likely to be reluctant to switch drugs. Which is why drug company reps also like to leave samples wherever they go, especially at hospitals. It's cost-effective to hand out enough expensive drugs to treat a patient for a week, knowing that once the patient has left the hospital, the treatment will be continued and paid for over the next however-many months.

Then there is Continuing Medical Education. As government health-care budgets are slashed and insurance-based health-care systems fight to keep costs down, CME has suffered. It's still required for various board certifications and access to some hospitals, and it is encouraged for self-advancement. So Big Pharma has moved quickly to fill the void.

Under the guise of CME, the companies reinforce the message of the marketers by offering physicians a trade-off. Big Pharma pays for the lectures and seminars that earn doctors CME credits, and pays for the food, and maybe throws in golf, or sailing, or skiing, or whatever. In exchange, doctors allow the drug companies to set the curriculum, select the speakers, and, as long as they're not too obvious about promoting their own drugs, to convince them that they're being educated with no strings attached.

Nobody says, "Oh by the way, in exchange for our hospitality, you should prescribe our product." It isn't stated because it doesn't need to be stated. Everyone understands. As one executive at Aventis admitted, "Continuing Medical Education is now determined by what the marketing department wants, not what the doctors need."

The pharmaceutical industry's own code of ethics preaches restraint. Most serious professional organizations also try to define what's acceptable. The American Medical Association, for instance, says that CME must be about education. So the drug companies make sure there is just enough science for the doctors to feel that everyone is complying with professional standards. These are not supposed to be vacations, but that doesn't mean they can't be held in vacation settings. At no point during a CME event should the sponsoring drug company exert control over the content in any speaker's presentation. So the drug companies talk about "hands-off sponsorship," yet hire speakers they can count on to be favourable to the company's products.

Bluntly put, drug companies run junkets cloaked as education to sell their drugs to doctors much the same way that casinos offer complimentary airfare and hotel suites to bring high-rollers to Las Vegas while all the time insisting that they discourage compulsive gambling.

Furthermore, drug company generosity is so readily available to doctors seeking freebies that, according to the *Lancet*, one British doctor working in a senior post at a teaching hospital managed to spend fifty days during 1998 away from his desk and patients as a guest of drug companies in the United States, the Middle East, the Orient, and no fewer than a dozen European countries.

This is not to condemn all CME as a lark. Serious meetings have a serious educational component. Many of them are on weekends because that's generally the only time people are available. Doctors arrive on a Friday night. They have lectures that night, more lectures and workshops on Saturday, and work on Sunday until the time they leave. There may be some good meals involved, but independent agencies look at the educational content of a particular meeting and approve it so that the doctors can get postgraduate educational points. In such cases, spouses are not allowed. There is no golf.

Yet, more often than not, there's got to be some sort of trade-off to get doctors to give up their free time. One major pharmaceutical company regularly invites a group of French cardiologists to be its guest at the annual meeting of the American College of Cardiologists. The doctors selected are heavy prescribers of the company's drugs. In 2000, a group of them were flown from France to Los Angeles, put up at a beachside hotel, wined, dined, and Disneyland-ed for six days. There were side trips to Tijuana and Las Vegas. Yes, there was carte blanche to all of the various professional meetings and lectures. And yes, the doctors were encouraged to attend. But those professional meetings and lectures were held in English, without translation facilities, and most of the French cardiologists didn't speak enough English to understand what was being said.

Most of the time, this type of CME is better camouflaged. One company regularly invites small groups of high prescribers and their spouses to a fancy hotel for a weekend. There are lunches and dinners and pool parties. The price the doctors are asked to pay is simply to sit still for a three-hour slide show on Saturday morning.

"There was a study done in the United States," explains Dr. Joel Lexchin, who has become one of the most vocal opponents of drug company marketing in North America. "They looked at what happened to prescribing after twenty doctors were flown by a drug company to a meeting in some resort area. When these people got home, the prescribing of that product took off. It's simple, whether you call it Continuing Medical Education or you call it marketing, the more a doctor has to do with drug company people, the more likely that doctor is to prescribe the company's drugs and to request that those drugs are put onto his hospital formulary. This isn't saying that the drugs are bad, but are they the best value for the money? If doctors don't think they're being influenced by drug company hospitality, under whatever guise, then they're being incredibly naïve. After all, the drug companies aren't stupid, they don't spend their money on things that don't work."

Nor do they waste their money on meetings that doctors won't attend. The rule of thumb is "The more glamorous the hospitality, the longer the list of doctors willing to show up." The fact the high-end glamorous hospitality might be against the pharmaceutical industry's own codes of practice is rarely a problem.

Lexchin continues, "Companies still break the rules and get away with it because one of the things about voluntary regulation, which is the main form of regulating drug company promotion, is that the associations don't do any active monitoring, they wait for complaints. Now, if I'm flown for free to a meeting, I'm hardly likely to complain that the drug company that flew me there is breaking the rules."

When Pfizer's idea of CME upset Joshua Sharfstein, a Massachusetts physician, he complained about it in a letter to the *New England Journal of Medicine*. In response, the company got defensive. Sharfstein explained how he'd come across a small poster on a bulletin board in the hospital where he works, proclaiming, "PFIZER NIGHT RETURNS." It was an invitation to physicians to meet a new team of Pfizer reps at a Boston billiards parlour. The theme of the evening was "Rack 'em up & Toss 'em down." Sharfstein felt that such an event was unethical and contrary to the AMA's guidelines, which allowed modest meals and trinkets only insofar as they benefit patients and are related to the physician's work. He couldn't see how beer and billiards qualified.

"For aggressive drug-company representatives," he wrote, "such inappropriate promotions, which also violate the Pharmaceutical Manufacturers Association's code of ethical marketing practices, may be just a way of doing business. But for doctors, they violate a basic principle: that we are advocates for our patients and not on the make for ourselves."

Refusing to admit that the company had been caught red-handed, Dr. Joseph Feczko, speaking for Pfizer, shot back a reply. "There were three slide presentations that we believe provided useful medical information to attendees."

Careful not to fall into the same trap, Merck took a different approach. Larry Sasich at Public Citizen says that his son, a resident at a hospital in St. Louis, was invited to attend a continuing education program for the company's latest asthma drug. It was the summer of 1999, right in the middle of baseball star Mark McGwire's quest to beat Roger Maris's sixty-one-home-run record. By sheer coincidence, the CME program fell on a Sunday when his team, the Cardinals, were playing a double-header at home. So, Sasich notes, Merck invited the doctors to Busch Stadium, hosted a tailgate barbecue before the game, gave them plenty to eat during the game, and delivered its spiel about its asthma drug in between games.

Occasionally, CME events create headlines. When Bristol-Myers Squibb announced a weekend program on AIDS therapy that it was sponsoring at a plush resort, one doctor complained about it to the College of Physicians and Surgeons of Ontario. While the college recognized that it might violate its own guidelines, it had to admit that it was powerless to act. So the doctor blew the whistle to the media and, in the face of negative publicity, BMS agreed that a change of venue, to a hotel in downtown Toronto, was more appropriate.

Another company hired a PR firm to invite three hundred doctors for a weekend in the Bahamas to discuss off-label uses for its product. This was a clear violation of everybody's rules, and the junket was cancelled. Instead, the company invited the same three hundred doctors to visit its corporate offices. Two-thirds of them stayed home.

Then again, not all CME programs are events.

One drug company sent literature on antihistamines to doctors, along with forms they were asked to fill out in exchange for CME credit. The forms were both a test of the doctors' understanding of the literature and a history of the doctors' experiences prescribing the drug. In other words, they didn't get the CME credit unless they completed the form and they couldn't complete the form unless they prescribed the drug.

A variation on that theme are Product Familiarization Programs (PFP), which are little more than glorified sales pitches disguised as postmarketing studies. Shortly after the FDA has approved a drug but before it's brought to market, a group of potential prescribers is brought together in an attempt to establish a large customer base on which to launch the drug. To help doctors compile whatever statistics the company pretended to want in one particular PFP, the company supplied each doctor with a brand-new fax machine, paid for a fax line to be installed, and also paid for the monthly line rental.

Because drug companies are always looking inside the medical profession for celebrities to endorse their products – well known or successful physicians – another gimmick is the public-speaking clinic. Here, doctors who show a friendly bent towards the company are whisked away to some resort to attend a two-day workshop in the art of public speaking. The drug company then certifies these doctors as official spokespersons at events and meetings set up by the drug company. To the doctors in the audience at those events, these doctors are leaders in the field and frequently published peer reviewers. It is almost never disclosed either that these doctors have been trained by the drug company or that they are receiving an honorarium for their appearance.

The physician's desk was littered with drug-company-logoed pens, calendars, calculators, notepads, flashlights, golf balls, chocolates, rulers, and letter openers.

The question was, "Where did you get all this stuff?"

His answer, "They give it to you."

"Who?"

"The drug companies. The reps. They always hand you something."

"And what do you do for them?"

"Nothing."

"Then why do they give this stuff to you?"

"Don't ask me, ask them."

So the same question was asked of an American Home Products marketing fellow minding a stand filled with corporate-logoed trinkets at a huge biotech fair.

"Why do you give all this stuff away?"

"They're harmless reminder items."

"By harmless you mean they're not bribes."

"Bribes are absolutely not our style. That's not what this is all about. If you're insinuating that we expect something in return, you're dead wrong. If we give a doc a coffee mug that has our logo on it, it's just a friendly gesture to remind him who we are. If we give him a cheap plastic ruler that has our drug's name and dosage information on it, that just makes it easier for him to remember how much to prescribe."

"What about tickets to football games . . . *aide-mémoire*?"

He shrugs, "It keeps the door open."

Wyeth–Ayerst broke the mould with Travel for Knowledge, a "frequent flyer" program designed specifically to promote Inderalo LA, the company's hypertension drug. A physician writing fifty prescriptions would be awarded a roundtrip airplane ticket to any destination in the United States. By the time the program was stopped, more than twenty thousand doctors had subscribed. Wyeth–Ayerst was subsequently fined nearly $1 million by federal and state authorities for its efforts.

A variation on the theme was Connaught Pharmaceuticals' Very Important Purchaser (VIP) program with points awarded for each purchase of a company vaccine. Those points could then be exchanged for cash or gifts.

Some years ago, ten companies banded together to form The Physicians' Computer Network, which they designed to deal with many day-to-day office tasks. In exchange for agreeing to review thirty-two e-mailed promotional messages per month and making their prescribing information available to the ten companies, the doctors were given $35,000 worth of computer hardware.

Along the same lines, one company offered high-prescribing doctors office equipment, including laser printers and fax machines.

Another company, Searle of Canada, took the novel approach of linking drug sales with altruism. Every time a doctor prescribed Searle's oral contraceptives, the company made a contribution to a charity for battered women.

Believing that charity begins at home, Roche Pharmaceuticals offered physicians $1,200 to prescribe the company's antibiotic Rocephin to twenty patients. Roche had hoped to pass it off as a research project to test the efficacy of the drug by asking physicians what type of infection they were treating and the result of that treatment. The jig was up when U.S. Senate hearings revealed that the payments were not coming out of the R&D budget but from the marketing department.

More recently, accusations were lodged in the Spanish parliament against Abbott Laboratories for allegedly handing out $2.7 million in the form of gifts, trips, and cash to doctors for prescribing Abbott's drugs.

Today most countries have tightened up their guidelines when it comes to gifts from drug companies. The Canadian Medical Association stipulates no gifts. The American Medical Association allows them, but only when they are "of minimal value."

The Australians have amended their rules to say that gifts must either be brand-name reminders or somehow otherwise related to medical education. Any hospitality to doctors must be subordinate to an educational function. Almost as soon as the rules were adopted, the *Sydney Morning Herald* reported that ICI had offered doctors a choice of a $1,000 travel voucher, ten dinners for two at $120 each, or ten bottles of champagne for providing certain information that would assist ICI in promoting its drugs. And not to leave out the doctors' staff, there were also perfume packs, worth $130, for receptionists.

In Britain, abuses piled up throughout the 1980s as drug companies flouted self-regulation. So parliament banned expensive gifts, including medical equipment and foreign trips. Inexpensive gifts would be permitted, as long as they were relevant to the practice of medicine or pharmacy and the cost to the company did not exceed £4.99 (C$10).

That put an end to mountain bikes, stereos, and photographic equipment, although in most countries items like that show up instead as raffle prizes. Doctors who qualify – which means they've filled in a few forms that pretend to be a survey – have their name thrown into the hat.

Still, one doctor who eventually stopped seeing drug reps noted in a letter to the *BMJ* that by the time he called it quits, his entire black bag was filled with drug-company-supplied equipment.

Besides the fact that gifts of any size – including trinkets – give the impression of influence, the cost of the pen, pad, calculator, weekend of golf, whatever, is ultimately passed on to the public, hidden inside the price of the drugs.

"Many doctors are insulted when you tell them they can be influenced," Eric Rose concedes, "especially by a ballpoint pen or a coffee mug. And yet, in a survey of one hundred third-year medical students, 85 per cent thought it was inappropriate for a public official to accept a $50 gift from a contractor, but less than 50 per cent thought it inappropriate for physicians to receive the same gift from a pharmaceutical company."

Rose personally finds it absurd that somebody with a doctorate in medical science would willingly give up an hour of time to listen to somebody who doesn't know what they're talking about just so that he or she can get a plastic pocket protector and a souvenir ballpoint pen.

"A drug company's job is to make products that are safe and effective and, at the same time, to make money for their stockholders. That's what they're supposed to do, which is why I don't point a finger at them for marketing drugs the way they do. No, I can't blame a predatory animal for acting like a predatory animal. I put the onus on doctors. They're the ones I blame. It's the docs who have a fiduciary responsibility to their patients to be objective and impartial and not be bribed."

Which is why he doesn't see drug reps.

David Griffith, the author of that editorial in the *BMJ*, stopped seeing reps too. "We may not earn as much as doctors in America, but we have a decent salary, more than enough that we can afford to buy our own ballpoint pens."

A successful internist on Long Island made a similar point: "There was a never-ending line of people trying to sell me stuff. A few of them knew what they were talking about, especially the ones who had studied to be pharmacists. But the majority of them had simply rehearsed a routine. They were reciting a script to me. I couldn't justify the time they wasted, so I cut them off. I told my secretary, no more."

At least he thought he did.

"They kept coming, trying to get in to see me, and when they were told no, they left their promotional aids anyway. Not just leaflets and tearsheets of articles but all the usual trinkets. They did whatever they could to bribe their way past the front door. They continued to show up with candy and other goodies."

It took a while but eventually, he says, most of them got the message. Leaflets, brochures, and tear sheets continued to show up in the mail, along with non-peer-reviewed magazines touting the company's drugs, but at least the doorstep visits slowed to a trickle.

Except they didn't get turned off completely.

Alarmed at losing an important prescriber, Big Pharma sent in the big guns. Someone arrived at the doctor's office one morning asking for an appointment, and offered another physician's name as a reference. The new patient filled in the usual questionnaire and was worked into the appointment schedule. The doctor cordially greeted his new patient, who quickly confessed this wasn't really a medical visit.

"The company had upped the stakes," he recalls. "This rep was wearing a short skirt and a frilly blouse, she had a lot of hair and a big smile. She wanted to know why I stopped seeing her company's reps and if I would allow her to stop by every now and then, just to say hello. I threw her out. But you know what amazed me? Some of my male colleagues who'd also announced they wouldn't see reps, a few of those jerks fell for it. Sex sells. Far be it for a pharmaceutical company to let a doctor escape for the sake of a short skirt."

So the question becomes, "If you walk into a physician's office and find his or her desk littered with drug-company-logoed pens, calendars, calculators, notepads, flashlights, golf balls, chocolates, rulers, and letter openers, what should you do?"

Joel Lexchin suggests, "I would walk out. But then I know where to go to get another opinion. Short of that, I would certainly be more skeptical of what that person prescribes for me."

Peter Mansfield draws a medical analogy: "If you look at the way drug companies market their products directly to doctors and think of those ways as risk factors in the same way we think of cholesterol and blood pressure being risk factors in heart attacks, then trusting in drug company information is a more powerful risk factor for inappropriate belief. And if you see inappropriate belief as a heart attack, then trust in drug companies is a bigger factor than cholesterol."

In other words, he says, drug-company-logoed stuff scattered around a doctor's office is cause for real concern.

"Yes, and I think a patient should express that concern. It's only the doctors who don't seem to be aware that there's a problem. For whatever reason, many doctors just don't understand that this whole issue of trust, which is so vital in the doctor-patient relationship, is being undermined."

Eric Rose is equally frank. "What patients should be worried about is not how many trinkets are on the doctor's desk, but the source of that doctor's information. I think a very legitimate question for a patient to ask a doctor is how do you keep up with new developments in medicine? There's nothing wrong with asking that and I don't think any doc should demur to answer that. Hopefully, the answer will involve peer-reviewed literature and other scientifically sound sources of information. If a doc says, 'Sure I see drugs reps and I read all these magazines that come to my house even though I never subscribe to them, and look at all the neat stuff they give me,' then you might want to reconsider your relationship with that doctor."

EPILOGUE

The global pharmaceutical industry has emerged from the twentieth century as a hugely powerful economic force. Granted, it is filled with highly intelligent, highly motivated people who, with monumental dedication, are trying to change the world, trying to make this planet a healthier one, and in so doing, without any doubt, are enriching each of our lives.

Granted, too, as a result of such dedication, we are the first people on the planet who can be cured of disease. Our ancestors could be comforted, have their pain relieved, and made to feel better. But we can be healed. That journey started, perhaps, with penicillin and has, in a short period of time, come all the way to the mapping of the human genome. We are, therefore, perhaps the last generation to live three score and ten. Our grandchildren could easily live to twice that. And if they do, that will be testament to the men and women who have dedicated their lives to finding and developing the science that unlocks the keys and opens the doors of better health.

But in the pursuit of good, there has been evil.

If the recklessness of some people in this industry were mirrored in, say, the airline business, we would surely stop flying. If the dishonesty – or at least the reliance on quasi-truths – of some people in this industry were mirrored in the financial sector, we would not entrust our money there. If the greed of some people in this industry were mirrored in our elected officials, what little respect politicians can still command would evaporate.

No, the pharmaceutical industry is not like any other.

Because we cannot stop taking medication, we are asked to tolerate recklessness in the name of progress, to accept dishonesty in the name of research and development, and to turn a blind eye to greed in the name of shareholder satisfaction.

We are also faced with the sad truth that there is no indication, anywhere, that things will get any better.

Even though drugs in Canada are less expensive than they are in the United States, they are not necessarily cheap. Sure, Americans come across the border to buy in Canada the same drugs they may have to pay 50 per cent more for in the United States. But Canadians are now paying more for drugs than for doctors, and drug prices are increasing at around 15 per cent a year.

Now consider three vital points.

First, the fact that drug prices are under threat in the United States and that will have ramifications in Canada. A bill allowing cheaper pharmaceuticals to be reimported will reduce some prescription costs in the States. Consequently, Big Pharma can be expected to opt for the knock-on effect, raising drug prices in markets such as Canada to assure that price discrepancies are erased.

Second, if drug prices fall considerably in the States, Big Pharma's profits will have to be sustained through price rises in other markets. Here, Canada is a sitting duck.

And third, Big Pharma's assault on the ban against direct-to-consumer advertising in Canada is guaranteed, eventually, to succeed. Whether it's the slow-drip leak of American media heading north or the sure-fire power of the Internet, in due time Canada will be flooded by DTCA. The pharmaceutical lobby will argue that unless it is allowed to educate Canadians, the country will be overrun with American-based information that may or may not apply to Canada. If Ottawa can't stop it, they'll look for ways of allowing it and taxing it. Doctors still intent on prescribing generics will find their advice short-circuited.

Critics of the industry in Canada point to drug prices and note that while they are going up much faster than any other element of health care, jobs in the industry are decreasing. Since 1993, pharmaceutical sales in Canada are up, now running around C$12 billion a year retail, or about C$9 billion a year wholesale. Looking at the ratio of dollars to jobs, it means there are some 15,000 people employed taking in C$9 billion. In many other industries, the ratio runs closer to C$1 billion for every 10,000 to 15,000 employees.

That leaves some critics to insist that C$9 billion for the same number of employees indicates that prices are nine times what they should be.

Canada's generic sector employs 6,000 people and takes in C$1 billion. By the same ratio, those critics suggest, generic drugs are much cheaper than they should be to keep the industry alive.

Then they point to the balance of payments. The trade deficit in pharmaceuticals has grown from C$1 billion to C$3 billion. The question those critics ask is, "How could there be a C$1 billion to C$3 billion trade deficit in pharmaceuticals when it's a C$9 billion industry and the cost of goods is under C$1 billion?"

Even then, if this was only about money, one might not worry about an industry that feels the need to hire two lobbyists for every lawmaker in Washington. Or one's belief in an industry that has the gall to ask us to feel good about huge sums spent on R&D when that same industry spends even more money on marketing its products to us. Or our pride in ourselves as a society when one of the most powerful influences in that society turns its back on the less fortunate who simply cannot afford to pay artificially high prices for essential medicines?

Should any of us fully trust – as we are asked to do – any corporation with our health when that same corporation is fast to remind its shareholders where its true allegiance lies?

No doubt there are responsible voices in the industry who would want to earn the public's respect – not just for the science but for every aspect of industry – especially the way it does business.

But those voices seem, sadly, few and far between.

Instead, all too often, the noise the industry makes sounds more like chants of "Kill the messenger."

"You have a lot to answer for," came my criticism to a senior marketing executive at one of the world's largest pharmaceutical companies.

He responded simply, "We're in business."

"You're different."

"Not as far as our shareholders are concerned."

"Ask the people who can't afford to pay ten bucks for a pill that costs ten cents."

"Don't tell me that the glass is half empty when it's almost full."

"I'm telling you that people are dying."

"The truth of the matter is that, thanks to us, people are living."

"The truth of the matter is that good people sometimes, collectively, do evil things and, in this case, the overriding theme is collective corporate greed."

He warned, "You realize, I'm sure, that if you come after us, we'll come after you."

"What does that mean?"

"You're welcome to interpret that anyway you care to."

"How about if I care to quote you as threatening me."

Now he suggested, "I wouldn't, if I were you."

And I warned, "But you're not me."

ACKNOWLEDGEMENTS

For their cooperation and input, I am indebted to: Dr. Nancy Olivieri, Barry Sherman of Apotex, Jack Kay of Apotex, Professor Trudo Lemmons at the University of Toronto, Dr. Joel Lexchin, Jim Keon of the Canadian Drug Manufacturers Association, Dr. Michele Brill-Edwards, attorney Lori Stoltz, and Dr. Arnold Naimark.

To that list I add my thanks to: Dr. Richard C. Davis of Guelph, Ontario; Dr. Alex Arrow, Cyril Beck, Dr. Alastair Benbow; Dean Boyd, Phil Reed, and Kevin Della-Colli at U.S. Customs; attorneys Ezequiel Camerini, Mark Kleiman, Peter Reichertz, Dan Sigelman, D'Lisa Simmons, Mike Williams, and to Jim Griffin of the U.S. Justice Department; Jon Close, Guy Dehn at Public Concern at Work; Bruce Downey and Carol Cox at Barr Laboratories; Linda Foster of Bioglan, Dr. Martin Goldman at Pharmax, Dr. David Griffith, Dr. John Gueriguian, Dr. Susan Horwitz at Albert Einstein College of Medicine, Richard Jennings of Cambridge University, Dr. Sheldon Krimsky at Tufts University, Dr. Graeme Laver, Richard Liwicki of Oxford University, Dr. Peter Mansfield of MaLAM, Dr. Andrew Millar, Dr. Robert Misbin, Duncan Moore of Morgan Stanley Dean Witter, Dr. David Nathan of the Dana Farber Cancer Institute, Russell Mokhiber at Corporate Crime Reporter, Eugene Reed, Dr. Drummond Rennie of *Journal of the American Medical Association*, Dr. Eric Rose, Dr. Michael Ryan of Georgetown University, Dr. Larry

Sasich of Public Citizen, Dr. Stephen Schondelmeyer of the Prime Institute, Dr. David Shimm, Warwick Smith of the British Generic Manufacturers Association, Dr. P. Roy Vagelos, Richard Walden of Operation USA, Diane Walker at the Food and Drug Administration, Dr. Monroe Wall, Sir David Weatherall of Oxford University, Bob Weisman of Multinational Monitor, Dr. Frank Wells, Paul Whybrow, Dr. Gavin Yamey of the *British Medical Journal*.

Additionally, I am grateful to several members of the U.S. Congress and their staff, including: the Honorable Marion Berry, the Honorable Henry Waxman, the Honorable Bernard Sanders, Paul Kim, Dustin May, and Tate Heuer.

I also owe thanks to: the American Medical Association, the Canadian Medical Association, the British Medical Association, Doctors for Research Integrity, the Hospital for Sick Children and the University of Toronto, the U.K. Medicines Control Agency, the European Agency for the Evaluation of Medicinal Products, the General Medical Council of the United Kingdom, the U.K. National Institute for Clinical Excellence, the Royal Pharmaceutical Society of Great Britain, the U.K. Ministry of Health, the British Prescription Medicines Code of Practice Authority; the editors of *La Revue Prescrire* in Paris, the *Lancet*, the *New England Journal of Medicine*, and the *Canadian Medical Association Journal*; the International Federation of Pharmaceutical Manufacturers Associations, the Pharmaceutical Research Manufacturers Association, the National Association of Pharmaceutical Manufacturers, Médecins Sans Frontières, the Department of Health and Human Services Food and Drug Administration, American Home Products, AstraZeneca, Aventis, Bayer, Bristol-Myers Squibb, Glaxo-Wellcome, Hoffmann-La Roche, HMR, Eli Lilly and Company, Merck & Co, Novartis, Parke-Davis, Pfizer, Pharmacia & UpJohn, Schering-Plough, Searle, SmithKline Beecham, Sanofi-Winthrop, Warner-Lambert, Wyeth-Ayerst, the Technology Vision Group, and Cipla Pharmaceuticals.

The sheer abundance of information available on the World Wide Web is such that no serious researcher can afford to disregard it. While it goes without saying that the quality of the material available online runs the gamut from richly outstanding to totally unreliable, I wish to acknowledge my appreciation to the individuals who participate in and the organizations who make information and sources available on four exceptional sites: The E-Drug discussion group (www.healthnet.org), MaLAM (www.camtech.net.au/malam), Médecins Sans Frontières (www.msf.org), and Health Action International (www.haiweb.org).

Many special thanks, as well, to Jonathan Webb at McClelland & Stewart for his always expert advice, my agents Milly Marmur in New York and Linda McKnight in Toronto, and, of course, La Benayoun.

SELECTED BIBLIOGRAPHY

BOOKS

Abraham, John. *Science, Politics and the Pharmaceutical Industry: Controversy and Bias in Drug Regulation.* New York: St. Martin's Press, 1995.

Arno, Peter S., and Karyn L. Feiden. *Against the Odds: The Story of AIDS Drug Development, Politics and Profits.* New York: HarperCollins, 1992.

Barlow, Maude, and Bruce Campbell. *Take Back the Nation.* Toronto: Key Porter Books, 1991.

Basara, Lisa Ruby, and Michael Montagne. *Searching for Magic Bullets: Orphan Drugs, Consumer Activism and Pharmaceutical Development.* New York: Haworth Press, 1994.

Beauchamp, Tom L., and Norman E. Bowie, eds. *Ethical Theory and Business.* New Jersey: Prentice Hall, 1993.

Bian, Tonda R. *Drug Lords: America's Pharmaceutical Cartel.* Michigan: No Barriers Publishing, 1997.

Bogner, W., and H. Thomas. *Drugs to Market: Creating Value and Advantage in the Pharmaceutical Industry.* London: Pergamon, 1996.

Bork, Robert H. *The Antitrust Paradox.* New York: Basic Books, 1978.

Burkholz, Herbert. *The FDA Follies.* New York: Basic Books, 1994.

Cookson, William. *The Gene Hunters.* London: Aurum Press, 1994.

Danzon, P. M. *Pharmaceutical Price Regulation: National Policies Versus Global Interests.* Washington, D.C.: American Enterprise Institute Press, 1997.

Davis, P. *Managing Medicines: Public Policy and Therapeutic Drugs.* Buckingham: Open University Press, 1997.

Drake, Donald, and Marian Uhlman. *Making Medicine – Making Money*. Kansas City: Andrews & McMeel, 1993.

Gambardella, Alfonso. *Science and Innovation: The U.S. Pharmaceutical Industry During the 1980s*. New York: Cambridge University Press, 1995.

Helms, Robert B., ed. *Competitive Strategies in the Pharmaceutical Industry*. Washington, D.C.: American Enterprise Institute Press, 1996.

Helms, Robert B., ed. *Drug Development and Marketing*. Washington, D.C.: American Enterprise Institute Press, 1975.

Hurtig, Mel. *The Betrayal of Canada*. Toronto: Stoddart Publishing, 1991.

Kenney, M. *Bio-Technology: The University-Industrial Complex*. New Haven: Yale University Press, 1986.

Kwitney, Jonathan. *Acceptable Risks*. New York: Simon & Schuster, 1992.

Lapierre, Dominique. *Beyond Love*. London: Century, 1991.

Maren, Michael. *The Road to Hell: The Ravaging Effects of Foreign Aid and International Charity*. New York: Free Press, 1997.

McCormick, Dr. Joseph B., Dr. Susan Fisher-Hoch, and Leslie Alan Horvitz. *Virus Hunters of the CDC*. Atlanta: Turner Publishing, 1996.

McDonald, Marci. *Yankee Doodle Dandy*. Toronto: Stoddart Publishing, 1995.

Mintzes, Barbara. *Blurring the Boundaries: New Trends in Drug Promotion*. Amsterdam: HAI, 1998.

Mokhiber, Russell, and Robert Weissman. *Corporate Predators: The Hunt for Mega-Profits and the Attack on Democracy*. Maine: Common Courage Press, 1999.

Peters, C. J., and Mark Olshaker. *Virus Hunter*. New York: Anchor Books, 1997.

Preston, Richard. *The Hot Zone*. New York: Doubleday, 1994.

Rachlis, Michael, M.D., and Carol Kushner. *Strong Medicine*. Toronto: HarperCollins, 1994.

Robinson, Jeffrey. *The Manipulators: Unmasking the Hidden Persuaders*. London: Pocket Books, 1999.

Ryan, Michael P. *Knowledge Diplomacy: Global Competition and the Politics of Intellectual Property*. Washington, D.C.: Brookings Institution Press, 1998.

Schweitzer, S. *Pharmaceutical Economics and Policy*. New York: Oxford University Press, 1997.

Sjöström, H., and R. Nilsson. *Thalidomide and the Power of the Drug Companies*. London: Penguin Books, 1972.

Smith, H. *Principles and Methods of Pharmacy Management*. Philadelphia: Lea and Febiger, 1975.

Spece, R., D. Shimm, and A. Buchanan, eds. *Conflict of Interest in Clinical Medicine and Biomedical Research*. New York: Oxford University Press, 1996.

Sullivan, Donald L. *Consumer's Guide to Generic Drugs*. New York: Berkley Books, 1996.

Sunday Times Insight Team. *Suffer the Children: The Story of Thalidomide*. London: Andre Deutsch, 1979.

Sutherland, M. *Advertising and the Mind of the Consumer: What Works, What Doesn't and Why.* London: Allen & Unwin, 1993.

Watson, James D. *The Double Helix.* London: Penguin Books, 1997.

Werth, Barry. *The Billion Dollar Molecule: One Company's Quest for the Perfect Drug.* New York: Touchstone, 1994.

Young, James Harvey. *The Toadstool Millionaires: A Social History of Patent Medicines in America Before Federal Regulations.* New Jersey: Princeton University Press, 1972.

NEWSPAPERS AND NEWS AGENCIES

ADVERTISING AGE

September 29, 1993: Freeman, L., "Consumer Ads for Rx Drugs Take Off"

ASSOCIATED PRESS

September 21, 2000: "Senator's Roles Prompt Hypocrisy Cry"

September 18, 2000: "Bayer Makes Tentative Deal in Probe"

September 15, 2000: "Lawsuits Accuse Ritalin Makers"

July 4, 2000: Galewitz, Phil, "Pharmaceutical Giant Glaxo Hits Setbacks on Road to No. 1"

May 22, 2000: Moulson, Geir, "AIDS Strategy Needs to Look Beyond Price-Cutting, Africans Say"

May 16, 2000: Neergaard, Lauran, "FDA Prepares to Overhaul Warnings"

May 16, 2000: "American Home Products Investigated"

May 3, 2000: Holland, Jesse J., "Medical Research Deaths Probed"

January 18, 2000: Galewitz, Phil, "Drug-Company Mergers Could Raise Prices for Consumers"

December 29, 1999: Gullo, Karen, "Drugs in Research Lightly Monitored"

June 17, 1999: Galewitz, Phil, "Drugmaker Ads Can Backfire"

May 24, 1999: "Diet Drug Company Accused of Funding Favorable Journal Articles"

BOSTON GLOBE

June 11, 2000: Zuckoff, Mitchell, "Prozac – New Directions – Science, Money Drive a Makeover"

May 12, 2000: Rosenberg, Ronald, "Transplant Drug Makers Request Refused by State"

January 26, 1999: Sager, Alan, and Deborah Socolar, "A Fairer Prescription Plan"

December 26, 1999: Anderson, C., "Drug Firms Said to Pay Less in Taxes"

November 27, 1999: Hoffmann, V., "Health Groups Say Poor Nations Need Access to Generic Drugs"

March 6, 1999: Knox, R. A., "Drug-Coverage Crisis Hurting Elderly"

January 4, 1999: Trager, Ellen Lutch, "Cheaper Rx's for Seniors"

April 7, 1998: Zuckoff, Mitchell, et al., "Public Research-Private Profit: Tax Dollars Fuel University Spinoffs"

April 7, 1998: Zuckoff, Mitchell, et al., "Public Research-Private Profit: UMass Nearly Cut Out of Lucrative 'Pharming' Market"

April 7, 1998: Globe Spotlight Team, "Public Research-Private Profit: MIT Unrivaled in Reaping Rewards of Its Inventions"

April 6, 1998: O'Neill, Gerard, et al., "Public Research-Private Profit: Self-Dealing Scientists"

April 7, 1998: Globe Spotlight Team, "Public Research-Private Profit: A 'Helper' Who Calls the Shots and Holds the Money"

April 5, 1998: Dembner, Alice, et al., "Public Handouts Enrich Drug Makers, Scientists"

CAPE TIMES (SOUTH AFRICA)

May 10, 2000: "Manufacturers Coin Billions on AIDS Drug"

CHICAGO TRIBUNE

March 27, 1999: "FDA Allows Qualified Use of Warner-Lambert Diabetes Drug"

U.S. FEDERAL REGISTER

October 8, 1998: "Food and Drug Administration: List of Drug Products That Have Been Withdrawn or Removed from the Market for Reasons of Safety or Effectiveness"

FINANCIAL TIMES

July 30, 2000: Pilling, David, "Malaria Study Given $40M"

July 17, 2000: Pilling, David, "Glaxo Wins Malarone Approval"

June 17, 2000: "Breast Cancer Drugs Recommended"

May 6, 2000: "Ovarian Cancer Treatment Drug Gets Go-Ahead"

May 3, 2000: "Clinical Body Looks at More Cancer Drugs"

March 27, 1999: "FDA May Restrict Rezulin"

March 15, 1999: "Consolidation Enters More Frantic Phase: Pharmaceutical Companies Face Increasing Pressures to Merge"

June 14, 1998: "Biotech Sues Sacked Employee: Company Alleges Former Head of Clinical Trials Breached Confidentiality Agreement"

May 5, 1998: "Agency Releases Details About Biotech Report"

May 1, 1998: "The Changing Fortunes of British Biotech: Fateful Phone Call that Unbottled Dr Millar's Tale"

April 28, 1998: "Millar's Motives in British Biotech Disclosures"

April 27, 1998: "Sacked Director Says Biotech Board Upgraded Status of Trials"

April 26, 1998: "Sacked Biotech Boss Reveals Doubts"

THE GUARDIAN
August 2, 2000: Palast, Gregory, "Keep Taking Our Tablets: No One Else's"
June 17, 2000: "NHS 'Should Use Best Breast Cancer Drugs'"
May 6, 2000: "Ovarian Cancer Drug Cleared for Wider Use"
April 12, 2000: "Controls Eased on 'Too Costly' Cancer Drugs"
August 18, 1999: Boseley, Sarah, "Drug Firm's TV Adverts Test Industry Rules"
July 27, 1999: Boseley, Sarah, "Drug Trials Risk to Patients"

HARTFORD COURANT (CONNECTICUT)
April 11, 2000: Kauffman, Matthew, and Andrew Julien, "Industry Cash a Potent Habit"
April 9, 2000: Kauffman, Matthew, and Andrew Julien, "Surge in Corporate Cash Taints Integrity of Academic Science"

THE INDEPENDENT
June 17, 2000: "Postcode Lottery for New Breast Cancer Drug"
April 12, 2000: "NHS Restrictions on Cancer Drug Due to Be Lifted"
January 27, 2000: "One in Three Authorities in Breach of Cancer Guidelines"

INDIANAPOLIS STAR
April 22, 2000: Swiatek, Jeff, "Lilly's Legal Strategy Disarmed Prozac Lawyers' Secret Deals, Hardball Tactics Limited Drugmaker's Liability for Top-Selling Antidepressant"

INTERNATIONAL HERALD TRIBUNE
November 18, 1998: de Aenlle, Conrad, "Mergers Give Industry Boost in Developing New Products"
July 2, 1997: Elliott, S., "Anti-Depressant Makes Sunny Pitch to Public"

LE MONDE DIPLOMATIQUE
July 1999: Maréchal, Jean-Paul, "Making Merchandise of Biodiversity"

LOS ANGELES TIMES
January 31, 1999: Bernstein, S., "Drug Makers Face Evolving Marketplace"

MALAM NEWSLETTER
March/April 1999: "Memoirs of Methods Used to Sell Drugs"
July/August 1997: Sweet, M., "Healthy Profits: An Overview of Promotion in Australia"

THE MEDICAL POST (TORONTO)
September 8, 1998: Wysong, Pippa, "Time with Drug Reps Affects Prescribing"
January 21, 1997: Jeffrey, Susan, "Research Conflict – Doctor May Be in Legal Battle after Reporting Negative Findings of Drug Company Study"

NEW YORK TIMES

August 27, 2000: Peterson, Melody, "What's Black and White and Sells Medicine?"

July 23, 2000: Stolberg, Sheryl Gay, and Jeff Gerth, "In a Drug's Journey to Market, Discovery Is Just the First of Many Steps"

July 23, 2000: Stolberg, Sheryl Gay, and Jeff Gerth, "Holding Down the Competition: How Companies Stall Generics and Keep Themselves Healthy"

July 18, 2000: Goode, Erica, "Once Again, Prozac Takes Center Stage, in Furor"

June 17, 2000: McNeil, Donald G., Jr., "Prices for Medicine Are Exorbitant in Africa, Study Says"

May 21, 2000: McNeil, Donald G., Jr., "Medicine Merchants: Drug Companies and the Third World, a Case Study in Neglect"

May 18, 2000: McNeil, Donald G., Jr., "Patent Holders Fight Proposal on Generic AIDS Drugs for Poor"

April 23, 2000: Gerth, Jeff, and Sheryl Gay Stolberg, "Medicine Merchants: Drug Companies Profit from Research Supported by Taxpayers"

April 23, 2000: "From the Lab to the Pharmacy"

October 29, 1999: Steinhauer, Jennifer, "Rising Cost of Drugs Take a Bigger Share of Health Insurance Outlays"

October 8, 1999: Morrow, David J., "Fen-Phen Maker to Pay Billions in Settlement of Diet: Injury Cases"

June 29, 1999: Abelson, Reed, "Among U.S. Donations, Tons of Worthless Drugs"

June 16, 1999: Toner, Robin, "Drug Coverage Dominates Fight Brewing on Medicine"

May 16, 1999: Eichenwald, K., and G. Kolata, "Drug Trials Hide Conflicts for Doctors"

January 11, 1999: Zuger, Abigail, "Fever Pitch: Getting Doctors to Prescribe Is Big Business"

November 17, 1998: Freudenheim, Milt, "Influencing Doctor's Orders"

September 11, 1997: Freudenheim, Milt, "Cleaning Out the Medicine Cabinet: Prescription Drug Makers Reconsider Generics"

June 24, 1997: Freudenheim, Milt, "Lilly Cuts Distribution Unit's Book Value By $2.4 Billion"

October 8, 1996: Freudenheim, Milt, "Not Quite What Doctor Ordered: Drug Substitutions Add to Discord Over Managed Care"

October 4, 1994: Altman, Lawrence K., "Some Authors in Medical Journals May Be Paid by 'Spin Doctors'"

November 18, 1991: Freudenheim, M., "Merck Reports Major Shift in Its Marketing on Drugs"

PHILADELPHIA INQUIRER

June 16, 1999: Greve, Frank, "Drug Donations: A Bitter Pill? Some Medications Shipped Abroad Provide More Relief for the Manufacturers Than for Those Who Are Suffering"

April 20, 1999: Collins, Huntly, "Drug Firm's CEO Showed a New Way"
August 18, 1997: Gelles, J., "Critics Warn Ads for Prescription Drugs Are Flawed"

PITTSBURGH POST-GAZETTE
March 8, 1998: "Drug Makers Guard Patents Lawsuits, Other Delaying Tactics Make It Tough for Generics to Break Brand-Name Grip"

PR NEWSWIRE
July 6, 2000: Publication of Glaxo SmithKline Merger Documentation

REUTERS
May 15, 2000: "AstraZeneca Sues U.S. Generic Drug Makers"
July 17, 1998: "Researchers Say Drug Companies, Politics Cheat Mental Health Research"

SAN JOSE MERCURY NEWS
May 16, 1999: Krieger, Lisa M., "Patients Feeling Squeezed"

SCOTLAND ON SUNDAY
January 16, 2000: "Executive Denying Women Access to New Cancer Drugs"

SCOTSMAN
June 17, 2000: "Cancer Patients to Get Drug Following English Ruling"
April 12, 2000: "Doubt Over Access to Cancer Drugs for Scots"
April 12, 2000: "Drugs Worth Paying For"

SUNDAY MIRROR (U.K.)
July 3, 1994: "Thalidomide Dad's Tragedy"

SUNDAY TIMES (U.K.)
July 16, 2000: Rogers, Lois, "Doctors Cut Down Patients' Drug Doses to Save on Costs"

SYDNEY MORNING HERALD
October 25, 1997: Sweet, Melissa, "Healthy Profits"

TIMES HIGHER EDUCATION SUPPLEMENT (U.K.)
October 22, 1999: "Wellcome Pioneers"
October 22, 1999: "Canada Tempts U.S. with Cut-Price Fees"

TALLAHASSEE TIMES-UNION
March 21, 2000: Pendleton, Randolph, "Medicaid Pill Prices at Issue, Legislators Debate Restrictions on Expensive Drugs as Costs Soar"

TAMPA TRIBUNE
March 20, 2000: Forgrieve, Janet, "Buying Science"

TORONTO GLOBE AND MAIL
November 2, 1998: "Salvage Group Tackles Sick Kids' Image Disaster"
September 7, 1998: "Letter to the Editor: To Tell the Truth"
August 28, 1998: "Researchers at Sick Kids Threaten to Leave"
August 21, 1998: "Sick Kids Plans External Review of Clinical Trials"
August 13, 1998: Taylor, P., "A Doctor Takes on a Drug Company"
January 8, 1998: Immen, W., "Heart-Drug Supporters Financed by Makers: Study
    Links Research to Doctors' Funding"
March 20, 1997: Berger, P., "The Industry Is Acting Improperly in Promoting HIV
    Drugs"
May 20, 1996: McKenna, B., "Generics Press Ottawa for Relief"
March 16, 1996; Coutts, J., "Drug Giant Seeks to Delay Sale of Generic Prozac"

TORONTO STAR
May 4, 2000: Levy, Harold, "Doctor Deemed Too Good to Fire for Harassment"

USA TODAY
January 19, 2000: Sternberg, Steve, "Drug Firms Buy Results from Doctors"
November 10, 1999: Cauchon, Dennis, "Americans Pay More: Here's Why"

VANCOUVER SUN
August 15, 1997: Pharmaceutical Industry Job Vacancies Ad

WALL STREET JOURNAL
July 6, 2000: Harris, Gardoner, "Drug Firms Stymied in the Lab, Become
    Marketing Machines"
May 24, 2000: Harris, G., "Drug Makers Pair Up to Fight Key Patent Losses"
May 11, 2000: Murray, S., and L. Lagnado, "Drug Companies Face Assault on
    Prices"
March 29, 2000: "Rezulin Proves the System Works"
March 24, 2000: Waldholz, Michael, "Pfizer Weighs Requests to Cut Price of
    Drug"
December 9, 1999: Adams, Chris, "A Determined Doctor Decides to Write a
    New Prescription for Drug Research"
February 19, 1999: "Dose of Reality: Idea of Having Medicare Pay for Elderly's
    Drugs Is Roiling the Industry"
February 2, 1999: "Medical Journals Rarely Disclose Researchers' Ties"
November 16, 1998: Langreth, R., "Drug Marketing Drives Many Clinical Trials"
November 16, 1998: Tanouye, E., "Drug Dependency: U.S. Has Developed an
    Expensive Habit, Now, How to Pay for It?"

July 21, 1997: Schatz, Tom, and Leslie Paige, "Politics Trumps Science at the FDA"

July 1, 1997: Burton, T. M., and Y. Ono, "Campaign for Prozac Targets Consumers"

May 6, 1997: Ingersoll, Bruce, "American Home Products Gets a Boost as FDA Rejects Generics of Premarin"

February 13, 1997: Tanouye, Elyse, "Prices of Drugs Increase Faster Than Inflation"

January 18, 1996: Cohen, Laurie P., and Elyse Tanouye, "Bitter Pill"

August 31, 1995: Tanouye, Elyse, "Drug Makers Seek Relaxed Restrictions on Marketing"

August 12, 1994: Tanouye, Elyse, "Drug Marketers May Use Illegal Tactics to Sell"

August 1, 1994: Anders, George, "Drug Resistance: Costly Medicine Meets Its Match, Hospitals Just Use Lower Doses"

May 31, 1994: Tanouye, Elyse, "Owning Medco, Merck Takes Drug Marketing the Next Logical Step"

April 27, 1994: Miller, M. W., "Creating a Buzz: With Remedy in Hand, Drug Firms Get Ready to Popularize Illness"

April 5, 1994: "Druggist Payments Ending"

September 10, 1993: Anders, G., "Managed Health Care Jeopardizes Outlook for Drug Detailers"

August 3, 1993: Gutfeld, R., "FDA Attacks Drug Makers' Ads to Doctors"

February 26, 1993: Racz, G., "Drug Companies' Profit Margins Top Most Industries, Study Says"

January 22, 1993: Rosewicz, Barbara, "Science Posts Pose a Puzzle for President"

May 26, 1992: Waldholz, Michael, "Stymied Science: New Discoveries Dim Drug Makers' Hopes for Quick AIDS Cure"

November 14, 1989: Ingersoll, Brice, "Chief of FDA to Step Aside after Five Years"

October 22, 1987: Waldholz, M., "Merck, in Unusual Gesture, Will Donate Drug to Fight Leading Cause of Blindness"

WASHINGTON POST

May 11, 2000: Burgess, John, "Africa Gets AIDS Drug Exception"

March 23, 1999: Schwartz, John, "Is FDA Too Quick to Clear Drugs?"

February 15, 1998: O'Harrow, R., "Prescription Sales, Privacy Fears: CVS, Giant Share Customer Records with Drug Marketing Firm"

August 22, 1997: "Schering-Plough Is Told to Halt Claritin TV Ads"

April 16, 1997: Weiss, Rick, "Data on Drug's Generic Rivals Suppressed"

January 30, 1997: Baker, Donald P., "Virginia Bill Would Bar Cash Incentives for Persuasive Druggists"

March 26, 1996: Auerbach, Stuart, "Study Finds Cheap Drugs Can Be Costly in Long Run"

December 10, 1995: Sakson, Steve, "Drug Discounts for HMOs May Shift Costs to Others"

July 31, 1990: Spolar, Chris, "New Schizophrenia Drug Arouses Furor Over Cost"

MAGAZINES AND JOURNALS

ACADEMIC MEDICINE

Frankel, Mark S. "Perception, Reality, and the Political Context of Conflict of Interest in University–Industry Relationships," December 1996.

ACP-ASIM OBSERVER (American College of Physicians–American Society of Internal Medicine)

Maguire, Phyllis. "Community-Based Trials Under Scrutiny: Critics Worry About Conflicts of Interest and Quality of Research," July–August 1999.

Wiebe, Christine. "Drug Representatives and Residents: Dangerous Liaison?" September 1995.

ALIVE: CANADIAN JOURNAL OF HEALTH AND NUTRITION

Wolfson, Richard. "Pharmaceutical Money Drives the Medical Profession," March 1998.

AMERICAN DRUGGIST

"Mail Order Drug Sales Leap 10 Percent," July 1, 1999.

Vaczek, David. "The Rise of the Generic Drug Industry," April 1996.

AMERICAN ECONOMIC REVIEW

Baker, Laurence C., and Kenneth S. Corts. "HMO Penetration and the Cost of Health Care: Market Discipline or Market Segmentation," May 1996.

Griliches, Zvi, and Iain Cockburn. "Generics and New Goods in Pharmaceutical Price Indexes," December 1994.

Grabowski, Henry, and John Vernon. "Longer Patents for Lower Imitation Barriers: The 1984 Drug Act," May 1986.

AMERICAN JOURNAL OF MEDICINE

Avorn, J., M.D.; M. Chen, and R. Hartley. "Scientific Versus Commercial Sources of Influence on the Prescribing Behavior of Physicians," July 1982.

AMERICAN MEDICAL NEWS

Greene, Jay. "Policing CME a Tough, Complex Job," October 11, 1999.

AMERICAN PROSPECT

Love, James. "The Other Drug War: How Industry Exploits Pharm Subsidies," Summer 1993.

ANNALS OF INTERNAL MEDICINE

Shuchman, Miriam, M.D. "Secrecy in Science: The Flock Worker's Lung Investigation," August 15, 1998.

Davidoff, Frank. "New Disease, Old Story," August 15, 1998.

Kern, David G., et al. "Flock Worker's Lung: Chronic Interstitial Lung Disease in the Nylon Flocking Industry," August 15, 1998.

Cho, Mildred, and Lisa Bero. "The Quality of Drug Studies Published in Symposium Proceedings," March 1, 1996.

Wilkes, M. S., B. H. Doblin, and M. F. Shapiro. "Pharmaceutical Advertisements in Leading Medical Journals: Experts' Assessments," June 1, 1992.

ANTITRUST REPORT

Bloch, Robert, Scott Perlman, and Myles Hansen. "Product Market Definition in Pharmaceutical Mergers," September 1997.

APPLIED ECONOMICS

Alexander, Donald, Joseph Flynn, and Linda Linkins. "Estimates of the Demand for Ethical Pharmaceutical Drugs Across Countries and Time," August 1994.

Hudson, John. "Pricing Dynamics in the Pharmaceutical Industry," January 1992.

THE ATLANTIC

Graham, Mary. "The Quiet Drug Revolution," January 1991.

BEST'S REVIEW

Jones, John D., "A Look at Formularies: Prescription for Success?" June 1996.

BRITISH MEDICAL JOURNAL

Editorial, "Protecting Whistleblowers," January 8, 2000.

"Study into Medical Errors Planned for the U.K.," October 23, 1999.

Ciment, James. "Study Finds that Most Drug Donations to Developing Countries Are Appropriate," October 9, 1999.

Hopkins, Tanne J. "Direct to Consumer Drug Advertising Is Billion Dollar Business in U.S.," September 25, 1999.

"American Medical Association Guidelines on Direct to Consumer Advertising," September 25, 1999.

Griffith, David, M.D. "Reasons for Not Seeing Drug Representatives," July 10, 1999.

Letters. "Regulating the Pharmaceutical Industry," January 17, 1998.

Smith, R. "Beyond Conflict of Interest: Transparency Is the Key," February 13, 1998.

Campbell, Duncan. "Medicine Needs Its MI-5," December 20, 1997.

Editorial. "Hazardous Drugs in Developing Countries," December 13, 1997.

Shaughnessy, A. F., and D. C. Slawson. "Pharmaceutical Representatives: Effective If Used With Caution," June 15, 1996.

Dyer, Owen. "GP Struck Off for Fraud in Drug Trials," March 30, 1996.

Roberts, John, and Richard Smith. Editorial. "Publishing Research Supported by the Tobacco Industry, Journals Should Reverse Ban on Industry Sponsored Research," January 20, 1996.

Kingman, Sharon. "Drug Companies Are Censured by Watchdog," March 26, 1994.

BUSINESS & HEALTH

Gemignani, Janet. "PBMs: Why this exponential growth?" March 1996.

BUSINESS WEEK

Capell, Kerry, Heidi Dawley, and Amy Barrett. "Deals: Burying the Hatchet Buys a Lot of Drug Research," January 31, 2000.

"Year 2000 Pharmaceutical Sales," January 31, 2000.

"R&D by the Numbers," December 6, 1999.

Barrett, Amy, Ellen Licking, John Carey, and Kerry Capell. "Pharmaceuticals: Addicted to Mergers?" December 6, 1999.

Weber, Joseph. "The Doctor Vs the Drugmaker," November 30, 1998.

Weber, Joseph. "Drug-Merger Mania," May 16, 1994.

CANADIAN FAMILY PHYSICIAN

Lexchin, Joel, M.D. "What Information Do Physicians Receive From Pharmaceutical Representatives," June 1997.

Lexchin, Joel, M.D. "Consequences of Direct-to-Consumer Advertising of Prescription Drugs," April 1997.

Tong, K. L. and C. Y. Lien. "Do Pharmaceutical Representatives Misuse Their Drug Samples?" August 1991.

CANADIAN MEDICAL ASSOCIATION JOURNAL

Hailey, David. "Scientific Harassment by Pharmaceutical Companies: Time to Stop," January 25, 2000.

Lexchin, Joel, M.D. "Rethinking the Numbers on Adverse Drug Reactions," May 18, 1999.

Shuchman, Miriam, M.D. "Independent Review Adds to Controversy at Sick Kids," February 9, 1999.

Lexchin, Joel, M.D. "Making Drug Data More Transparent," January 26, 1999.

Hoey, John. "Placing the Ads," October 20, 1998.

Lexchin, Joel, M.D. "Placing the Ads," October 20, 1998.

Phillips, Robert A., and John Hoey. "Constraints of Interest: Lessons at the Hospital for Sick Children," October 20, 1998.

Shuchman, Miriam, M.D. "Legal issues surrounding privately funded research cause furore in Toronto," October 20, 1998.

Lexchin, Joel, M.D. "Can Drug Companies Have It Both Ways?" April 1, 1997.

Desjardins, Jean G., M.D. "The PMAC Code of Marketing Practices: Time for Improvement?" February 1, 1997.

Lexchin, Joel, M.D. "Enforcement of Codes Governing Pharmaceutical Promotion," February 1, 1997.

Shapiro, Martin F., M.D. "Regulating Pharmaceutical Advertising: What Will Work?" February 1, 1997.

Lexchin, Joel, M.D. "Interactions Between Physicians and the Pharmaceutical Industry: What Does the Literature Say?" November 15, 1993.

CHEMISTRY AND INDUSTRY

Gilvert, David. "Drug Firms Promoting Choice?" London, England: January 18, 1999.

CHEST

Orlowski, J. P. and L. Wateska. "The Effects of Pharmaceutical Firm Enticements on Physician Prescribing Patterns: There's No Such Thing as a Free Lunch," July 1992.

CHRONICLE FOR HIGHER EDUCATION

Strosnider, Kim. "Medical Professor Charges Brown U. With Failing to Protect His Academic Freedom," July 18, 1997.

Wheeler, David L. "Journal Publishes Thyroid-Study Report That Had Been Blocked by Drug Company," April 17, 1997.

CLINICAL PHARMACOLOGY AND THERAPEUTICS

DiMasi, Joseph A., Mark A. Seibring, and Louis Lasagna. "New Drug Development in the United States from 1963 to 1992," June 1994.

CLINICAL THERAPEUTICS

Dickson, M. "The Pricing of Pharmaceuticals: An International Comparison," April 1992.

CONSUMER POLICY REVIEW

Gilbert, D., and A. Chetley. "New Trends in Drug Promotion," June 1996.

CONSUMER REPORTS

"Relief for the Rx Blues," October 1999.

"Drug Advertising: Is This Good Medicine?" June 1996.

"Wasted Health Care Dollars," July 1992.

"Pushing Drugs to Doctors," February 1992.

DISEASE MANAGEMENT HEALTH OUTCOMES

Lexchin, Joel, M.D. "Direct-to-Consumer Advertising: Impact on Patient Expectations Regarding Disease Management," May 5, 1999.

DRUG INFORMATION JOURNAL
DiMasi, Joseph A. "New Drug Development: Cost, Risk and Complexity," May
1995.

DRUG TOPICS
Glaser, M. "Boom Year," April 5, 1999.
Gebhart, F. "Annual Rx Survey: The New Golden Age," March 16 1998.
Muirhead, Greg. "Consenting Adults: PCS' Pilot Program for Rx Compliance
Looks Promising," September 2, 1996.
Conlan, M. F. "In-Your-Face Pharmacy," July 8, 1996.
Muirhead, Greg. "Chain PBMS," July 8, 1996.
Sheetz, Patricia. "Drug Compliance Program Can Boost Refills," June 24, 1996.
Muirhead, Greg. "Discount Program Targets Patients without Rx Benefit,"
September 4, 1995.
Muirhead, Greg. "Disease Management," August 7, 1995.
Muirhead, Greg. "HMOs More Willing to Pay Pharmacists for Extra Services,"
July 24, 1995.
Conlan, Michael F. "Prior-Authorization Programs Can Save Money –
Sometimes," July 10, 1995.
Conlan, Michael F. "Pharmacy and Manufacturers Spar over Drug Discounts,"
April 24, 1995.
Conlan, Michael F. "Patent Law Changes Could Help or Hurt Drugmakers,"
March 20, 1995.
Muirhead, Greg. "HMOs Are Controlling More and More Prescriptions,"
November 7, 1994.
Muirhead, Greg. "Generics Market to Reach $5.9 Billion by 2000," Sep-
tember 19, 1994.
Ukens, Carol. "Shaping the Future," July 25, 1994.
Ukens, Carol. "Drug Switch Reimbursement: Really Pharmaceutical Care?,"
May 23, 1994.
Ukens, Carol. "Under Legal Fire, Miles Ends Drug Switch Payments," April 25,
1994.
Ukens, Carol. "Buying Group Offers Consumer Discount Card," February 21,
1994.
Gebhart, Fred. "New Pharmacist Pricing Suit Adds to the Turmoil," February 7,
1994.

ECONOMIST
"The New Alchemy: The Drug Industry's Flurry of Mergers Is Based on a Big
Gamble," January 22, 2000.
"A Dose of History," December 31, 1999.
"Survey on the Pharmaceutical Industry," February 21, 1998.
"Drug Mergers: Popping the Question," January 24, 1998.
"The Doctors' Dilemma," January 27, 1990.

EDUCATIONAL HEALTH PROFESSIONAL
Bowman, M.A., and D.L. Pearle. "Changes in Drug Prescribing Patterns Related to Commercial Company Funding of Continuing Medical Education," August 1988.

FAMILIES USA
"Hard to Swallow: Rising Drug Prices for America's Seniors," November 1999.

FDA CONSUMER
Henkel, John. "How TV Launched the Orphan Drug Act," May 1, 1999.
Special Report. "New Drug Development in the United States," January 1995.

FOOD AND DRUG LAW JOURNAL
Balto, David A. "A Whole New World?" January 1997.

FORBES
Brimelow, Peter, and Leslie Spencer. "Food and Drugs and Politics," November 22, 1993.

FORTUNE
"How the Industries Stack Up," April 17, 2000.
"Fortune 500," March 1998.
Guyson, Janet. "A Mangled Merger," March 30, 1998.
"The Mother of All Mergers," February 7, 1998.
Tully, Shawn. "The Plots to Keep Drug Prices High," December 27, 1993.

GERONTOLOGIST
Rogowski, J., L.A. Lillard, and R. Kington. "The Financial Burden of Prescription Drug Use Among Elderly Persons," April 1997.
Lillard, L. A., J. Rogowski, and R. Kington. "Long-Term Determinants of Patterns of Health Insurance Coverage in the Medicare Population," March 1997.

HAI NEWS
Sagoo, Kiran, and Lisa Hayes. "Public Health First: Revised Drug Strategy Addresses Trade & Health," June 1999.
Balasubramaniam, K. "Impact of WTO on National Drug Policies," October 1998.
Balasubramaniam, K. "The Revised Drug Strategy," June 1998.
Balasubramaniam K., O. Lanza, and S. Kaur. "Retail Drug Prices: The Law of the Jungle," April 1998.
Balasubramaniam, K. "Retail Drug Prices in the Asia-Pacific Region," December 1995.
Balasubramaniam, K. "Pharmacoeconomics," December 1992.

HARVARD BUSINESS REVIEW

Brenner, S. N., and E. A. Molander. "Is the Ethics of Business Changing?" January–February 1977.

HEALTH AFFAIRS

Davis. M., J. Poisal, G. Chulis, C. Zarabozo, and B. Cooper. "Prescription Drug Coverage, Utilization, and Spending Among Medicare Beneficiaries," January 18, 1999.

Smith, S., M. Freeland, S. Heffler, et al. "The Next Ten Years of Health Spending: What Does the Future Hold?" May 1998.

Long, S. "Prescription Drugs and the Elderly: Issues and Options," February 1994.

HEALTH CARE FINANCING REVIEW

Poisal, J. A., L. A. Murray, G. S. Chulis, and B. S. Cooper. "Prescription Drug Coverage and Spending for Medicare Beneficiaries," March 1999.

HEALTH MARKETING QUARTERLY

Mehta, Subhash, and Sanjay Mehta. "Strategic Options for Brand-Name Prescription Drugs When Patents Expire," Autumn 1997.

INTERNATIONAL JOURNAL OF THE ECONOMICS OF BUSINESS

Danzon, Patricia. "Price Discrimination for Pharmaceuticals: Welfare Effects in the U.S. and the E.U.," November 1997.

Reekie, W. Duncan. "Cartels, Spontaneous Price Discrimination and International Pharmacy Retailing," November 1997.

Elzinga, Kenneth, and David Mills. "The Distribution and Pricing of Prescription Drugs," November 1997.

INTERNATIONAL JOURNAL OF PHARMACEUTICAL COMPOUNDING

"Proposed List of Agents Not to be Compounded Due to Withdrawal for Safety/Efficiency Concerns," October 8, 1998.

INTERNATIONAL JOURNAL OF STRATEGIC MANAGEMENT

Jones, J., and M. Pollitt. "From Promise to Compliance: The Development of Integrity at Smithkline Beecham," April 1999.

JOURNAL OF THE AMERICAN MEDICAL ASSOCIATION

Wazana, A., M.D. "Physicians and the Pharmaceutical Industry," January 19, 2000.

Rennie, Drummond, Dr. "Thyroid Storm," April 16, 1997.

Dong, Betty J., et al. "Bioequivalence of Generic Brand-name Levothyroxine Products in the Treatment of Hypothyroidism," April 16, 1997.

Blumenthal, David, et al. "Withholding Research Results in Academic Life Science: Evidence from a National Survey of Faculty," April 16, 1997.

Pécoul, Bernard, Pierre Chirac, Patrice Trouille, and Jacques Pinel. "Access to Essential Drugs in Poor Countries: A Lost Battle?" January 27, 1997.

Ziegler, M. G., P. Lew, and B. C. Singer. "The Accuracy of Drug Information from Pharmaceutical Sales Representatives," April 26, 1995.

Chren, M. M., and C. S. Landefeld. "Physicians' Behavior and Their Interactions with Drug Companies," March 2, 1994.

McKinney, W. P., D. L. Schiedermayer, N. Lurie, D. E. Simpson, J. L. Goodman, and E. C. Rich. "Attitudes of Internal Medicine Faculty and Residents Toward Professional Interaction with Pharmaceutical Sales Representatives," October 3, 1990.

JOURNAL OF BUSINESS

Cocks, Douglas, and John Virts. "Pricing Behavior of the Ethical Pharmaceutical Industry," July 1974.

JOURNAL OF COMMERCE

Sutter, Mary. "U.S. Drug Makers Fear Generics Law in Mexico: Brand-Name Sales Considered at Risk," March 2, 1998.

JOURNAL OF DRUG ISSUES

Morris, L. A., and J. P. Griffin. "The Evolving Role of FDA in Prescription Drug Promotion," February 1992.

Basara, L. R. "Direct-to-Consumer Advertising: Today's Issues and Tomorrow's Outlook," February 1992.

JOURNAL OF ECONOMIC LITERATURE

Comanor, William S. "The Political Economy of the Pharmaceutical Industry," September 1986.

JOURNAL OF ECONOMICS AND MANAGEMENT STRATEGY

Frank, Richard G., and David S. Salkever. "Generic Entry and the Pricing of Pharmaceuticals," Spring 1997.

Cockburn, Iain, and Rebecca Henderson. "Racing to Invest? The Dynamics of Competition in Ethical Drug Discovery," Fall 1994.

JOURNAL OF THE FAMILY PRACTITIONER

Brotzman, G. L., and D. H. Mark. "Policies Regulating the Activities of Pharmaceutical Representatives in Residency Programs," January 1992.

JOURNAL OF GENERAL INTERNAL MEDICINE

Gibbons, R. V., F. J. Landry, D. L. Blouch, D. L. Jones, F. K. Williams, C. R. Lucey, and K. Kroenke. "A Comparison of Physicians' and Patients' Attitudes Toward Pharmaceutical Industry Gifts," March 13, 1998.

Wolfe, Sidney, M.D. "Why Do American Drug Companies Spend More Than $12 Billion a Year Pushing Drugs? Is It Education or Promotion?" November 1996.

Stryer, D., and L. A. Bero. "Characteristics of Materials Distributed by Drug Companies: An Evaluation of Appropriateness," October 11, 1996.

Shaughnessy, A. F., D. C. Slawson, and J. H. Bennet. "Separating the Wheat from the Chaff: Identifying Fallacies in Pharmaceutical Promotion," September 1994.

Lurie, N., and E. C. Rich. "Pharmaceutical Representatives in Academic Medical Centers: Interaction with Faculty and Housestaff," May 1990.

Davidson, R. A. "Source of Funding and Outcome of Clinical Trials," January 1986.

JOURNAL OF HEALTHCARE MARKETING

Williams, James, and Paul Hensel. "Direct-to-Consumer Advertising of Prescription Drugs," Spring 1995.

JOURNAL OF HEALTH ECONOMICS

Garber, Alan, and Charles Phelps. "Economic Foundations of Cost-Effectiveness Analysis," February 1997.

DiMasi, Joseph, and Ronald Hansen. "Cost of Innovation in the Pharmaceutical Industry," July 1991.

JOURNAL OF INDUSTRIAL ECONOMICS

Jensen, Elizabeth J. "Research Expenditures and the Discovery of New Drugs," September 1987.

Reekie, W. Duncan. "Price and Quality Competition in the United States Drug Industry," March 1978.

JOURNAL OF THE INSTITUTE FOR FISCAL STUDIES

Bloom, N., and J. Van Reene. "Regulating Drug Prices: Where Do We Go From Here?" March 1999.

JOURNAL OF LAW AND COMMERCE

Davis, Melissa K. "Monopolistic Tendencies of Brand-Name Drug Companies in the Pharmaceutical Industry," Fall 1995.

JOURNAL OF LAW AND ECONOMICS

Manning, Richard L. "Products Liability and Prescription Drug Prices in Canada and the United States," April 1997.

Grabowski, Henry G., and John M. Vernon. "Brand Loyalty, Entry, and Price Competition in Pharmaceuticals after the 1984 Drug Act," October 1992.

Dranove, David. "Medicaid Drug Formulary Restrictions," April 1989.

Hurwitz, Mark, and Richard Caves. "Persuasion or Information? Promotion and the Shares of Brand Name and Generic Pharmaceuticals," October 1988.
Leffler, Keith B. "Persuasion or Information? The Economics of Prescription Drug Advertising," April 1981.

JOURNAL OF RESEARCH IN PHARMACEUTICAL ECONOMICS
Kucukarslan, Suzan. "In Search of an Understanding of Pharmaceutical Prices," July 1996.
Pathak, Dev, and Alan Escovitz. "Managed Competition and Pharmaceutical Care: An Answer to Market Failure?" July 1996.
Shah, Hemant K. "Redefining the Pharmaceutical Industry," July 1996.
Bobula, Joel D. "A New Era in Pharmaceutical Pricing," July 1996.
Cohen, Kenneth R. "Managed Competition: Implications for the U.S. Pharmaceutical Industry," July 1996.
Kolassa, E. M. "Physicians' Perceptions of Prescription Drug Prices: Their Accuracy and Effect on the Prescribing Decision," June 1995.
Mullins, C. Daniel. "Toward an Understanding of Pharmaceutical Pricing Strategies through the Use of Simple Game Theoretic Models," June 1995.

LANCET
"*NEJM* Conflict-of-Interest Policy Under Scrutiny," October 30, 1999.
"Spain Investigates 'Bribery' of Doctors," October 30, 1999.
"Canadian Universities Go Shopping for Research Scientists," October 23, 1999.
Editorial. "A Meeting Too Many," October 10, 1998.
Editorial. "Pushing Ethical Pharmaceuticals Direct to the Public," March 28, 1998.
Editorial. "Good Manners for the Pharmaceutical Industry," June 7, 1997.
Firshein, J. "Drug Firm Buys Up Chain of U.S. Cancer Clinics," April 26, 1997.
Sheldon, T. A., and G. D. Smith. "Consensus Conferences as Drug Promotion," January 9, 1993.

MANAGING INTELLECTUAL PROPERTY
Wild, Joff. "Pharmaceutical Trademarks in a Hostile World," May 1995.

MARKETING INTELLIGENCE AND PLANNING
Blackett, Tom. "Branding and the Rise of the Generic Drug," October 1992.

MEDICAL CARE
Lillard, L. A., J. Rogowski, and R. Kington. "Insurance Coverage for Prescription Drugs: Effects on Use and Expenditures in the Medicare Population," September 1999.
Stuart, B., and J. Grana. "Ability to Pay and the Decision to Medicate," February 1998.

Stuart, B., and J. Grana. "Are Prescribed and Over-the-Counter Medicines Economic Substitutes? A Study of the Effects of Health Insurance on Medicine Choices by the Elderly," May 1995.

MEDICAL MARKETING AND MEDIA

Goldberg, Gene L. "Problems Ahead in Generic Marketing," April 1997.

Hodnett, J. "Targeting Consumers," November 1995.

Gray, Michael. "PBMS: Can't Live with 'Em, Can't Live without 'Em," September 1995.

Castagnoli, William G. "Is Disease State Management Good Therapy for an Ailing Industry?" January 1995.

Matalia, N. "Journal Advertising Works! Three Studies Say So!" May 1994.

Goldberg, Gene L. "Will There Be a Generic Industry Five Years From Now?" April 1994.

Paul, C. Marshall. "Time to Cut Back on Detailing," October 1993.

MERGERS AND ACQUISITIONS

Harrison, Joan. "Going Upstream in Drug Marketing," September/October 1994.

MONEY MAGAZINE

Rock, Andrea. "A Dose of Trouble," December 1998.

Keating, Peter. "Drugmakers Pressuring Medical Pros to Prescribe Their Products," June 1997.

Keating, Peter. "Why You May be Getting the Wrong Medicine," June 1997.

THE NATION

Finkelstein, Katherine Eban. "Medical Rebels: When Caring for Patients Means Breaking the Rules," February 21, 2000.

NATURE

"Dangers of Over-Dependence on Peer Reviewed Publication," October 21, 1999.

"U.S. Guidelines Widen the Net on Scientific Misconduct," October 21, 1999.

Bonetta, Laura. "A Duty to Publish," October 1998.

NEW ENGLAND JOURNAL OF MEDICINE

Angell, Marcia, M.D. "The Pharmaceutical Industry: To Whom Is It Accountable?" June 22, 2000.

Angell, Marcia, M.D. "Is Academic Medicine for Sale?" May 18, 2000.

Bodenheimer, Thomas. "Uneasy Alliance: Clinical Investigators and the Pharmaceutical Industry," May 18, 2000.

Olivieri, N. F., G. M. Brittenham, C. E. McLaren, et al. "Long-Term Safety and

Effectiveness of Iron-Chelation Therapy with Deferiprone for Thalassemia Major," August 13, 1998.

Stelfox, H.T., G. Chua, K. O'Rourke, and A. S. Detsky. "Conflict of Interest in the Debate over Calcium-Channel Antagonists," January 8, 1998.

Letter to the Editor, "Pfizer Night at Boston Billiards," July 10, 1997.

Angell, M., J. P. Kassirer. "Editorials and Conflicts of Interest," October 3, 1996.

Rosenberg, Steven A. "Secrecy in Medical Research," February 8, 1996.

Olivieri, N. F., G. M. Brittenham, D. Matsui, et al. "Iron-Chelation Therapy with Oral Deferiprone in Patients with Thalassemia Major," April 6, 1995.

Kessler, David, Janet Rose, Robert Temple, Renie Schapiro, and Griffin Joseph. "Therapeutic-Class Wars-Drug Promotion in a Competitive Marketplace," November 17, 1994.

Brennan, T. A. "Buying Editorials," September 8, 1994.

NEW MEDICINE

Nader, Francois. "When Should Pharmaceutical Companies Be Involved in Disease Management Programs?" January 1997.

NEW YORK TIMES MAGAZINE

Wilkes, M. S., and M. Shuchman. "Pitching Doctors," November 5, 1989.

OUR TIMES MAGAZINE

Nore, Gordon. "Pop Goes Education: No Choice for a New Generation of Students," June-July 1994.

OUTLOOK ON SCIENCE POLICY

"U.K. Government Use of Science and Technology," October 21, 1999.

"Report Assesses Australia's R&D Policy," October 21, 1999.

"New Zealand's Blueprint for Science and Technology," October 21, 1999.

PERSPECTIVES IN BIOLOGY AND MEDICINE

Laver, G., N. Bischofberger, and R. Webster. "The Origin and Control of Pandemic Influenza," Winter 2000.

PHARMACOECONOMICS

Lyles, A., and F. Palumbo. "The Effect of Managed Care on Prescription Drug Costs and Benefits," February 1999.

Dickson, M., and H. Redwood. "Pharmaceutical Reference Prices: How Do They Work in Practice?" May 1998.

Towse, A. "The U.K. Pharmaceutical Market," October 1996.

Le Pen, C. "Drug Pricing and Reimbursement in France: Towards a New Model?" October 1996.

Denig, P., and F. M. Haaijer-Ruskamp. "Do Physicians Take Cost Into Account When Making Prescribing Decisions?" August 1995.

PHARMACY TIMES

Salmo, Rose. "Market Forces Usher in a Golden Age of Generic Drugs," January 1994.

POLICY STUDIES

Earl, Slater. "A Study of Pharmaceutical Policies in the E.U.," March–April 1997.

PRESCRIRE INTERNATIONAL

Becel, B., D. Bardelay, and E. 't Hoen. "A French Physician's Network Monitoring Medical Representatives," 1997.

"Calcium Antagonists: Overused and Inadequately Assessed," May 1996.

Bardelay, D. "Visits from Medical Representatives: Fine Principals, Poor Practice," April 1995.

PSYCHIATRIC NEWS

"Ethics of Pizza, Prozac, and Profits Challenge Residents to Think Twice," June 7, 1996.

PSYCHIATRIC TIMES

Klein, Donald F., M.D. "Current Obstacles to Drug Development," June 1997.

PUBLIC CITIZEN MAGAZINE

Atkinson, Carla, and John Geiger. "Just Say No? When Drug Companies Make Offers Doctors Can't Refuse," March–April 1991.

PUBLIC INTEREST

Weidenbaum, Murray. "Are drug prices too high?" Summer 1993.

REPORT ON BUSINESS MAGAZINE

"Ivy-League Hustle," June 1998.

REVIEW OF ECONOMICS AND STATISTICS

Lu, Z. John, and William Comanor. "Strategic Pricing of New Pharmaceuticals," February 1998.

RISK MANAGEMENT

Jones, John D. "Easier to Swallow," February 1996.

ROYAL COLLEGE OF GENERAL PRACTITIONERS INTERNATIONAL NEWSLETTER

Hickey, Kevin, M.D. "MaLAM: An End to Exaggerol?" June 1999.

SCIENCE
"A Misconduct Definition That Finally Sticks?" October 15, 1999.
"Philanthropy's Rising Tide Lifts Science," October 8, 1999.
Marshall, Eliot. "NIH, DuPont Declare Truce in Mouse War," August 28, 1998.
Cohen, Jon. "Exclusive License Rankles Genome Researchers," June 6, 1997.
Marshall, Eliot. "Secretiveness Found Widespread in Life Sciences," April 25, 1997.
Pennisi, Elizabeth. "Merck Gives Researchers Knockout Deal," April 25, 1997.
Vogel, Gretchen. "Long-Suppressed Study Finally Sees Light of Day," April 25, 1997.
Roush, Wade. "Secrecy Dispute Pits Brown Researcher Against Company," April 25, 1997.
Holden, Constance. "Company Secrets Don't Stop Science," March 8, 1996.
Cohen, Jon. "Share and Share Alike Isn't Always the Rule in Science," June 23, 1995.

SCIENCE AND PUBLIC AFFAIRS
"A Glimpse of the Future," October 1999.
"Taking part in the political process," October 1999.

SCIENCE, TECHNOLOGY, AND HUMAN VALUES
"Secrecy in University-Based Research: Who Controls? Who Tells?" Spring 1985.

SCIENTIFIC AMERICAN
Laver, G., N. Bischofberger, and R. Webster. "Disarming Flu Viruses," January 1999.
Kessler, David A., M.D., and Karyn I. Feiden. "Faster Evaluation of Vital Drugs," March 1995.

THE SCIENTIST
Gwynn, Peter. "Corporate Collaborations Scientists Can Face Publishing Constraint," May 24, 1999.
Kreeger, Karen Young. "Industry Support of Societies Under Fire," June 23, 1997.
Benowitz, Steven. "Is Corporate Research Funding Leading to Secrecy in Science?" April 1, 1996.
Watanabe, Myrna E. "Merger Mania Among Drug Firms Raises Concern About Commitment to Discovery," October 2, 1995.
Watanabe, Myrna E. "The Urge to Merge," October 2, 1995.
Benowitz, Steven. "Wave of the Future: Interdisciplinary Collaborations," June 26, 1995.
Kahn, Robert L., and Denis J. Prager. "Interdisciplinary Collaborations Are a Scientific and Social Imperative," July 11, 1994.

SCRIP

Saunders, Philippa. "It's Time to Call a Halt to Poor Drug Donation Practice," September 1999.

"Troglitazone Suspended in U.K. After More Adverse Events," December 1997.

"U.K. Pilot Disease Management Scheme," June 3, 1997.

"Self-Medication Increasing in India," May 27, 1997.

"Who to Look at Internet Pharmaceuticals Trade," May 23, 1997.

"EC Commission to Revisit DTC Advertising Ban," May 20, 1997.

"New U.S. Direct-to-Consumer Campaigns," April 8, 1997.

"PhRMA to Continue Ad Campaign," February 28, 1997.

"U.S. DTC Campaigns-Caverject, Effexor," February 21, 1997.

"U.S. DTC Advertising Spend Tops $700 Million," February 4, 1997.

"Evaluating Marketing Measures in Eastern Europe," February 1997.

Mansfield, Peter, M.D. "Pharmaceutical Customers: Prey or Partners?" June 1995.

Branthwaite, A., and T. Downing. "Marketing to Doctors – The Human Factor," March 1995.

SOCIAL SCIENCE MEDICINE

Grabowski, H., and C. D. Mullins. "Pharmacy Benefit Management, Cost-Effectiveness Analysis and Drug Formulary Decisions," April 1997.

Leibowitz, Arleen, Willard Manning, and Joseph Newhouse. "The Demand for Prescription Drugs as a Function of Cost-Sharing," October 1985.

SOUTHERN ECONOMIC JOURNAL

Frank, Richard, and David Salkever. "Pricing, Patent Loss and the Market for Pharmaceuticals," October 1992.

THIS MAGAZINE

Schmidt, Sarah. "The University of Toronto Is Selling Its Classrooms, Its Programs, Even Its Washrooms, to the Highest Bidder – But the Corporate Takeover of the Academy Goes Much Further," September-October 1998.

TIME

Several Authors. "Swallowing Bitter Pills Fake and Adulterated Medicines Are Posing Health Risks Greater than the Diseases They're Meant To Cure," January 26, 1998.

Purvis, Andrew. "The Goodwill Pill Mess: Eli Lilly and Other Firms Give Away Medicine to Places Like Rwanda. Trouble Is, It's Not Always of Use," April 29, 1996.

Gorman, C. "Oh, My Aching Head!" June 30, 1997.

Greenwald, John. "The Pain of Pricey Pills," March 8, 1993.

Gorman, Christine, Mary Cronin, and Peter Shaw. "The Price Isn't Right:

Drug Firms Start to Feel the Heat as the Cost of Medication Spirals,"
January 8, 1990.

UNIVERSITY OF CINCINNATI LAW REVIEW
Dodd, Christine. "Comments: The Merck–Medco Merger: An Isolated Incident
or a Catalyst for the Transformation of an Industry?" Summer 1995.

U.S. NEWS & WORLD REPORT
Podolski, D., and R. Newman. "Prescription Prizes," March 29, 1993.

MONOGRAPHS AND SPEECHES

AMERICAN ASSOCIATION OF RETIRED PERSONS: Gibson, M., N. Brangan,
D. Gross, et al. "How Much Are Medicare Beneficiaries Paying Out-of-
Pocket for Prescription Drugs?" Washington, D.C., 1999.
ASSOCIATION OF THE BRITISH PHARMACEUTICAL INDUSTRY, Code of
Practice Authority. *Code of Practice Review*, London, May 2000.
ASSOCIATION OF THE BRITISH PHARMACEUTICAL INDUSTRY, Code of
Practice Authority. *Code of Practice Review*, London, February 2000.
ASSOCIATION OF THE BRITISH PHARMACEUTICAL INDUSTRY, Code of
Practice Authority. *Code of Practice Review*, London, November 1999.
ASSOCIATION OF THE BRITISH PHARMACEUTICAL INDUSTRY, Code of
Practice Authority. *Code of Practice Review*, London, August 1999.
ASSOCIATION OF THE BRITISH PHARMACEUTICAL INDUSTRY, Code of
Practice Authority. *Code of Practice Review: The Internet and the Code of Practice
for the Pharmaceutical Industry*, London, May 1996.
CONGRESSIONAL RESEARCH SERVICE: Morrison, Sylvia. "Prescription Drug
Prices: The Effects of Generics, Formularies, and Other Market Changes."
Washington, D.C., August 17, 1993.
EASTMAN, H. C. "The MRC of Canada and the Pharmaceutical Patent Legislation,"
Medical Research Council of Canada, Ottawa, 1987.
EASTMAN, H. C. "Report of the Commission of Inquiry on the Pharmaceutical
Industry," Commission of Inquiry on the Pharmaceutical Industry, Ottawa,
1985.
ECONOMIC REPORT TO THE PRESIDENT OF THE UNITED STATES:
Edwards, Charles C. "The Competitive Status of the U.S. Pharmaceutical
Industry," Washington, D.C., 1998.
GENERIC PHARMACEUTICAL INDUSTRY ASSOCIATION. "Facts and Figures,"
Washington, D.C., 1998.
HEALTH ACTION INTERNATIONAL: Chetley, A., and B. Mintzes, eds. "Pro-
moting Health or Pushing Drugs? A Critical Examination of Marketing of
Pharmaceuticals," Amsterdam, 1992.

HOSPITAL FOR SICK CHILDREN: Naimark, Arnold, Dr. "Clinical Trials of L1 (Deferiprone) at the Hospital for Sick Children: A Review of Facts and Circumstances," Toronto, December 1999.

INTERNATIONAL FEDERATION OF PHARMACEUTICAL MANUFACTURERS' ASSOCIATIONS. "Code of Pharmaceutical Marketing Practices," Geneva, 1994.

KERN, DAVID G., M.D. "A Recent Case Study," MIT, Cambridge, MA, March 29, 1999.

KESSLER, DAVID A., M.D., Commissioner of Food and Drugs. Speech Before the FDLI Annual Meeting, Washington, D.C., December 13, 1994.

KESSLER, DAVID A., M.D., Commissioner of Food and Drugs. Speech Before the National Food Editors and Writers Association, Washington, D.C., October 3, 1991.

LEVY, ROY. "The Pharmaceutical Industry: A Discussion of Competitive and Antitrust Issues in an Environment of Change," Bureau of Economics, Federal Trade Commission, Washington, D.C., 1999.

MEDICAL RESEARCH COUNCIL OF CANADA, Natural Sciences and Engineering Research Council of Canada, Social Sciences and Humanities Research Council of Canada, Tri-Council policy statement: "Ethical Conduct for Research Involving Humans," Ottawa, 1998.

NATIONAL ACADEMY OF SOCIAL INSURANCE: Gluck, M. "A Medicare Prescription Drug Benefit," Washington, D.C., 1999.

NATIONAL INSTITUTES OF HEALTH. "Estimates of National Support for Health Care R&D by Source of Funds," Washington, D.C., 1999.

NATIONAL PHARMACEUTICAL COUNCIL. "Pharmaceutical Benefits Under State Medical Assistance Programs," Reston, Virginia, 1998.

NATIONAL WHOLESALE DRUGGISTS' ASSOCIATION (NWDA). "Industry Profile and Health Care Fact Book," Washington, D.C., 1999.

NOVARTIS. "Pharmacy Benefit Report Facts and Figures," New Jersey, 1999.

ORGANIZATION FOR ECONOMIC COOPERATION AND DEVELOPMENT (OECD): Jacobzone, S. "How Can Pharmaceutical Policy Reconcile Social Objectives and Industrial Efficiency? A View from the Recent Experience of OECD Countries," Paris, 1999.

ORGANIZATION FOR ECONOMIC COOPERATION AND DEVELOPMENT (OECD). "Social and Health Policies in OECD: A Survey of Current Programmes and Recent Developments," Paris, 1998.

PARKE-DAVIS. Dear Healthcare Professional Letter: Important Drug Warning, October 28, 1997.

PARKE-DAVIS. Dear Healthcare Professional Letter, December 1, 1997.

PHARMACEUTICAL MANUFACTURERS' ASSOCIATION OF CANADA. "Towards a Better Informed Consumer of Prescription Medicines," Toronto, 1997.

PhRMA, Pharmaceutical Research and Manufacturers of America. "Pharmaceutical Industry Profile," Washington, D.C., 1999.

PhRMA, Pharmaceutical Research and Manufacturers of America. "Pharmaceutical Industry Profile,"Washington, D.C., 1998.

PhRMA, Pharmaceutical Research and Manufacturers of America. "The Drug Development and Approval Process,"Washington, D.C., 1996.

PhRMA, Pharmaceutical Research and Manufacturers of America. "Corporate Welfare and the Pharmaceutical Industry,"Washington, D.C., 1996.

PUBLIC CITIZEN: Sasich, Larry, and Dr. E. Fuller Torrey. "International Comparison of Prices for Antidepressant and Antipsychotic Drugs,"Washington, D.C., 1998.

PUBLIC CITIZEN: Sasich, Larry. "False and Misleading Promotion of the Nonsteroidal Anti-Inflammatory Drug (Nsaid) Nabumetone (Relafen). Worst Pills Best Pills News,"April 1997.

REICH, MICHAEL R., ED. "An Assessment of U.S. Pharmaceutical Donations: Players, Processes and Products," Harvard School of Public Health, Boston, 1999.

ROSE, ERIC, M.D. "Pharmaceutical Marketing in the United States: A Critical Analysis," Seattle, 1997.

SCHONDELMEYER, STEPHEN. "The Cost of Bill C-91: An Economic Analysis of the Elimination of Compulsory Licensing of Pharmaceuticals in Canada," Prime Institute, University of Minnesota, Minneapolis, 1993.

SHIMM, DAVID, DR. "Attitudes Towards Industry Capitation Payments for Entering Patients into Clinical Trials," 39th Annual Meeting of the American Society for Therapeutic Radiology and Oncology, Florida, October 1997.

SMITH, M. "Patent Protection for Pharmaceutical Products," Library of Parliament Research Branch, Ottawa, 1993.

UNITED KINGDOM, Department of Health. "Pharmaceutical Price Regulation," London, 2000.

UNITED KINGDOM, HOUSE OF COMMONS, Science and Technology Committee."Fifth Report, British Biotech,Volumes I and II," London, August, 1998.

UNITED NATIONS. "The TRIPS Agreement and Developing Countries," New York, 1996.

UNITED STATES BUREAU OF LABOR STATISTICS. "Producer Price Index Revision: Current Series for Pharmaceutical Preparations, Prescriptions," Washington, D.C., 1999.

UNITED STATES CENTRAL INTELLIGENCE AGENCY. "National Intelligence Estimate: The Global Infectious Disease Threat and Its Implications for the United States,"Washington, D.C., 2000.

UNITED STATES CONGRESS, Office of Technology Assessment."Pharmaceutical R&D: Costs, Risks and Rewards,"Washington, D.C., 1993.

UNITED STATES CONGRESS, Office of Technology Assessment. "Drug Labeling in Developing Countries,"Washington, D.C., 1993.

UNITED STATES CONGRESS, Office of the Budget. "How Increased Competition from Generic Drugs Has Affected Prices and Returns in the Pharmaceutical Industry," Washington, D.C., 1998.

UNITED STATES CONGRESS, Office of the Budget. "How Health Care Reform Affects Pharmaceutical Research and Development," Washington, D.C., June 1994.

UNITED STATES DEPARTMENT OF HEALTH AND HUMAN SERVICES, Food and Drug Administration. "FDA Talk Paper: Rezulin Labeling Changes," November 3, 1997.

UNITED STATES DEPARTMENT OF HEALTH AND HUMAN SERVICES, Food and Drug Administration. "FDA Talk Paper: Patient Testing and Labeling Strengthened for Rezulin," December 1, 1997.

UNITED STATES DEPARTMENT OF HEALTH AND HUMAN SERVICES, Food and Drug Administration. "Code of Federal Regulation: Prescription Drug Advertising," Washington, D.C., 1996.

UNITED STATES DEPARTMENT OF HEALTH AND HUMAN SERVICES, Food and Drug Administration, Center for Drug Evaluation and Research (CDER). "Report to the Nation: Improving Public Health through Human Drugs," Washington, D.C., 1998.

UNITED STATES DEPARTMENT OF HEALTH AND HUMAN SERVICES, Food and Drug Administration, Center for Drug Evaluation and Research (CDER). "Approved Drug Products with Therapeutic Equivalence Evaluations," Washington, D.C., 1998.

UNITED STATES DEPARTMENT OF HEALTH AND HUMAN SERVICES, Office of Inspector General. "Experience of Health Maintenance Organizations with Pharmacy Benefit Management Companies," Washington, D.C., 1997.

UNITED STATES DEPARTMENT OF HEALTH AND HUMAN SERVICES, Office of Inspector General. "Special Fraud Alert: Prescription Drug Marketing Schemes," Washington, D.C., 1994.

UNITED STATES FEDERAL TRADE COMMISSION: Bond, Ronald, and David Lean. "Sales, Promotion and Product Differentiation in Two Prescription Drug Markets," Bureau of Economics Staff Report, Washington, D.C., 1977.

UNITED STATES GENERAL ACCOUNTING OFFICE. "Prescription Drug Benefits: Implication for Beneficiaries of Medicare HMO Use of Formularies," Washington, D.C., 1999.

UNITED STATES GENERAL ACCOUNTING OFFICE. "Pharmacy Benefit Managers: FEHBP Plans Satisfied with Savings and Services, But Retail Pharmacies Have Concerns," Washington, D.C., 1997.

UNITED STATES GENERAL ACCOUNTING OFFICE. "Pharmacy Benefit Managers, Early Results on Ventures with Drug Manufacturers," Washington, D.C., 1996.

UNITED STATES GENERAL ACCOUNTING OFFICE. "Prescription Drug Pricing: Implications for Retail Pharmacies," Washington, D.C., 1996.

UNITED STATES GENERAL ACCOUNTING OFFICE. "Prescription Drugs: Companies Typically Charge More in the United States Than in the United Kingdom," Washington, D.C., 1994.

UNITED STATES GENERAL ACCOUNTING OFFICE. "Prescription Drugs: Spending Controls in Four European Countries,"Washington, D.C., 1994.

UNITED STATES GENERAL ACCOUNTING OFFICE. "Prescription Drugs: Companies Typically Charge More in the United States Than in Canada," Washington, D.C., 1992.

UNITED STATES HOUSE OF REPRESENTATIVES, Committee on Government Reform, Minority Staff. "Prescription Drug Pricing in the United States: Drug Companies Profit at the Expense of Older Americans," Washington, D.C., November 9, 1999.

UNITED STATES HOUSE OF REPRESENTATIVES, Prescription Drug Task Force. "Affordable Medications for Americans: Problems, Causes and Solutions,"Washington, D.C., 1999.

UNITED STATES HOUSE OF REPRESENTATIVES, Subcommittee on Courts and Intellectual Property of the Committee on the Judiciary. "Testimony of Andrew M. Berdon,"Washington, D.C., July 1, 1999.

UNITED STATES HOUSE OF REPRESENTATIVES, Subcommittee on Courts and Intellectual Property of the Committee on the Judiciary. "Testimony of Gordon Binder,"Washington, D.C., July 1, 1999.

UNITED STATES HOUSE OF REPRESENTATIVES, Subcommittee on Courts and Intellectual Property of the Committee on the Judiciary. "Testimony of Richard P. Burgoon Jr,"Washington, D.C., July 1, 1999.

UNITED STATES HOUSE OF REPRESENTATIVES, Subcommittee on Courts and Intellectual Property of the Committee on the Judiciary. "Testimony of Peter Barton Hutt,"Washington, D.C., July 1, 1999.

UNITED STATES HOUSE OF REPRESENTATIVES, Subcommittee on Courts and Intellectual Property of the Committee on the Judiciary. "Testimony of Maura Kealey,"Washington, D.C., July 1, 1999.

UNITED STATES HOUSE OF REPRESENTATIVES, Subcommittee on Courts and Intellectual Property of the Committee on the Judiciary. "Testimony of Gerald F. Meyer,"Washington, D.C., July 1, 1999.

UNITED STATES HOUSE OF REPRESENTATIVES, Subcommittee on Courts and Intellectual Property of the Committee on the Judiciary. "Testimony of Dr. Richard F. Selden,"Washington, D.C., July 1, 1999.

UNITED STATES HOUSE OF REPRESENTATIVES, Subcommittee on Courts and Intellectual Property of the Committee on the Judiciary. "Testimony of Jonathan Spicehandler M.D.,"Washington, D.C., July 1, 1999.

UNITED STATES HOUSE OF REPRESENTATIVES, Subcommittee on Courts and Intellectual Property of the Committee on the Judiciary. "Statement of Congressman Pete Stark,"Washington, D.C., July 1, 1999.

UNITED STATES HOUSE OF REPRESENTATIVES, Subcommittee on Courts and Intellectual Property of the Committee on the Judiciary. "Statement of Congressman Henry A. Waxman,"Washington, D.C., July 1, 1999.

UNITED STATES HOUSE OF REPRESENTATIVES, Committee on the Budget. "Testimony of Ralph Nader,"Washington, D.C., June 30, 1999.

UNITED STATES HOUSE OF REPRESENTATIVES, Committee on Government Reform and Oversight. "Prescription Drug Pricing in the U.S.: Drug Companies Profit at the Expense of Older Americans," Washington, D.C., February 1998 and October 1998.

UNITED STATES HOUSE OF REPRESENTATIVES, Committee on Government Reform and Oversight, Minority Staff Report. "Prescription Drug Pricing in the United States: Drug Companies Profit at the Expense of Older Americans," Washington, D.C., 1998.

UNITED STATES HOUSE OF REPRESENTATIVES, Subcommittee on Regulation, Business Opportunities and Technology of the Committee on Small Business. "Testimony of James P. Love, Director, Consumer Project on Technology: Comments on the Need for Better Federal Government Oversight of Taxpayer Supported Research and Development," Washington, D.C., July 11, 1994.

UNITED STATES HOUSE OF REPRESENTATIVES, Subcommittee on Regulation, Business Opportunities and Technology, Committee on Small Business. "Pricing of Drugs Codeveloped by Federal Laboratories and Private Companies," Washington, D.C., January 25, 1993.

UNITED STATES SENATE, Special Committee on Aging. "Federally Funded Pharmaceutical Inventions, Testimony of Ralph Nader and James Love," Washington, D.C., February 24, 1993.

UNITED STATES SENATE, Committee on the Judiciary, Subcommittee on Antitrust, Monopolies and Business Rights. "Anticompetitive Abuse of the Orphan Drug Act: Invitation to High Prices," Washington, D.C., January 21, 1992.

UNITED STATES SENATE, Committee on Labor and Human Resources, Hearings Before the Committee on Labor and Human Resources of the United States Senate. "Examining Practices of United States Pharmaceutical Companies and How Drug Prices and Prescriptions are Affected," Washington, D.C., December 11-12, 1990.

WORLD HEALTH ORGANIZATION. "Globalization and Access to Drugs, Perspectives on the WTO/TRIPS Agreement," Geneva, 1999.

WORLD HEALTH ORGANIZATION. "Clinical Pharmacological Evaluation in Drug Control," Copenhagen, 1993.

INDEX

Abbott Laboratories, 110, 212
Aberman, Dr. Arnold, 123
Actos, 9, 47, 60
Adbusters, 184-85
advertising, 101, 174-88; and
  categories of drugs, 177; Internet,
  189, 217; and physicians, 178, 179-80,
  181-82, 183, 197
Affordable Prescription Drugs Act,
  90-91
Africa, need for help with drugs, 1-2,
  15, 16, 84-86, 91
AIDS drugs, 37, 110; prices in Africa,
  1-2, 84, 86, 91
Alberta Medical Association, 133-34
Allegra, 177, 181
allergy drugs, 176-77, 181
American Home Products (AHP), 10,
  33, 45, 51-54, 57, 58-59, 61, 211
American Medical Association, 206
Angell, Dr. Marcia, 71-72, 133
Annan, Kofi, 85
antibiotics, 18
Apotex, 40-42, 115, 118-35, 137,
  139-44, 165

Apotex Foundation, 130
approval process, 30-31
AstraZeneca, 10, 30, 33, 137-38,
  185-86
Avandia, 9, 47, 60
Aventis, 10, 14, 33, 206
Avorn, Dr. Jerry, 181-82
"awareness weeks," 188
Aziz, Mohammed, 105, 106

Barr Laboratories, 140, 144-47
Bayer Pharmaceutical, 14, 163, 164,
  172, 173, 180, 195
Bayh-Dole Act (U.S., 1980), 74
Benbow, Dr. Alastair, 196, 202-3
Berry, Marion, 88-89
Betnasol, 91-92
Bill and Melinda Gates Foundation,
  15
Bilstad, Dr. James, 46, 48
biopharmaceutical research, 18
biotech sector, 19, 74
bisacodyl, 181
black Africa, 83-86
blackfly, 105-6, 113

blockbuster drugs, 11-12
Boots Pharmaceuticals, 80, 81
Brereton, G.G., 32-33
Brill-Edwards, Dr. Michele, 24-26,
    118, 129
Briner, Kurt, 16
Bristol-Myers Squibb, 10, 21, 37, 111,
    114, 180, 184-85, 209
British Biotech, 77
British Medical Journal (BMJ), 68, 189,
    201
Brittenham, Dr. Gary, 117, 118, 120,
    123
Brown, Sherrod, 90-91
Brown University, 78, 79
Bush, George, 36
Business Week, 35

calcium-channel blockers, 67-68
Canadian Drug Manufacturers
    Association, 148
Canadian Medical Association Journal,
    132, 133
cancer drugs, 1, 37, 100, 103-5, 111-12,
    114
Cangene Corp., 134-35
Carratu International, 160-61, 162,
    164
Carter, Jimmy, 113
Celebrex, 9
charity see donations
Chemie Grünenthal, 22-23
cholesterol-lowering drugs, 21, 101,
    176, 177, 180, 198
Chrétien, Jean, 42, 149, 152; and
    generic drug firms, 140, 149, 150,
    152
Ciba-Geigy, 3
Cipla Pharmaceuticals, 32
Claritin, 10, 30-31, 84, 176-77, 181
class-action suits, 55, 57, 61, 81, 82
Clinton, Bill, 85
Combivir, 2, 86, 92

Committee on Publication Ethics
    (COPE), 68
competition, 8-9; lessened by mergers,
    35-36; lessened by patents *see* patents
compulsory licensing, 30, 85, 140, 149;
    in Canada, 38-42, 144; proposal
    defeated in U.S., 91; in South Africa,
    84-86
computers, 19; pricing compared with
    drug pricing, 89
confidentiality clause *see* gag clause or
    order; whistle blowers
conflicts of interest: drug companies
    and medical research, 64-74; manu-
    facturers' goals and public needs, 7,
    16; Naimark, 131-35; universities and
    private sector, 74-76, 78-79, 81-82
Connaught Pharmaceuticals, 211
Connolly, Dr. Heidi, 51-52, 53, 54
consumer groups *see* watchdog groups
Consumer Reports, 187, 200
Contergan, 22
Continuing Medical Education
    (CME), 206-10
contract research organizations
    (CROs), 70-71
contraindications: played down by
    reps, 5; *see also* side effects
Cooper, Dr. Glenn, 53
Cooperative Research and
    Development Agreement (CRADA),
    108, 109, 111, 114
Copaxone, 110
Cordarone, 58-59
Cortaid, 187
"cost-effective illnesses," 14
costs of developing and making drugs,
    7, 86-88, 111, 137
counterfeit drugs, 153-57, 191; under-
    cover work against, 154-55, 160-73

deferiprone, 116-35
Deitch, Dr. Marc, 53, 57

Della-Colli, Kevin, 190-91
Detsky, Dr. Allan, 67-68
developing countries: assistance with
    manufacturing, 102; diseases, 105-8;
    donations to, 15, 32-33, 92-97,
    106-8, 113, 114; drug prices and, 1-2,
    83-86, 91; and generic drugs, 37-38;
    and patents, 36-38; R&D not devoted
    to needs of, 13-16; unethical
    practices in, 4, 182-83
development of drugs, 1, 7; costs, 7,
    86-88; and mergers, 34, 35;
    "pipeline," 11; "rational drug
    development," 100-101
dexfenfluramine, 46, 51-54, 57, 61
diabetes drugs *see* troglitazone
Diflucan, 92
Dilantin (phenytoin), 46-47
direct-to-consumer advertising
    (DTCA), 174-88; not permitted in
    Canada, 182, 187, 217
"disease management" in competition,
    10
DNA, 19
doctors *see* physicians
Doctors for Research Integrity, 124-25
donations to developing countries, 15,
    32-33, 106-8, 113, 114; and inventory
    management, 96; Operation USA,
    92-97
Dong, Dr. Betty, 78, 79-82, 120, 122
dosages, 20, 197
Downey, Bruce, 89, 145-47
drug trials, 20-21, 72-74, 117; *see also*
    Olivieri, Dr. Nancy
Duovir, 32
Dupont, 113

Eastman Commission, 40, 142
Eastman, Dr. Richard, 50
Economic Council of Canada, 39
Eli Lilly, 9, 30, 36, 37, 60, 195; and
    Prozac, 145-47, 186

Empire Laboratories, 139
enalapril, 40, 41, 42
excipients, 20

Federal Drug Administration (FDA),
    21, 22, 59, 80, 117; approval process,
    30-31; controls on advertising,
    175-76; criticized, 61-62; and Fen-
    Phen, 53, 54, 61; generic approval
    by, 146; and Rezulin, 46-51, 55, 56,
    57, 60
Fen-Phen, 45-46, 51-54, 57, 58, 59-61
fenfluramine, 45, 51, 52-53, 54
"fifteen-year rule," 151
Flack, Mick, 164, 165, 166, 167-73
Fleming, Alexander, 17-18
Flint Pharmaceuticals, 79-80
"floor" for sales, 12-14
Florida State University, 111
fluconazole, 37-38
fluoxetine, 9, 11, 30, 68, 144-47, 151,
    183, 188
Food and Drug Act (U.S, 1906), 21
Food, Drug, and Cosmetic Act (U.S.),
    22, 23-24
Fortune magazine, 2
Fosamax, 186
Free Trade Agreement, 40, 41, 142
Frelinghuysen, Rodney, 84

gag clause or order, 77-79, 81, 120,
    122, 123, 124, 127, 130
GATT (General Agreement on Tariffs
    and Trade), 37, 38
generic drug firms, 39, 42, 89, 112,
    119, 137-38; Barr Laboratories, 140,
    144-47; Barry Sherman and Apotex,
    138-44, 147-53
generic drugs, 6, 9, 87, 137; in Canada,
    38-43, 218; and developing
    countries, 37-38; distinguished from
    counterfeit drugs, 155
genes, patents on, 28

genetic engineering, 35
genome, 28
genomics, 19
gifts from drug companies, 210-15
Glaxo, 49, 113, 188
Glaxo SmithKline, 10, 33, 143
Glaxo Wellcome, 157; assistance to
    poor countries, 2, 32-33, 86, 92
Global Infectious Disease Threat, 13
globalization, 141-44, 163, 189
Gore, Al, 84
Gorgei, Melissa, 202
grey market drugs, 163
Griffith, Dr. David, 201, 213
Gueriguian, Dr. John, 47-48

Harvard University, 75-76
Health Canada, 24, 54, 58-59
Health Protection Branch in Canada,
    24, 25, 26
heart valve problems with obesity
    drugs, 51-54
Henney, Dr. Jane, 56, 61-62
hepatitis B, 13, 102
hepatitis C, 13
HIV/AIDS, 13; see also AIDS drugs
HMR, 33
Holton, Dr. Robert, 111
Horwitz, Dr. Susan, 104-5
Hospital for Sick Children, Toronto,
    116, 118, 120, 124-30; Research
    Ethics Board (CREB), 120, 122
hospitals, price reductions to, 86
Hubertus, Gert, 202
human genome, 19

illegal prescription drugs: counterfeit
    drugs see counterfeit drugs; importing
    drugs illegally, 190-92; types of, 155
imitator drugs ("me-toos"), 8-9, 87
IMS Canada Ltd., 188
Infectious Disease Threat, 13
innovation, cost of, 7-8

intellectual property, 112; and Third
    World, 2
Internet: advertising on, 189, 217; sale
    of drugs on, 189-91; source of
    medical information, 175, 189
Interneuron, 46, 51-54, 61
investment banks, 34-35

Johnson & Johnson, 10, 60
"Jones," 160-61, 164, 165, 166-67, 171,
    173
Journal of the American Medical
    Association (JAMA), 80-81
journals of medicine: financial
    interests of authors, 66-69; industry-
    supported journals, 69-70

Kefauver, Sen. Estes, 23, 30
Kelsey, Dr. Frances, 23
Kern, Dr. David, 78-79, 120, 122
Knoll Pharmaceuticals, 80-82
Knoppers, Bartha, 131-32
Kopp, Dr. Christophe, 180
Koren, Dr. Gideon, 118-19, 121, 124,
    125, 126, 127-28, 130, 132
Krimsky, Dr. Sheldon, 35, 65, 68-70,
    75, 76, 90, 109

L1 (deferiprone), 116-35
labels, information required, 22, 50,
    58-59
Lancet, The, 23
lawsuits, 55, 57-61, 145; class-action
    suits, 55, 57, 61, 81, 82
leishmaniasis, 15
Lemoine, Bernard, 16
leprosy, 24
Levamisole, 88
Lexchin, Dr. Joel, 182, 214
lifestyle medications, 12, 177
"line extensions," 9
Lipitor, 11-12, 21, 178, 180, 198
lobbying see political lobbying

Losec (omeprazole), 11, 30, 137–38
Lowy, Dr. Frederick, 132

McMaster University, 205
malaria, 13, 14, 15, 113
Malarone, 14, 15
Manley, John, 147-48, 149, 150-51
Mansfield, Dr. Peter, 4–5, 185, 194,
 214-15
marketing, 16, 100, 101; effectiveness
 of promotion, 176-78, 181–82,
 198-99; gifts to doctors, 210-15;
 separated from R&D, 3; *see also*
 Continuing Medical Education
 (CME); direct-to-consumer
 advertising; physicians; sales reps
"me-too" drugs, 8-9, 30, 87
Mectizan, 106, 113, 114
Medical Information Department
 (MID), 196
Medical Lobby for Appropriate
 Marketing (MaLAM), 4, 185
Medical Marketing & Media, 183
medical research and drug companies,
 64-74
Medicines Control Agency
 (MCA)(U.K.), 49, 189
Medrol, 88
Memorial Hospital, Pawtucket, 78-79
meningitis, 15, 37
Merck, 10, 21, 30, 34, 100-103, 105,
 114, 137, 143, 151; *Apotex v. Merck*,
 40-42; donations to developing
 countries, 106-8, 113, 114;
 marketing, 9, 180, 195, 209
mergers, 5, 33-36
Mevacor, 21, 101, 144, 180
Microfibers Inc., 78-79
Millar, Dr. Andrew, 76-77
Misbin, Dr. Robert, 48-49, 56-57,
 61-62
monoclonal antibodies, 18
Moore, Duncan, 174-75

Morris, Dr. David Evan, 202
Mulroney, Brian, 40, 41, 139, 148
multinational drug companies, 141-44;
 fight against illegal drugs, 157

Naimark, Dr. Arnold, 131-35
Nathan, Dr. David, 126-28
National Cancer Institute (NCI), 98,
 99, 100, 104
National Institutes of Health (NIH),
 45, 105, 111
Nevirapine, 91
New England Journal of Medicine
 (*NEJM*), 52, 53, 66-67, 120, 124, 184
North American Free Trade
 Agreement (NAFTA), 37, 41
Norvasc, 11
Norvir, 110
Novartis, 3, 10, 33, 182
NSAIDs, studies of, 64, 65

obesity drugs, 45-46, 51-54, 57, 58,
 59-61
off-label uses, 58, 145, 200
Olivieri, Dr. Nancy, 115-35
omeprazole, 11, 30, 137-38
onchocerciasis, 105-8
Operation USA, 93-97
Oraflex, 175-76
Orphan Drug Program, 110
orphan drugs, 112

packaging: of Internet drugs, 191; to
 fight counterfeit drugs, 157
paclitaxel, 1, 37, 99-100, 103-5,
 111-12, 114
parasitic diseases, 105-8
Patent Act (Canada, 1923), 38
Patented Medicines Notice of
 Compliance Regulations, 41
patents, 6, 26-31, 36, 89-90, 137;
 Canada, 38-43; categories, 27-28,
 146; defences against expiration, 9;

and developing countries, 36–38; on
genes, 28; length of protection, 28;
Prozac, 145–47; and research, 142;
royalties to patent holders proposed,
91; and universities, 74–75
patient groups, 188
patient input into treatment, 174–88,
217
penicillin, 17–18
Pfizer, 10, 34, 37, 38, 113, 208–9
Pharmaceutical Research and
Manufacturers of America (PhRMA),
109–10
Pharmaceutical Security Institute
(PSI), 157
Pharmacia & Upjohn, 10, 33, 34, 186–87
pharmacies, information sold to drug
firms, 188, 204
phenolphthalein, 180–81
phentermine, 45
phenytoin, 46–47
PhRMA, 84, 86, 109–10, 179
physicians: databases kept by sales reps,
203–4; and drug advertising, 178,
179–80, 181–82, 183, 197; prescribing
influenced, 197, 198, 199, 200, 201,
204–5, 208; price and choice of
drug, 5–6; recruiting patients for
drug trials, 63–64, 72–74; research
for profit, 70, 74–78; sources of
information for, 194, 197, 201, 202,
210, 215
Physicians' Computer Network, 211
"pipeline," 11
plants: drugs from, 98, 99–100; patents
on, 28; see also Taxol
polio vaccine, 27
political lobbying, 25, 28, 30–31, 37–38,
84, 86, 90, 112, 218
politics, 25–26, 36–37; Mulroney and
compulsory licensing, 40–42;
"politics of disease," 90; Quebec and
drug industry, 39, 151

Pondimin (fenfluramine), 45, 51,
52–53, 54
poor countries see developing
countries
Pravachol, 21, 144, 180, 184–85
Prepulsid, 60
prices, 8, 86–92, 102–3, 114, 217–19;
Canada's attempts to lower, 38–42;
and choice of drug by doctors, 5–6;
in different countries, compared, 91;
and manufacturing costs, 7, 86–88,
89, 111; Vagelos' efforts to stabilize,
102–3
Prilosec, 186
problem drugs: Cordarone, 58–59;
damage-control by companies,
44–45; Fen-Phen, 45–46, 51–54, 57,
58, 59, 60–61; questions about L1
(deferiprone), 120–28; Rezulin, 9,
46–51, 54–57, 60, 61–62;
Thalidomide, 22–24
Product Familiarization Programs
(FPF), 210
product samples, 205–6
profit rates, 2; effects of greed, 3–4;
"floor" for sales, 12–14; see also prices
Proleukin, 110
proton-pump inhibitors, 175
Prozac (fluoxetine), 9, 11, 30, 68,
144–47, 183, 188, 190; generic
versions, 145–47, 151
pseudogenerics, 140
Public Citizen, 6, 30, 31, 55, 65, 179,
183, 209
public good, 6, 108–14
public-speaking clinic, 210

Quayle, Sen. Dan, 37
Quebec and drug industry, 39, 151

Reagan, Ronald, 40
Redux (dexfenfluramine), 46, 51–54,
57, 61

Rees, Dr. Harvey, 201
Regan, Donald, 36-37, 107
Reich, Michael, 96
Reidbord, Dr. Steven, 202
Relenza, 66
removing a drug from the market,
   55
Rennie, Dr. Drummond, 66, 125-26
research and development, 7-16; in
   Canada, 151-52; deferiprone and
   Dr. Olivieri, 116-35; and develop-
   ment of new drugs, 88; drug trials,
   63-64, 72-74; focused on developed
   countries, 13, 14; and patents, 142;
   phases in process, 19-21; possible
   influence on research, 64-72, 74-78;
   separated from marketing, 3
Revue Prescrire, La, 180, 199-200
Rezulin (troglitazone), 9, 46-51,
   54-57, 60, 61-62
river blindness, 105-8, 114
Roche Pharmaceutical, 212
Rogaine, 177, 186-87
Romozin, 49
Rose, Dr. Eric, 178, 179-80, 197, 213,
   215
royalties to patent holders, 39, 91
Ryan, Dr. Michael, 29

sales, minimum projections ("floors"),
   12-13
sales reps, 194-206, 210-11; accuracy
   questioned, 5, 199-200, 201; databases on doctors, 203-4; job descrip-
   tions, 195; product samples, 205-6;
   susceptibility of young doctors,
   204-5
Salk, Jonas, 27
Sanders, Bernard, 88
Sasich, Dr. Larry, 6-7, 14, 30, 65
Schafer, Dr. Arthur, 132-33
Schering-Plough, 10, 30-31, 84, 176,
   180-81

Schondelmeyer, Dr. Stephen, 6, 14,
   27-28, 87-88, 176-77
Scrip magazine, 189
S.E. Massengill Pharmaceutical
   Company, 21-22
Searle, 8-9, 212
secrecy *see* gag clause or order; whistle
   blowers
Sedergreen, Dr. Chris, 201-2
seniors, and drug prices, 8, 90, 91
share price, 11
Sharfstein, Dr. Joshua, 208-9
shelf life of drugs, 92
Sherman, Barry, 89-90, 115, 119, 120,
   128, 131, 135, 136, 138-44, 147-53,
   165-66
Shimm, Dr. David, 72-74
Sick Kids *see* Hospital for Sick
   Children
side effects: deemphasized by sales
   reps, 5; heart valve problems with
   obesity drugs, 51-54; liver damage
   with Rezulin, 48-50, 54-56; *see also*
   problem drugs
Sigelman, Dan, 60
sleeping sickness, 13-14
SmithKline, 9, 60, 188
SmithKline Beecham, 33, 113, 143,
   196
smuggling and the Internet, 190-91
Soberman, Dan, 127
South Africa, 84-85
Spino, Dr. Michael, 118-19, 120-23,
   130, 135
Stahl, Leslie, 128
Strofolino, Michael, 130
Synthroid, 79-82

Tagamet, 27, 174-75
Tamoxifen, 91
taxation, 143
Taxol (paclitaxel), 1, 37, 99-100, 103-5,
   111-12, 114

taxpayers' money, 90, 108, 109–11,
110, 114
television advertising, 189
testing of drugs, 20–21, 117
Teva Pharmaceutical Industries, 110
thalassemia, 116
Thalidomide, 22–24
Third World *see* developing countries
Time magazine, 181
Timoptic, 101
top firms, 10
transfer pricing, 143
trials of drugs, 20–21, 117
Triflucan, 37–38
TRIPS agreement, 37, 38
TRIPS-PLUS, 37, 38
troglitazone, 9, 46–51, 54–57, 60,
61–62
tuberculosis, 13, 15
Turk, James, 130

United States Department of
Agriculture (USDA), 98, 99
universities: and corporate money,
70–71, 74–76, 78–79, 81–82; patent
awards, 74
University of California in San
Francisco, 81–82
University of Manitoba, 134–35
University of Toronto, 124, 129–30
University of Toronto Faculty
Association, 130
USA Today, 61–62

Vagelos, Dr. Roy, 34, 98–99, 100–103,
105–8, 113, 114
Valium, 190
Vasotec, 40, 150
Viagra, 16, 177, 190
Viral Hepatitis Prevention Board, 188

Walden, Richard, 92–97
Wall, Dr. Monroe, 99–100, 103–4
Wani, Dr. M.D., 99, 103
Warner-Lambert, 10, 34; Rezulin, 9,
46–51, 54–57
warnings on labels, 50, 58–59
watchdog groups, 4, 6, 49; *see also*
Public Citizen
Waxman, Henry, 50, 51
Wazana, Dr. Ashley, 197
Weatherall, Sir David, 126
whistle blowers, 76–77
Whybrow, Paul, 154–55, 157–73
Williams, Mike, 57–59
Wonke, Dr. Beatrice, 123
World Health Organization (WHO), 7,
97, 105, 107, 113, 155, 156
World Trade Organization, 28, 112
"worried well", prescriptions to, 178
Wyeth-Ayerst, 51–54, 61, 185, 196,
197–98, 211

Zantac, 33, 175
Zlotkin, Dr. Stanley, 122
Zocor, 11, 21, 30, 91, 101, 180, 198
Zyrtec, 177, 181